A HISTORY
OF MODERN
BRITAIN
IN TWENTY
MURDERS

ALSO BY DAVID WILSON

The Prison Governor: Theory and Practice (with Shane Bryans)

*What Everyone in Britain Should Know About
Crime and Punishment* (with John Ashton)

What Everyone in Britain Should Know About the Police
(with John Ashton and Douglas Sharp)

The Longest Injustice: The Strange Story of Alex Alexandrovich
(with Alex Alexandrovich)

Prison(er) Education: Stories of Change and Transformation
(with Anne Reuss)

Innocence Betrayed: Paedophilia, the Media and Society
(with John Silverman)

Death at the Hands of the State

Serial Killers: Hunting Britons and Their Victims, 1960–2006

Hunting Evil: Inside the Ipswich Serial Murders
(with Paul Harrison)

A History of British Serial Killing

*The Lost British Serial Killer: Closing the Case on
Peter Tobin and Bible John* (with Paul Harrison)

Mary Ann Cotton: Britain's First Female Serial Killer

*Pain and Retribution: A Short History of British Prisons,
1066 to the Present*

*Female Serial Killers in Social Context: Criminological
Institutionalism and the Case of Mary Ann Cotton*
(with Elizabeth Yardley)

*My Life with Murderers: Behind Bars with the
World's Most Violent Men*

*Signs of Murder: A Small Town in Scotland,
a Miscarriage of Justice and the Search for Truth*

*A Plot to Kill: A True Story of Deception, Betrayal
and Murder in a Quiet English Town*

*Murder at Home: How Our Safest Space
is Where We're Most in Danger*

A HISTORY OF MODERN BRITAIN IN TWENTY MURDERS

1885–2025

DAVID WILSON

SPHERE

SPHERE

First published in Great Britain in 2025 by Sphere

1 3 5 7 9 10 8 6 4 2

Extract on page 6 from 'The Scalpel House' by George MacBeth,
in *The Cleaver Garden* (London: Secker & Warburg, 1986).

A CIP catalogue record for this book
is available from the British Library.

Hardback ISBN 978-1-4087-3451-3
Trade paperback ISBN 978-1-4087-3452-0

Typeset in Warnock by M Rules
Printed and bound in Great Britain by Clays Ltd, Elcograf S.p.A.

Papers used by Sphere are from well-managed forests
and other responsible sources.

Sphere
An imprint of
Little, Brown Book Group
Carmelite House
50 Victoria Embankment
London EC4Y 0DZ

The authorised representative
in the EEA is
Hachette Ireland
8 Castlecourt Centre
Dublin 15, D15 XTP3, Ireland
(email: info@hbgi.ie)

An Hachette UK Company
www.hachette.co.uk

www.littlebrown.co.uk

For Sue & Neil, and Liz & Brian

The one duty we owe to history is to rewrite it.

OSCAR WILDE,
'The Critic as Artist' (1891)

All crib from skulls and bones
who push a pen.
Readers crave bodies. We're the
resurrection men.

GEORGE MACBETH,
'The Scalpel House' (1986)

Introduction

As a criminologist I've written several books, sometimes about individual murder cases and others about 'serial killers', who kill repeatedly over a period of time until they're finally caught. My interest within these accounts has always been about the mechanics of the murder, the victim who was chosen and then killed, and the underlying personality of the perpetrator. But then the subtitle of a book inspired me to consider a new direction, and I started to wonder if I could explore murder cases not just as a criminologist, but as a trained historian.

In 2004 Nicci Gerrard, a novelist who has always taken a keen interest in true crime, wrote about the murders of ten-year-olds Holly Wells and Jessica Chapman in Soham, Cambridgeshire in August 2002. She called her book *Soham*, which seemed logical enough, but it was the subtitle that really got me thinking: *A Story of Our Times*.[1] What did this shocking case of a double child murder by a predatory paedophile tell us about Britain at the turn of the millennium? Could we, as Gerrard argued, 'extrapolate wider meanings' from this one story?

Most murders don't attract the attention that was devoted to what happened in Soham. The nation's very public and understandable displays of compassion about these murders, which dominated the summer of 2002, were at least in part because of Holly and Jessica's status as 'ideal victims'.[2] Young, white, pretty girls (both wearing iconic Manchester United shirts in the last photograph taken of them), living in a picture-perfect town where nothing much ever happened, were always going to grab the headlines. It's a cruel reality, but a similar murder of two young black boys living on an inner-city 'sink estate' would never have received the same attention.

But that still left me with a question – what was it, then, that these murders told us about ourselves? What was the 'story of our times'?

It was suggested the 'meaning of Soham' lay both within and beyond the specific horrors of the murders themselves. That there was something wider to learn from our 'hysteria and terror and a euphoria of sadness; with sentimentality, acute empathy and a collective mourning that was like a spasm of religious fervour in our post secular age'.

That conclusion caught my attention. As someone who's made a career of working with and studying violent offenders, many of whom committed murder (sometimes multiple times), could other murders – and not necessarily just those that involved 'ideal victims' – do the same? And, if that was possible, could this be sustained over a longer period of time to tell the story of Britain? I think that they can because researching and then writing this book allowed me to see that murder really does offer a unique and compelling way to tell a history of Britain, rather than simply a history of murder.[3]

If pushed, I'd describe what follows as a form of micro-history[4] – a history which prioritises the experiences of ordinary people. Micro-history uses the 'dots in the big picture' in order to 'unearth evidence of human consciousness, both familiar and extraordinary'.[5] This reminds me of William Blake attempting to 'see a world in a grain of sand'. Yet there's always a tension about how these everyday lives might relate to grander historical forces such as industrialisation, economic development, changes in foreign policy, war and so forth. The journalist Ian Jack, for example, in trying to make sense of his father's life – a Scottish working-class man born as the Boer War ended and who died just before the Falklands War began – acknowledged that he'd 'met nobody who mattered very much and lived far removed from the centre of great events'. His father had:

> Never owned a house and he never drove a car, and today there is very little public evidence that he ever lived. I mean by that those symbols of 'continuity' which the British make so much of, items such as tombstones, memorial benches, educational bequests, country property, private copses, ancient colleges, law firms or literary agencies that can be pointed out as 'father's' or 'the family's'.[6]

What Jack describes is true for most people. Unless we're very lucky (or indeed unfortunate), we're all just tiny dots in a much bigger picture. History, as the cliché goes, is written by winners. Winners, as I was to discover, not just in the lottery of life, but certain types of winners doing very specific things, whose story is then harnessed to tell a particular, consciously constructed narrative about Britain and the British.[7]

There are still more tensions when we consider murder, but these create an opportunity. After all, murder is – thankfully – extraordinary and exceptional. So, a murder gets investigated and then recorded by the state and sometimes also reported in the media. A story is told about the killer and their victim – about what happened, and how they came to be in contact with one another. If we're really lucky, we also discover what their lives had been like, which allows us to peer through the historical gloom that tends to cloak everyday life. And because most murderers and their victims rarely feature in general histories, this gives the historian and the criminologist alike a chance to discuss individuals and events that have all too often been overlooked or, more bluntly, ignored. Even Ian Jack's father's life is described only because he had a skilled and successful son who was able to bring him to life for a much wider audience. As callous as it sounds, for those who don't have a family member with Jack's ability and connections, murder is one of the most common ways a public record of an ordinary life will be created and then survive across the generations.

I'm encouraged in my approach by the fact that many 're-visionist' historians have begun to move away from rather sterile (my polite way of saying 'boring') debates about whether British 'decline' was the dominant narrative of the twentieth century, albeit pluckily punctuated by two wars. These historians explore stories rooted in gender, class, ethnicity, the arts, the development of science and technology, misogyny, sexuality, mass media, politics and culture. Their fresh thinking has inspired me to believe that while this is a history embedded in the most dreadful of crimes, it can use those wrongs to reflect more broadly on who we once were, what we have since become, and who we might be in the future.

But be warned.

Accounts of British history tend to cluster around the usual suspects. I discuss new and very different characters, events and settings. At the same time, I also reassess the roles played by some of these traditional figures and reconsider several set-piece events that have served to create our sense of ourselves and the country where we live. So, not only am I trying to tell different stories, but I'm also unravelling some of the ones we usually tell about ourselves as a nation and as a people and deliberately ignoring others altogether. This disregarding or re-writing of some familiar (but not necessarily accurate) events is, as Professor David Olusoga has put it, 'literally the job of professional historians'.[8]

I've chosen as my time frame 1885–2025, and so this is a history of 'modern' Britain. That choice of dates is both pragmatic and criminological.

The first murders that I'll examine will be those committed by the serial killer known as 'Jack the Ripper' in Whitechapel in 1888. However, the roots of these murders, as historian Hallie Rubenhold has pointed out, can be traced back to several years before the Ripper's victims died.[9] I use the murders to reflect on Britain at a particular time, and the bigger picture that these 'dots' can offer to us. This zooming in to consider a murder and then zooming out to look at Britain more broadly will recur throughout the narrative.

1885 is also the year of the Criminal Law Amendment Act,

which came hard on the heels of a media-generated cause célèbre about young girls being sold into prostitution. During its passage through the Commons, an infamous amendment to the Act would outlaw same-sex activities between men,[10] even if these took place in private. Historical cultural concerns about prostitution and homosexuality remind us that the past has a living and active existence in the present.

The book is written chronologically, like a 'traditional' history, but at times I also look forwards (and backwards) to make links with other murders outside the specific period under discussion. I might use a decade to frame the narrative of each chapter, but I try to avoid being too 'decadist', especially as I move closer to the present day, when the narrative becomes more thematic. As a guide, I identify the particular murder or murders that I want to consider at the start of each chapter. Writing about these twenty cases made me realise that exploring historical events is rather like trying to make sense of a crime scene. They're both exercises which seek to comprehend what's happened in the past, and who might have been responsible. And, like all history, I use the stories of these murders to piece together what happened 'back then', so as to serve those who are living in the here and now.

The choice of 2025 is as pragmatic as it is criminological. I wanted to choose a murder closest to 'now' which would be able to sustain a wider meaning beyond the crime itself. The last case that I consider is the murder of Sarah Everard by Wayne Couzens, an off-duty Metropolitan Police officer, in London in 2021. I accept that this murder is somewhat distanced from 2025. However, I think my use of it is justified as it continues to raise questions about women's safety in the twenty-first century, misogyny more generally and the demands in some quarters for the police to be 'de-funded' – a call which intersects with the Black Lives Matter movement both in Britain and, especially, the USA.

As I've chosen these murders, I can hardly pretend that this history is objective. It is, after all, *a* history of modern Britain, and not *the* history of modern Britain. I doubt any history can be objective – a thought that seems to upset and offend some people. However, I've never seen history purely as a science dedicated to seeking out historical truths through uncovering neutral, objective facts. I think of it as an art and 'an exercise in intellectual empathy'.[11] Of course, I'm going to show the evidence that I've used to form my conclusions. That way readers can walk in my research footsteps and decide if my inferences are fair and my analysis is sound. For me, history has always been about spending time in archives reading primary sources, while also consuming vast amounts of secondary literature, then using my 'intellectual empathy' in a systematic way to come to an understanding about what has happened. Fair enough. However, that does mean the past becomes a creation of the present, and so I've long accepted that history tells us as much about ourselves as it does about our ancestors.

Throughout the book and consistent with my approach as a criminologist, I try to use the first names of victims but the surnames of the perpetrators, where they are known, although I do use the first name of a killer if this helps to make the narrative clearer. My work as a criminologist has also always involved talking to people and visiting crime scenes, and I use several field trips and interviews that I conducted during my research in the final chapters. So too I discuss photographs, popular literature from the period and the published reminiscences of former psychologists, pathologists, detectives and organised crime bosses to throw light onto these murder cases.

There are some remarkable continuities over my time frame, and these provide a thematic spine. Chief among these is how Britain is a profoundly unequal society; how it has an almost clinically bipolar view towards women, which seeks to both sexualise and persecute their bodies; and is a country characterised by both historical amnesia and excessive secrecy. Here I'm not just thinking about the Official Secrets Acts, but more generally. Perhaps my ongoing work in criminology and, before that, as a prison governor, which involved me signing confidentiality agreements and dealing with official documents and government agencies, has rather coloured my view. However, it's clear to me that our culture is far from open and I'm not alone in thinking this. One journalist has even gone as far as to state that secrecy is a 'very British disease', which has been 'more than two hundred years in the making'.[12] Such secrecy might originally have been intended to deter foreign spies, but it now seems to me to be equally applied – if not more so – to deterring ordinary citizens from asking awkward questions, or at least having them answered. This is something I've become much more conscious of in my work as an author and through my roles within the print and broadcast media.[13]

There's another continuity, one which has been almost riven into our sense of who we are, and where we live. It's in the DNA of what we imagine Britain and the British to be. We like to think of ourselves as a tolerant, peace-loving people living in a place that follows the rule of law; a nation where we can take pride from the fact that our police – 'the best in the world' – aren't routinely armed, even if they are now rarely on the beat; and where the end of the British Empire was peaceable. (It's been suggested that this makes us sound a bit like hobbits, and Britain like the Shire.[14]) If we do have problems they must have been caused by something alien to the culture of Britain, to the British and to the apparatus of the state.

This sense of 'othering' our own difficulties and clinging to a more benign story of how we see ourselves seems to be omnipresent over my time frame, although who those 'others'[15] might be changes at various points in the narrative. What's also clear is that we begin to understand the world and ourselves through these 'origin myths' and, in their re-telling, sustain an idea about Britain and what it means to be British, conveniently forgetting those people or events that don't conform to that story.[16]

I should acknowledge some sweeping economic and social transformations over this time frame, which have had a clear impact on Britain and British culture.[17] In 1900 Britain was a cosmopolitan and free-trading nation that imported nearly half of its food from the rest of the world. Almost anything could be imported into Britain free of tariff duties between 1900 and 1945. It paid for these goods primarily by exporting coal, and unsurprisingly given its importing of foodstuffs, was the most urbanised and industrialised nation in the world, with the lowest agricultural population of any major nation. The importance of free trade became a moral as well as an ideological cause as it involved Britain being internationalist – some might even claim anti-imperialist in its outlook – and hostile to nationalism. This would change fundamentally as my time frame moved closer to the present, when different concerns began to dominate and nationalism, rather than internationalism, gained ascendancy, especially in England.

This might seem to suggest that this is a book that seeks to 'bash Britain' and denigrate what British culture is all about. Nothing could be further from the truth. The Britain that emerges is one in which its people continue to value family, community, democracy, fairness, honesty and decency, and, above all, despite the many obstacles that are put in their way, they want to hold those in power accountable for the decisions that they make.

Finally, briefly, I should say something about what I mean by the term 'Britain'. As I've specifically excluded murders that took place within the confines of Northern Ireland, I don't use the term 'United Kingdom'. I'm therefore using 'Britain' and 'British' to reflect only England, Scotland and Wales, although I do reflect upon murders that have connections to the Troubles in Northern Ireland.

Of course, the sense of there being a unified Britain that's possible to describe and give meaning to has never been under greater stress, and, frankly, it's likely to disappear in the years to come. It almost feels as if I'm swimming against the cultural and political tide even to include 'Britain' in the title of the book. However, I'll happily use the term in this very specific context as a Scot who was educated in and has lived in England for most of my life, and who's therefore also acutely aware that many others who have gone before me essentially saw 'Britain' as 'England'.[18] That's certainly not my intention and, if I'm honest, it still genuinely annoys me when it's presumed that 'England' is 'Britain'. Where I can, I use several Scottish (although fewer Welsh) examples, although inevitably murders committed in England will dominate.

That really shouldn't be a surprise, as it's where most murder in Britain occurs.

CHAPTER ONE

Case One

The Murders Committed by Jack the Ripper, 1888

This very night in London, and every night, year
in and year out, not seven maidens only, but
many times seven ... will be offered up as the
Maiden Tribute of Modern Babylon. Maidens
they were when this morning dawned, but
to-night their ruin will be accomplished, and
to-morrow they will find themselves within
the portals of the maze of London brotheldom.
Within that labyrinth wander, like lost souls, the
vast host of London prostitutes, whose numbers
no man can compute, but who are probably not
much below 50,000 strong.

W. T. STEAD, *Pall Mall Gazette*, 6 July 1885

A sequence of murders of women – several of whom sold sexual services – committed in Whitechapel, London, between 7 August 1888 and 9 November 1888, and which have all been attributed to a serial killer popularly known as Jack the Ripper, offers an irresistible platform on which to build this history. The temptations of this serial of killings, within what I prefer to call 'the Whitechapel Murders',[1] are obvious. Not only do these notorious murders emerge from the iniquitous social, gender and economic conditions of the late Victorian period, but they also establish a range of phenomena that resonate throughout our time frame, such as: the power of the media to create and develop a story so that it comes to occupy public consciousness, and therefore becomes a pressing social issue; the ability – or failure – of the state to respond to crime; and how some crimes shine a light on aspects of our society that we would usually prefer to ignore – specifically glaring disparities of wealth.

The Whitechapel Murders echo across modern British history. For example, at the height of another serial murder of women – those committed by Peter Sutcliffe, popularly known as the 'Yorkshire Ripper' – Margaret Thatcher was so incensed by the failure to catch the killer that she threatened to take charge of the police investigation herself. There was a great deal at stake – the Conservatives, after all, were seen as being the party of law and order. Yet here was someone able to kill at least thirteen women and still avoid detection. Apparently, it was only William Whitelaw, Thatcher's genial Home Secretary, who was able to persuade her that it wouldn't be a good idea to have the Prime Minister stationed at Leeds police headquarters for days on end.[2]

The fact that the Whitechapel Murders remain unsolved, unlike those of the Yorkshire Ripper, means they continue to generate popular interest as one criminologist, historian or, more typically, 'Ripperologist' after another suggests a new theory as to who might've been responsible. On the other hand, Hallie Rubenhold, rather than attempting to unmask the killer, attempted in *The Five* to 'retrace the footsteps of five women, to consider their experiences within the context of their era, and to follow their paths through both the gloom and the light'.[3] Rubenhold persuasively reminds us that terms such as 'street walker' and 'walk the streets', which today would be euphemisms for prostitution, were not firmly established in this usage until the mid-twentieth century, and therefore that some of the victims of Jack the Ripper may have been mischaracterised. Above all, she reminds us of their humanity as people, and as women – beyond how they might, or might not, have earned their living. The success of *The Five*, which won the Baillie Gifford Prize for non-fiction in 2019, is indicative of the continuing interest in this series of murders, and how writing about them can become representative of more current preoccupations.

It's also possible to observe this cultural obsession from search engines. My typing 'Jack the Ripper' into Google generated just under twenty million hits while, by way of comparison, 'the Yorkshire Ripper' produced just under five million; there are some two thousand books with 'Jack the Ripper' in the title for sale on Amazon – as well as a hundred films and assorted TV programmes. There's a controversial Jack the Ripper Museum in Cable Street, 'in the heart of Whitechapel', and there are a number of walking tours offering tourists the opportunity to follow in the footsteps of the killer. One of the most popular of these tours on TripAdvisor boasts of having 'Ripper-Vision': 'your guide uses handheld projectors to accompany spine-chilling tales of the murders[.] As you explore the dimly lit back streets of Whitechapel, the images of Victorian London are projected onto buildings to guarantee a highly atmospheric experience.'[4] When Madame Tussauds re-opened their Chamber of Horrors in London in October 2022, Jack the Ripper was, unsurprisingly, the main attraction.

In historical terms we might view what I've been describing as the 'after', but of course I'm also interested in the 'before', as well as the crimes themselves. Prior to discussing the murders, it's important to understand how they emerged from a distinct period within late Victorian England.

*

It's always difficult to identify when an event, a movement, or indeed a sequence of murders started. History can sometimes remind me of talking to witnesses of a crime – looking at the same incident, they usually have a different analysis of what had taken place, and who might have been responsible. The 'truth', in other words, is often partial and incomplete. For me, the Whitechapel Murders' 'origin story' begins with the Criminal Law Amendment Act of 1885. This Act of Parliament and the very public controversies that surrounded it helps to make sense of the events in Whitechapel three years later, and specifically the power of the press to create a scandal that could cross party political lines and class boundaries.[5]

This Bill was a formal attempt by the state to counter concerns that a growing number of women and girls were selling sexual services, and a sense that there had been a decline in moral standards that seemed to have accompanied the country's rapid industrialisation. It was also a way of responding to a fear that children and young women were being sold into an organised international trade known as 'white slavery', which coerced them into prostitution. In 1881 a House of Lords select committee had recommended that the age of consent should be raised from thirteen to sixteen, and the subsequent Criminal Law Amendment Bill was then introduced to Parliament. It passed the Lords but failed in the House of Commons in 1883. The Bill was re-introduced in 1884, and again in 1885 when Lord Salisbury took office with a minority government after the resignation of Gladstone, although it seemed that the Bill would fail once more.

It was at this point that the editor of the *Pall Mall Gazette* entered the fray.[6] William Thomas (W. T.) Stead was a northern Nonconformist, a radical liberal who wanted real social change and justice, and who saw the class system as preventing that change from happening. One of the most controversial figures of the nineteenth century, Stead was born in the Northumberland village of Embleton in 1849 and would die on the *Titanic* in 1912.[7] He was the son of a Congregationalist minister, suitably pious, a rebel, a free-thinker, and virtually single-handedly invented what we'd now call tabloid journalism. At the time this was called 'the new journalism', which involved reporting on issues that stemmed from Stead's personal, religious and moral beliefs, using emotive, sensational language and illustrations.

Early in his career he'd written about prostitution for the *Northern Echo*. In one of his first editorials for that newspaper he described it as 'the ghastliest curse which haunts civilised society, which is steadily sapping the very foundations of our morality'. He'd also covered the case of the female serial killer Mary Ann Cotton. Cotton had murdered her way through various husbands, partners, children and stepchildren in the Durham area, and Stead recognised that reporting her case improved the paper's circulation.[8]

Having moved to London, Stead was horrified by what he saw on the streets of the capital and was equally intolerant of the seeming inability of politicians to do something about the 'evils of the sex trade'. Stead believed that through the 'justifiable sensation' of what he wrote, he could harness the power of people to create social change and thought that this type of journalism was a 'glorious opportunity of attacking the devil'. His most perceptive biographer has described him as 'an evangelist; a minister's son who saw the editor's chair as a pulpit and the reading public as his congregation'.[9] So he used the *Pall Mall Gazette*, a hitherto sedate gentleman's magazine, as a platform to expose the reality of child prostitution in London.

'The Maiden Tribute of Modern Babylon' was published in July 1885. It was written in instalments, with provocative headings proclaiming such things as 'The Violation of Virgins', 'Confessions with Brothel Keeper' and 'Strapping Girls Down'. It caused outrage and, virtually overnight, Stead successfully turned the issue of the trafficking of women and girls into a national, and indeed international, obsession with crowds demanding that action should be taken. Stead described this as 'government by journalism', and the subsequent passage of the Criminal Law Amendment Act not only led to the age of consent being raised but made the prosecution of brothels much easier. In celebration, anti-vice campaigners held a rally in Hyde Park that drew a crowd of three hundred thousand people. This, as the social historian Professor Julia Laite has observed, was a 'testament to the degree which Stead's exposé had truly rallied the public to the cause'.[10]

Stead also took direct action, and it's worth considering this more fully given that it reveals details rarely studied in our history. At its heart, 'The Maiden Tribute of Babylon' was a description of how Stead had commissioned a former sex worker called Rebecca Jarrett to purchase a child, to show how easy it was to procure a young girl and have her then sell sexual services. Stead graphically described how Jarrett was able to purchase 'Lily', a thirteen-year-old girl, from her mother for £5. Of course, 'Lily' is a name that serves to illustrate the girl's purity, as well as protect her identity. Lily's real name was in fact Eliza Armstrong. After being purchased by Jarrett, Eliza was 'certified' a virgin by an abortionist midwife, and then taken to a brothel. She was then drugged with chloroform before being sent to France in the care of the Salvation Army.

Eliza's mother recognised her daughter from the details contained within the article and, claiming that she'd been 'duped' by Jarrett, went to the police. Stead and Jarrett, and several other accomplices, including Bramwell Booth, Chief of Staff of the Salvation Army, were charged with the abduction and indecent assault of Eliza. Stead explained to the court that he'd been attempting to 'protect the children of the poor. Was that not the object that I did all this for? You know it was, and you know that was why Jarrett did it, and Bramwell Booth did it. It was not in order to abduct a girl, but to rescue her from what we believed was her inevitable doom.'[11] His pleas fell on deaf ears, and after two trials they were all found guilty. Stead was sentenced to three months in prison.

Despite his imprisonment and several other setbacks, Stead had established the ability of new journalism to engage the public in the social issues of the day, and in turn make politicians take notice of what was being reported. New journalism was a tool which could be harnessed to do good, as was always intended by the pious Stead, while at the same time selling ever greater numbers of newspapers.

Stead resigned from the *Pall Mall Gazette* in 1889. However, his literary invention was now firmly embedded in a range of other newspapers, in particular the *Star*, edited by an Irish radical called Thomas Power (T. P.) O'Connor. The *Star*'s reporting of the Whitechapel Murders took the new journalism to even greater extremes,[12] resulting in sales of some three hundred thousand copies per day – a circulation that was never remotely matched by the *Pall Mall Gazette*, even at the height of Stead's editorship. So, even before the first Whitechapel murder in 1888, the media had learned how to use a case to create maximum political impact, and in doing so generate huge public interest which could also be turned into profit. Sex work, policing, the incompetence of government and murder were therefore already the staple diet of many newspapers even before Jack the Ripper struck.

*

Ripperologists will have noticed that I stated the sequence of murders attributed to Jack the Ripper started on 7 August 1888. This is a few weeks before the murder of Mary Ann Nichols, the first of the so-called 'canonical five' victims usually ascribed to the Ripper. However, the first victim that I've identified is Martha Tabram, a thirty-seven-year-old woman who was also known as Martha Turner. She was stabbed thirty-nine times in George Yard Buildings, George Yard, Whitechapel, close to where she had been living at 19 George Street with a friend called Mary Ann Connelly, who also used the name 'Pearly Poll'. Both women were sex workers.

I've started with Martha for one simple reason: her murder was definitively identified as part of the sequence by HOLMES. This is the Home Office Large Major Enquiry System – the information retrieval system aimed at helping senior investigating officers (SIOs) in murder investigations. HOLMES was introduced in 1985 in the wake of the botched Yorkshire Ripper inquiry, which saw officers overwhelmed by the sheer amount of information being collected.[13] HOLMES provides a system that automates the process of collecting and collating information, and so helps the SIO see the wood for the trees.[14] In other words, what pieces of evidence are significant, and how might they be linked in a sequence of murders?

I was able to have the entire police file on the Whitechapel Murders entered into HOLMES by the police's lead trainer for a BBC documentary about Jack the Ripper.[15] This showed which of the various murders committed in Whitechapel between April 1888 and February 1891 might have been linked, and therefore likely to have been committed by the same perpetrator. Martha's murder was connected to the 'canonical five'. To be blunt, if these murders had taken place in the twenty-first century rather than 1888, the police would have viewed the sequence as involving six victims.

The circumstances surrounding Martha's murder also offer up clues about which of the various suspects might have been responsible. I'm only engaging in this parlour game here as it helps us to re-consider some of the stories that we like to tell ourselves about who might be responsible for serious, violent crime. The most widely considered suspects are James Maybrick, Francis Tumblety, Walter Sickert and, finally, a collection of suspects who might handily come under the heading of 'a royal conspiracy'. Why did these suspects emerge, and why does their story – or the story that is told about them – still resonate today? Each of these suspects has been proposed by authors of bestselling books. For example, Maybrick, a Liverpool-based cotton trader who died in 1889, is supposedly the author of a diary in which he 'confesses' to the murders.[16] However, the diary has become the subject of numerous claims and counterclaims in respect to its authenticity. Meanwhile, Tumblety emerged as a suspect through the research of Stewart Evans and his co-author Paul Gainey for *Jack the Ripper: First American Serial Killer* (1996). While he may have been suspected at one stage by Scotland Yard, he was a very unlikely Ripper: physically enormous, gay and with a distinctive moustache, Tumblety would have been very conspicuous and easily identified.

The artist Walter Sickert is put forward as a suspect in *Portrait of a Killer: Jack the Ripper – Case Closed* (2002) by the American novelist Patricia Cornwell, who states, 'I knew the identity of a murderer and I couldn't possibly avert my gaze.' Her use of modern forensic techniques to unmask her suspect is admirable, but she concentrates all her efforts on him, and this confirmation bias undermines her case. For instance, the last acknowledged Ripper victim, according to HOLMES, was Mary Jane Kelly, who was killed on 9 November 1888, but Sickert lived on well into the twentieth century, dying at the age of eighty-one in 1942. As Cornwell freely admits, most serial killers do not stop killing until they are apprehended or die, but she gets round this apparent paradox by suggesting that Sickert continued to kill and may have been responsible for some forty murders. She also claims that he killed children and young people as well as sex workers. I disagree. Cornwell produces convincing evidence that the artist was obsessed with Jack the Ripper and it's possible that he even wrote several letters to the police claiming to be the murderer. However, hoax letters are a common feature of many high-profile murder cases.[17] Perhaps the most telling argument against Sickert being Jack the Ripper is that he was out of the country for much of September 1888, when several of the murders occurred.

Another prime suspect is part of the 'royal conspiracy' – Prince Albert Victor, Queen Victoria's grandson. Some believe that the prince was himself the murderer; others that the killings were committed to protect his reputation. Notable among the books pointing the finger at Albert Victor is Stephen Knight's *Jack the Ripper: The Final Solution* (1976), and he also features in several films, most memorably *From Hell*, starring Johnny Depp. However, the prince wasn't in London when several of the murders were committed: he was in Yorkshire when Mary Ann Nichols was killed; in Scotland with his cousin Prince Henry of Battenburg when the 'double event' occurred – so called because Elizabeth Stride and Catherine Eddowes were killed on the same day – and in Norfolk when the final murder took place. Albert Victor couldn't have been Jack the Ripper, but Knight claims that a 'Freemasons' conspiracy' evolved to cover up the fact that the prince had fallen in love with a young Catholic woman called Annie Crook. They allegedly married in secret and had a child, who was put into the care of Mary Jane Kelly after the prince had been sent to India, and Annie Crook locked up in an asylum.

These books often draw unsupportable conclusions, but as a group they create a narrative about who's believed capable of such horribly iconic violence, and how these men may have escaped justice. Seemingly we've always liked to imagine that serial murderers must resemble the fictional and extraordinary Hannibal Lecter, a classical music-loving psychiatrist and a 'super predator', rather than the all-too-banal, weedy and needy Dennis Nilsen, a former police officer who killed young men in London in the late 1970s and early 1980s.

This popular understanding about who's capable of committing serial murder can also be found in a number of Edwardian biographies and autobiographies. These were written by a number of officials involved in the case and, in effect, are a rear-guard action on behalf of the police, essentially amounting to a defence of 'we knew all along who did it, but we just couldn't arrest him'. I discuss these accounts more fully below, but they include Robert Anderson's idiosyncratic *The Lighter Side of My Official Life* (1910), describing his time as Assistant Commissioner at Scotland Yard, which provides an almost authorised view of contemporary Jack the Ripper suspects. Walter Dew's *I Caught Crippen: Memoirs of Ex-Chief Inspector Walter Dew CID* (1938) covers the author's early career and his attendance at Miller's Court, where Mary Jane Kelly was murdered. Finally, Sir Melville Macnaghten's *Days of*

My Years (1914) is also useful as he was another senior official at Scotland Yard around the time of the murders.

Of the more recent books which have pushed our understanding forwards, David Canter's *Mapping Murder* (2003) explores whether the geography of Whitechapel might offer clues to the killer's identity – and 'geoprofiling'[18] more generally does help us to locate where the killer might have lived. And finally, today we are also able to construct a fairly sophisticated profile of the type of person who committed the murders based on which victims were chosen, what was done to them and how their bodies were discarded. This was attempted by 'the FBI's legendary mindhunter' John E. Douglas in *The Cases that Haunt Us: From Jack the Ripper to Jonbenet Ramsey* (2000), written with Mark Olshaker. While profiles of serial killers can often be very subjective, there's little doubt that Jack the Ripper's victims, and what happened to them, provide us with a number of clues that are worthy of consideration. However, before re-considering what all of this might tell us about plausible suspects, and the new importance of the murder of Martha Tabram as the first victim, let's look again at the 'canonical five'.

*

Most authors writing about Jack the Ripper have attributed five victims to him because of a confidential memorandum by Sir Melville Macnaghten in February 1894. Macnaghten, who'd joined the Metropolitan Police Force as Assistant Chief Constable CID in June 1889, wrote this memo in response to a newspaper claim that Jack the Ripper was a recently detained lunatic called Thomas Hayne Cutbush. In it Macnaghten states unequivocally that 'the Whitechapel murderer had five victims – & 5 victims only'. He then names the 'canonical five', and expressly dismisses Martha Tabram as a Ripper victim – he was wrong. However, we should note the striking degree of similarity between the five women: several were involved sporadically in the sex trade, although not all (Catherine Eddowes most obviously); each had problems with alcohol; some were homeless; and they were all, except for Mary Jane Kelly, in their forties.

What these women also had in common was that none was an 'ideal victim'; they didn't generate the sympathy of the public, as other murder victims might have done, because of their perceived lifestyles and personal circumstances. Instead, what was sensational was the idea of an unmasked killer, and the incompetence of the police in bringing him to justice. As Rubenhold has shown, this is grossly unfair to the women who were murdered, and reduces their lives to simply how they died, rather than giving them agency, autonomy and identity.

Mary Ann Nichols was also known as 'Polly'. She was born on 26 August 1845 to Edward Walker, a locksmith, and his wife Caroline, who worked as a laundress. The family lived in Shoe Lane, off Fleet Street. In January 1864 Mary Ann married an Oxford-born printer called William Nichols at St Bride's Parish Church in Fleet Street, and between 1866 and 1879 they had five children. While this indicates that their marriage was publicly fruitful, it was privately stormy, and broke down completely a year later. William said this was a result of Mary Ann's alcoholism, but her father denied that she was a heavy drinker, suggesting instead that the marriage failed as a result of William having an affair with the nurse who looked after Mary Ann during her last pregnancy. Whatever the truth,

Mary Ann moved out of the family home in September 1880 and went to live in the Lambeth Workhouse. She stayed there for some nine months and would return periodically over the next eight years. At first, after their separation, William continued to support Mary Ann, but he eventually stopped the payments. When the parish authorities tried to collect more maintenance money from him, he explained that his wife had deserted her children, taken up with another man, and was now earning her living as a prostitute. He won the case, and at the time of her death he hadn't seen Mary Ann for three years. However, it is important to note that men stood to benefit if they could paint their former partners in the worst possible light, and so their claims shouldn't be accepted at face value.

Between April and July 1888, Mary Ann worked as a domestic servant in the home of Mr and Mrs Cowdry in Wandsworth, a job secured for her by the matron of the Lambeth Workhouse. It seems logical to presume that the matron had placed Mary Ann in a good situation, but unfortunately – for whatever reason – this plan backfired. On 12 July Mrs Cowdry sent Mary Ann's father a postcard to say that she'd stolen clothing worth £3 10s. and absconded. At the time of her death, Mary Ann was living in a doss house known as the White House, in Flower and Dean Street in the East End, where men and women were allowed to sleep together.

Mary Ann was five feet two inches tall, with a dark complexion, brown eyes, greying brown hair, high cheekbones and discoloured teeth. Her associates viewed her as a very clean woman who tried to keep herself to herself and rarely talked about her affairs. This might suggest something of the regret she must have felt for the children she'd left behind. On the night that she died she went out drinking at the Frying Pan in Brick Lane, but by 1.20 a.m. she was in a lodging house in Thrawl Street, where she was asked for fourpence for her bed. She didn't have the money so was turned away. Later, Mary Ann was spotted by Mrs Emily Holland, with whom she had once shared a room in Thrawl Street. Emily described Mary Ann as having been drunk, and said she found her slumped against the wall of a grocer's shop. According to her statement, Emily tried to persuade Mary Ann to go home with her, but Mary Ann wanted to earn her doss money, so she staggered up Whitechapel Road and into Buck's Row – known today as Durward Street – where she met her death.

The circumstances in which Mary Ann was found don't need further elaboration. Of greater relevance are the injuries that she suffered, given that these might afford an insight into the state of mind of her killer. Mary Ann had two bruises on her face, one on each side. There were two cuts to her throat – one four inches long, the other eight inches – both of which were so deep as to reach the vertebrae of her neck. There was also bruising on her abdomen, and on her right side three or four cuts running downwards – according to a contemporary account, the 'lower part of the person was completely ripped open'. All the wounds had been inflicted with a sharp knife. While not commented upon by the coroner, several newspapers reported that Mary Ann might have been wearing a ring, which had been removed by the killer. Mary Ann seems to have turned her back to her murderer, possibly intending to have intercourse in this position, which gave him the opportunity to cut her throat. Cutting his victim's throat would have left her unable to scream, allowing him more time to mutilate his dying victim. This suggests that Jack the Ripper was 'act focused' – he wanted to kill his victims quickly – and wasn't interested in prolonging the process by which they died. He wanted his victim dead so he could feed his fantasies with an inert body.

The Ripperologist Paul Begg notes that all of the murders (with the exception of Elizabeth Stride's, when the Ripper was disturbed) were 'characterised by extensive mutilation of the victim, the womb being the target of his attacks'.[19] Dr Rees Ralph Llewellyn, who conducted the full post-mortem examination on Mary Ann, thought that her killer must have had at least some, albeit crude, anatomical knowledge. His opinion has been used by many commentators to propose doctors or people with a medical background as the murderer. However, as Patricia Cornwell points out, 'this isn't surgery; it is expediency, or grab and cut'. This 'grab and cut' added another layer to the horror of the story, which could be exploited by the press. Finally, there's no evidence that the killer engaged in sex with Mary Ann, or indeed with any of his later victims.

Annie Chapman, the second of the five, was born Annie Smith in September of either 1840 or 1841. Her father, George, was a soldier in the Life Guards. Annie's first job seems to have been as a domestic servant, and in May 1869 she married a coachman named John Chapman. Together they had three children. Annie drank heavily, which eventually led to the couple's separation in 1882. She was given an allowance of ten shillings a week by her ex-husband, but that ended abruptly when he died in 1886. Thereafter, Annie drifted from one relationship to another, and her friends described her at the time of her murder as 'addicted to drink'. She tried to support herself by selling matches and flowers bought at Stratford Market, but was forced into sex work, which reveals the precarious nature of life in late Victorian England for working-class women.

On the night of her murder Annie had been drinking in the Britannia public house on the corner of Dorset Street, near where she had been staying at a lodging house. She returned to her lodgings and, like Mary Ann Nichols, was asked for money for her bed. She didn't have it but told the warden – Tim Donovan – that he shouldn't let out her bed because she would return with the cash. Donovan stated that Annie was drunk but walking straight. There were also some unsubstantiated reports that she went on to the Ten Bells pub on the corner of Fournier Street. In any event, Annie was found dead, lying on her back, in the rear yard of 29 Hanbury Street. Her throat had been cut through to the spine, and a portion of her small intestine and abdomen was lying on the ground over her right shoulder, still attached to her body. The post-mortem report describes the remainder of her injuries: 'from the pelvis, the uterus and its appendages, with the upper portion of the vagina and the posterior two-thirds of the bladder, had been entirely removed'.

Elizabeth Stride and Catherine Eddowes were killed just over three weeks later, on the same night. This is often described as the 'double event', a phrase used in a postcard purportedly written by Jack the Ripper on 1 October 1888. Elizabeth was murdered first; then, just forty-five minutes later, Catherine was killed. Their murders are of particular significance because both seem to have been witnessed.

Elizabeth Gustafsdotter was born in Sweden in November

1843 and immigrated to London in February 1867. This seems to have been an attempt to put the past behind her, as she'd already been arrested by Swedish police for prostitution. She married a carpenter named John Stride in March 1869, and soon they were running a coffee shop together. However, John suffered ill-health, and in January 1879 Elizabeth asked the Swedish Church in London for financial assistance. John was admitted to Poplar Workhouse in August 1884 before being sent to the Poplar and Stepney Sick Asylum, where he died of heart disease two months later.

The Strides' marriage seems to have broken down three years before John's death, with Elizabeth's heavy drinking reportedly the principal cause. She spent time in the Whitechapel Workhouse infirmary and would eventually be sentenced to seven days' hard labour for being drunk and disorderly and soliciting on 13 November 1884. She liked to tell people that her husband and two of her children had died in a shipping accident in 1878, and Cornwell notes that Elizabeth had 'led a life of lies, most of them pitiful attempts to weave a brighter, more dramatic tale than the truth of her depressing, desperate life'. Paul Begg notes that she might also have masqueraded as another woman called Elizabeth Watts, and she certainly had a variety of nicknames – Long Liz, Hippy Lip Annie and Mother Gum.

After the collapse of her marriage, Elizabeth lived on and off with a man named Michael Kidney. By all accounts it was a stormy relationship, with Elizabeth disappearing for days or weeks at a time: 'It was the drink that made her go away,' claimed Kidney after her death. Support for this statement comes in the form of the numerous appearances Elizabeth made before the magistrates. For example, she was charged in February and October 1887, and again in February and September 1888, with being drunk and disorderly and using obscene language. Kidney and Elizabeth parted company for the last time on 25 September 1888, just five days before her death. As a result, he was initially suspected of her murder.

Elizabeth was seen drinking in the Bricklayer's Arms in Settles Street on the night of her death, and she may have been sold a bunch of grapes by a grocer, Matthew Packer, between 11 p.m. and midnight, although none were found in her stomach during her post-mortem. Her body was discovered in a passageway beside 40 Berner Street, home of the International Working Men's Educational Club. That night about a hundred people had turned up at the club to debate 'Why Jews Should Be Socialists', with most not leaving before 11.30 p.m. Several stayed on to drink until well after midnight. Clearly, then, people must have been around when Elizabeth was attacked. Israel Schwartz, for example, followed a man into Berner Street from Commercial Road. He saw the figure approach Elizabeth – who was standing outside the gates of the club – stop, exchange a few words with her and then assault her. Schwartz thought it was a domestic dispute, so he crossed the road to avoid becoming involved. He then saw a second man leave a pub on the corner and light his pipe. Next, he heard someone (perhaps the man with the pipe) shout 'Lipski' – a reference to Israel Lipski, who had been convicted for murder and executed in 1887 – which might have been intended to scare off Schwartz. He did indeed run away (as did the man with the pipe) but he reported all he'd witnessed the following day at Leman Street police station.

If Schwartz is to be believed, he undoubtedly saw the man who murdered Elizabeth Stride, and he provided the police with a description of Jack the Ripper. Schwartz stated that the man was approximately thirty, short – about five feet five inches tall – with broad shoulders, a fair complexion, dark hair, a full face and a small moustache. He was wearing a dark jacket and trousers, with a black peaked cap on his head. Because of the presence of Schwartz and/or the man with the pipe, or possibly due to the arrival several minutes later of Louis Diemshutz, who worked at the club as a steward, this time the killer didn't linger over his victim's body. He cut Elizabeth's throat, but her body wasn't mutilated in any way. Unfortunately for Catherine Eddowes, that meant the killer had unfinished business.

Catherine Eddowes, also known as Kate Kelly, was born in Wolverhampton on 14 April 1842. Her father was a tinplate worker and her mother a cook, and the family moved to London when Catherine was just one year old. She spent some of her childhood back in Wolverhampton and would eventually find work there as a tinplate stamper. Catherine was fired from that job and ran off to Birmingham, where she stayed with an uncle who made boots and shoes. This arrangement didn't work out, so she returned to Wolverhampton in 1861, where she met and set up home with a former soldier called Thomas Quinn. The couple had a son, moved to London, and three further children were born. However, Catherine's heavy drinking and fiery temperament seem to have been the cause of the relationship breaking down by 1880. She moved into a lodging house called Cooney's in Flower and Dean Street, where she met and started a relationship with John Kelly. He resolutely denied that Catherine was involved in sex work but admitted that she sometimes drank to excess – she was charged with being drunk and disorderly in September 1881.

On the day of her death, Catherine had again been drinking heavily enough to be arrested, by PC Louis Robinson at 8.30 p.m. She was taken to Bishopsgate police station to sleep it off. Just before one o'clock the following morning the station sergeant asked PC George Hutt to check if anyone could be released. Catherine was by now sober, so she was freed by Hutt, who asked her to shut the station door on her way out. 'All right. Good night, old cock,' she said as she walked into the early hours of the morning, just as Elizabeth Stride's body was being found.

Catherine seems to have gone in the opposite direction to Flower and Dean Street, and eventually she must have wandered into Mitre Square, where her body was found. By all accounts, the square was poorly lit, but the patrolling PC Watkins reported nothing unusual at 1.30 a.m. However, just five minutes later, a commercial traveller in the cigarette business named Joseph Lawende noticed a couple standing at the entrance of a passageway leading to the square. Lawende described a woman wearing clothes that matched those worn by Catherine that night. Strangely, at the inquest into Catherine's death he didn't give a description of the man who was with her, but *The Times* provided a brief pen picture, and the Home Office files contain a full description that can only have come from Lawende. Perhaps the police were trying to keep Lawende's information out of the public domain in the hope of using the intelligence he provided to trap the killer.

Catherine's body was discovered by PC Watkins when he

passed back through Mitre Square on his beat at 1.45 a.m. As he was later to tell the *Star* newspaper, Catherine had been 'ripped up like a pig in the market ... I have been in the force a long while, but I never saw such a sight.' The attack had been ferocious: her throat had been cut; after death her killer had mutilated her face and abdomen; her intestines had been cut out and placed over her right shoulder; and her left kidney and uterus had been removed. The damage to Catherine's face – the tip of her nose and her ear lobes had been cut off, and her cheeks slashed – was clearly deliberate. As Cornwell observes: 'The face is the person. To mutilate it is personal.' A search was made of the area near where Catherine's body was discovered, and some graffiti was found. This has again become part of Jack the Ripper folklore. It reportedly read, 'The Jews are the men that will not be blamed for nothing', but there's no way of knowing if this was connected to the murders or had been in existence for some time.

The last of the 'canonical five' was Mary Jane Kelly, also known as 'Black Mary', 'Ginger' and 'Marie Jeanette Kelly'. By far the youngest of the victims, her body was found at 13 Miller's Court, Dorset Street. Her murder was unusual because she wasn't murdered in public, and her extensive injuries indicate that the killer was able to spend some considerable time with Mary Jane's body after her death. More than any of the other murders, this one represents the ultimate expression of Jack the Ripper's hatred of his female victims. By the time of her death, Mary Jane would have been all too aware that there was a killer walking the streets of Whitechapel murdering prostitutes. However, she continued to sell sexual services, a simple fact that highlights the desperation of the young women who were involved in the sex industry in late Victorian Britain.

In his autobiography Walter Dew claimed that he knew Mary Jane by sight and said that most of her contemporaries would have described her as pretty. Born in Limerick, Ireland around 1863, she moved to Cardiff, where she first seems to have become involved in prostitution. Eventually she made her way to London. By April 1887, she was in a relationship with a porter called Joseph Barnett, but at the time of her murder their relationship had begun to cool, perhaps because Barnett disapproved of her work as a prostitute. As a result, Barnett lived apart from Mary Jane, who was renting a room in Miller's Court from a well-known East End pimp called John McCarthy.

There are several conflicting witness testimonies relating to when Mary Jane was last seen alive, and with whom she was seen entering Miller's Court. But there's no doubt about what happened to her after her death, as the police took photographs of both Mary Jane's body and the interior and exterior of 13 Miller's Court. Dew noted simply: 'There was little left of her, not much more than a skeleton. Her face was terribly scarred and mutilated.' Indeed, her ears, nose, cheeks and eyebrows had been partly removed. Dr Thomas Bond – who conducted Mary Jane's preliminary post-mortem at the crime scene – described the state of her body:

> The legs were wide apart, the left thigh at right angles to the trunk & the right forming an obtuse angle with the pubis. The whole surface of the abdomen & thighs was removed & the abdominal cavity emptied of its viscera. The breasts

were cut off, the arms mutilated by several jagged wounds & the face hacked beyond recognition of the features ... The viscera were found in various parts viz: the uterus & kidneys with one breast under the head, the other breast by the right foot, the liver between the feet, the intestines by the right side & the spleen by the left side of the body. The flaps removed from the abdomen & thighs were on a table ... the pericardium was open below & the heart absent.

When Mary Jane was buried ten days later at Shoreditch Church there were three large wreaths on her coffin, two crowns of artificial flowers and a cross that bore the words 'A last tribute of respect to Mary Kelly. May she rest in peace, and may her murderer be brought to justice.'

*

Today, if the police were faced with a series of murders such as these, there'd be a mass of DNA evidence available for analysis, fingerprints, CCTV footage and mobile phone records. The police would also be able to call on a range of experts, including profilers. The offence characteristics – how the crime was committed, why the victim was chosen and the manner in which the body was dismembered – would provide insight into the type of person that the offender was likely to be. In particular, a profiler would look at five areas: the crime scene; the nature of the attacks; forensic evidence; a medical examination of the victim; and, finally, the victim's characteristics.

In the case of Jack the Ripper I'd note that there was no evidence of sexual assault, and that he was 'act focused' – all of his victims were killed quickly. He didn't torture them while they were alive but, when he had time to be alone with a dead victim, he mutilated her abdomen and sometimes her face. He removed body parts and sometimes took other 'trophies', such as Mary Ann Nichols's ring. The mutilation of the abdomens has sexual overtones, but I'd suggest that Jack the Ripper wasn't sexually competent, and consequently was single. While he did murder several women who were involved in selling sex, his choice of victim doesn't seem to have stemmed from a desire to buy those services. Sex workers simply allowed him to get sufficiently close to commit his crimes. He committed most of his murders in the street, which meant that he often didn't have much opportunity to be alone with his dead victims for any length of time. As a result, he fully accomplished his goal only with Mary Jane Kelly, his final victim, whom he murdered indoors and so was able to mutilate at his leisure. He also never seemed to give much thought to his escape route, or indeed how he'd dispose of his victim's body. All of this suggests that he was a disorganised killer, who had no plan and merely sought out random opportunities to kill. When he did have the time to be alone with Mary Jane Kelly, the mutilation of her body was so comprehensive that her identity was virtually obliterated.

The timing of his attacks is also significant. They always occurred in the early hours of the morning on a Friday, Saturday or Sunday. This would suggest that he had some form of unskilled work that occupied him during the week, and no opportunity to be alone. In other words, it was only at the weekend that he was away from those who knew him, were related to him, or were living with him. All of the attacks occurred in a very narrow geographical area, which strongly suggests that he lived locally – he was too disorganised to travel any great distance. It seems reasonable to assume that he'd lodgings near to Buck's Row, where Mary Ann Nichols was killed. He undoubtedly had somewhere to return to after each attack, where he could clean himself and perhaps hide while the police conducted house-to-house searches.

Jack the Ripper was undoubtedly a white man of limited intelligence and education, under the age of forty-five. From the nature of his offences, it seems highly unlikely that he would've been interested in writing letters to the press. There's also no real evidence of any medical training or surgical knowledge in his crimes – he simply seems to have been curious about the internal organs of women. Finally, the nature of the murders he committed suggests that he was insane.

If we accept the broad parameters of this profile – which isn't far removed from others that have been conducted in the past – we can start to rule out some suspects. First, the prime suspect, James Maybrick, doesn't fit this profile in any way: he lived in Liverpool rather than locally; he was ill; he was older than the profile suggests; and he would've planned any attacks far more carefully than the man who was disturbed while murdering Elizabeth Stride and was seen with Catherine Eddowes. Whatever the truth about his diary – and in all likelihood it is a forgery – Maybrick is therefore a very unlikely candidate for Jack the Ripper. Nor, as I have indicated earlier in the chapter, should we 'close the case' and blame Walter Sickert. Even if he did write letters to the press claiming to be the Ripper, a profiler would suggest that such an action points more to his innocence than to his guilt.

So, having dismissed two of the principal suspects, who are

we left with? I'm keen to answer this question because it tells us so much about who we want a serial killer to be.

At least two people saw Jack the Ripper, and provided descriptions to the police: Israel Schwartz, who saw Elizabeth Stride being assaulted in Berner Street, and Joseph Lawende, who spotted Catherine Eddowes with her killer in Mitre Square. Their descriptions are remarkably similar. As we know, Schwartz recalled seeing a short, stocky thirty-year-old with a moustache, who was wearing a black cap with a peak. *The Times* reported that Lawende witnessed a man of shabby appearance, about thirty years of age, five feet nine inches tall, with a fair complexion and a small moustache, wearing a peaked grey cloth cap. The Home Office files relating to Lawende's description go into more detail (and knock an inch or two off the height, bringing it more in line with Schwartz's description): 'aged about thirty, five foot seven or eight, of fair complexion, with a fair moustache, of medium build, wearing a pepper-and-salt-coloured loose jacket, a grey cloth cap with peak of the same colour, and a reddish handkerchief tied in a knot around the neck, and having the appearance of a sailor'.

Based on these descriptions, Sir Robert Anderson outlined where the police's attention was focused:

> One did not need to be a Sherlock Holmes to discover that the criminal was a sexual maniac of a virulent type; that he was living in the immediate vicinity of the scenes of the murders; and that, if he was not living absolutely alone, his people knew of his guilt, and refused to give him up to justice. During my absence abroad the Police had made a house-to-house search for him, investigating the case of

every man in the district whose circumstances were such that he could go and come and get rid of bloodstains in secret. And the conclusion we came to was that he and his people were certain low-class Polish Jews; for it is a remarkable fact that people of that class in the East End will not give up one of their number to Gentile justice.

When his book was published, Anderson was criticised for the antisemitism of this passage, and he had to try to defend his observations in various newspapers and magazines. However, it does appear that he knew the identity of Jack the Ripper and, even acknowledging all the difficulties that now exist in being certain, I'm as convinced as I can be that he was correct. As we'll see, Anderson's problem comes not from the fact that he accuses a particular perpetrator but that he widens his point to imply that it would *always* and *only* be someone like this individual who was capable of serial murder. In other words, someone who was 'different', and not British.

Amid the controversy about Anderson's antisemitism, an even more significant passage was largely overlooked: 'the only person who had ever had a good view of the murderer unhesitatingly identified the suspect the instant he was confronted with him; but he refused to give evidence against him'.

In 1987 the so-called 'Swanson marginalia' were discovered and helped us to put a name to Jack the Ripper.

*

Chief Inspector Donald Swanson was placed in overall charge of the Whitechapel Murders inquiry in September 1888. He retired in 1903 but kept in touch with his former colleague Sir Robert Anderson, who later gave Swanson a presentation copy of his memoirs. At some point Swanson made a series of pencil comments in the margins, and of specific interest are those appended to the section quoted above, where he wrote: 'and after this identification which suspect knew, no other murder of this kind took place in London'. He also notes that 'this identification' took place at the 'Seaside Home where he had been sent by us with great difficulty in order to subject him to identification, and he knew he was identified'.

The 'Seaside Home' is presumed to be the Convalescent Police Seaside Home in Hove, which was opened in 1890. It seems that the police had a suspect and forced him to visit Hove, where he was officially identified, presumably by either Lawende or Schwartz. Swanson claims that this confrontation put an end to the murders because thereafter the suspect knew that he was being watched by the police. Further details are then given in the marginalia: 'in a very short time the suspect with his hands tied behind his back, he was sent to Stepney Workhouse and then to Colney Hatch and died shortly afterwards – Kosminski was the suspect – DSS'. Of course, if this is true – and we should note that Kosminski didn't die until 1919 – it answers a question that's often raised about Jack the Ripper: as he was never caught, why did the murders not continue into the 1890s?

Swanson's identification of Kosminski (no first name is given) brings us back to the confidential Macnaghten memorandum. In this, Macnaghten first states that 'no one ever saw the Whitechapel murderer' (which, of course, contradicts what has just been discussed), but then he mentions three people, 'any one of whom would have been more likely than Cutbush to have committed this series of murders': Montague Druitt, whom he describes as a doctor; Kosminski (like Swanson, Macnaghten doesn't include a first name); and, finally, Michael Ostrog. However, a generation of research has been able to demonstrate conclusively that neither Montague Druitt nor Michael Ostrog could have been Jack the Ripper. For example, although Druitt committed suicide in late 1888 and was in all likelihood insane, he seems to have taken his own life after being sacked from a teaching job at a school in Blackheath for sexual impropriety. While these issues make him an interesting suspect, his educational background and ability to hold down a job don't fit with the chaotic and disorganised behaviour of Jack the Ripper. We also know that Druitt had successfully represented the family business in court. None of this suggests the mental state of a man who had only recently obliterated Mary Jane Kelly. Whatever caused Druitt to take his own life, it seems unlikely that it was a result of his being a serial killer. Meanwhile, Ostrog was a career criminal who spent most of his life in prison for a series of opportunistic thefts. Nothing in his record suggests that he could display the type of violence that was perpetrated against the Ripper's victims, and Paul Begg goes as far as to say that 'it is a mystery is why anyone ever thought that he might have been [Jack the Ripper]'.

Macnaghten describes Kosminski as 'a Polish Jew, & resident in Whitechapel. This man became insane owing to many years' indulgence in solitary vices. He had a great hatred of women, especially of the prostitute class, & had strong homicidal tendencies; he was removed to a lunatic asylum about March 1889. There were many circs [sic] connected with this man which made him a strong suspect.'

*

Two primary sources – Anderson's autobiography and Swanson's marginalia – provide us with details about someone they strongly suspected of being Jack the Ripper. Allied to these we also have Macnaghten's memorandum. In effect all three tell the same story, even if the vague and often broad brush strokes that are employed jar as antisemitic. A Polish Jew living in the heart of the murder area who had people to look after him was responsible for the murders, and he was eventually committed to an asylum on account of his 'solitary vices' by his family in 1889. A thorough search of asylum records by the historian Martin Fido unearthed only one Kosminski who was admitted at this time – a young man named Aaron – and no one else with that surname has ever been located. So it's likely, although not certain, that this was Anderson and Swanson's suspect, although some of the details that each provides are at odds with historical records.

Aaron Kosminski was born in Poland in 1865 and came to England in 1882. He lived with his brother Woolf at 3 Sion Square, near Mulberry Street in Whitechapel. He was a barber, which would have given him access to various sharp instruments, Jewish and unmarried. In July 1890, and on the instruction of his brother, Kosminski was admitted to the Mile End Old Town Workhouse as a way of controlling his behaviour. The reason given was 'two years insane' – that is, since 1888 – with the cause being 'self abuse'. He was institutionalised for the rest of his life, dying in March 1919. Various medical notes catalogue Kosminski's time in several asylums, describing his 'mania', 'delusions', 'hallucinations' and 'incoherence'. One comments on Kosminski's belief that 'he is guided and his movements altogether controlled by an instinct that informs his mind'. Others record that he once threatened to kill his sister. When he was admitted to the Leavesden Asylum in April 1894, his next of kin was recorded as his mother, who was living at 63 New Street, off New Road in Whitechapel.

Unfortunately, the medical notes tell us little more about Kosminski, and they certainly don't provide an insight into his state of mind in 1888. They do suggest that he was incapable of looking after himself, and that his family could no longer cope with his mania, perhaps after he threatened to kill his sister. It's also worth pausing to consider the cause of his com-mittal – 'self-abuse', which clearly meant excessive (perhaps even public) masturbation. This would now be described as hypersexuality, known to the Victorians as 'satyriasis', and is characterised by an abnormal and compulsive need for fre-quent genital stimulation. However, no sexual or emotional satisfaction is ever gained by the sufferer, who may also suc-cumb to bipolar disorder during periods of mania.

This brings us back to the murder of Martha Tabram, and geo-profiling the sequence of murders. Martha had been soliciting on the night in question with her friend Mary Ann Connelly, aka 'Pearly Poll'. After Martha's murder Mary Ann reported to Commercial Street police station and gave an account of what they had been doing. She stated that she and Martha had been in the company of two soldiers – one a cor-poral, the other a private in the Guards – and that after a while she and Martha had gone their separate ways with their cli-ents. Mary Ann was confident that she would recognise both men if she saw them again. The police duly arranged to have guardsmen put on parade, but Mary Ann failed to identify any as the men with whom she and Martha had been spending time. Real efforts were made to discover who these soldiers might have been but, despite this, no one was ever identified. Of course, the soldiers could have closed ranks to protect one of their own, but there's another possibility too. We know that Aaron Kosminski lived with Woolf, and it doesn't seem too fanciful to suggest that perhaps, rather than two soldiers, Martha and Mary Ann had actually met the two brothers. Is it possible they merely suggested that they were soldiers and – as he was the most mentally stable – if Woolf did most of the talking, perhaps they could've kept up the charade? What's more, Sion Square is regularly identified as a geo-profiling 'hot-spot' when these crime scenes are analysed, and so rather than searching any number of army barracks, Sion Square would have been a much better place for the police to have conducted their house-to-house enquiries.

Was Aaron Kosminski Jack the Ripper? There's no way to be certain, although he was clearly a strong suspect at the time. He also fits our modern-day profile of Jack the Ripper, based on the crimes that he committed. Kosminski was sexually incompetent, insane and protected by people until they could do so no longer – just as Anderson had suggested. He also lived locally, which puts him in the same bracket as most serial killers. They're literally 'the bloke next door', rather than a prince, a famous artist or a Liverpudlian merchant who travelled to London to commit his crimes. We've tended not to notice that serial killers are embedded within our community, partly because, just like the 'Ripper industry' itself, the public's interest in serial killers has been built on and then maintained by myth and fantasy, with one wild hypothesis after another demanding our attention. However, a cold, rational look at the facts of these awful murders doesn't lead to a royal conspiracy or any other celebrity suspect, but rather to a disturbed, dangerous and anonymous immigrant living in the East End, who hated women.

Of course, Macnaghten's broader argument was that the killer couldn't possibly be British and that our problems stem from 'foreign' cultures with their different ways of behaving and acting – in this case 'low-class Polish Jews'. However, while serial killers might be psychologically different from the rest of us, they're really not glitches or anomalies but are instead part of our culture and society. 'Othering' their existence might offer some immediate consolation, for this mistakenly allows us to imagine that the source of our difficulties comes from somewhere else, rather than springing up closer to home. We can cover our eyes and close our ears and convince ourselves that Britain is a law-abiding and orderly place; that the 'British way of life' is peaceable and founded on reasonableness and civility. This somewhere else will change over the course of our time frame, although 'othering' our problems has remained a constant feature of our history and has thus helped to maintain a belief in where we live and who we are.

We can never be sure that Aaron Kosminski was Jack the Ripper, although it's of interest that he's named as such in the re-opened Chamber of Horrors at Madame Tussauds. We do, however, know the identities of his victims. Their stories reveal much about the risky nature of the lives being led by working-class women in late Victorian times, and how easy it was for them to slip from relative comfort to abject squalor.

The lives of Mary Ann Nichols and Annie Chapman changed dramatically when maintenance payments from their former husbands stopped. Their lives, and those of the Ripper's other victims, became dominated by the need to earn fourpence for a bed for the night, a task made even more difficult by their addiction to alcohol. This dependence also brought them into contact with the police and, even if she was not a sex worker, Catherine Eddowes had been arrested just before her murder because of what we would now call 'problem drinking'. In fact, all six were problem drinkers, and some of them were clearly alcoholic. Selling sexual services provided some of them with the means to keep their bodies and souls together, with just enough left over to buy more alcohol. Each of them, to borrow a phrase used by Patricia Cornwell, probably 'led a life of lies' in order to hide the desperation of a reality that kept some of them still working the streets, even when they knew there was a killer on the loose.

Six women's need to make money to feed an addiction made them vulnerable to attack by a serial killer. That's a pattern that has been repeated many times over the last 130 years, most dramatically in Ipswich in 2006. Homelessness and alcohol would be replaced there by heroin and crack,[20] but the simple need to earn enough cash for the next drink, or fix, and to find a bed for the night creates a sad and desperate connection between those who died at the hands of the Ripper and those who would become victims in the years that followed. Even in 2006 there were initially widespread rumours that the killer had to be a foreign lorry driver making his way through Ipswich to the ports of Felixstowe or Harwich, rather than someone who was in fact living in the heart of the town's red-light district. People continued to see local problems as coming from elsewhere and, in doing so, they could cling to a myth that we really are a 'green and pleasant land', where people respect the rule of law, and our bobbies are the best in the world. These myths existed before Jack the Ripper started to kill and they'd continue to be recycled by the mass media, popular entertainment and politics in the years after 1888.

CHAPTER TWO

Cases Two and Three

The Murder of Maud Clifford, 1914, and the Murders Committed by George Joseph Smith, 1912–14

[T]he wife is the actual bondservant of her
husband ... She can do no act whatever but by
his permission, at least tacit. She can acquire
no property but for him; the instant it becomes
hers, even if by inheritance, it becomes ipso facto
his. In this respect the wife's position under the
common law of England is worse than that of
slaves in the laws of many countries.

JOHN STUART MILL,
The Subjection of Women (1869)

T he philosopher John Stuart Mill's observation that the law
of England made the position of women 'worse than that

of slaves' seems like an exaggeration – a florid phrase designed simply to grab attention. It wasn't, and this chapter examines the cases of two men who exploited this dependent status to kill four women. Like the murderer in our first chapter, George Smith was a serial killer – in other words, he killed three or more of his victims in a period which exceeded thirty days, with a cooling-off period between each murder. His unique criminal 'signature' was to drown a new wife when she was having a bath. However, the first case that I consider involved a military veteran who killed his estranged wife in more prosaic circumstances – during a weekend in Brighton, just weeks before the outbreak of the First World War. What was supposed to be a holiday to patch things up didn't work out that way.

*

Percy Clifford was eighteen years old when he volunteered to join the Imperial Yeomanry in 1901. He became a private in the 94th Company (Metropolitan Mounted Rifles) and then went off to fight in South Africa. We don't know why Clifford enlisted – perhaps simply for adventure, the money, or feeling that he wanted to be part of something bigger than the life that he led in London. He was the son of a Jamaican immigrant called Albert Clifford, who'd come to England in 1871, originally to work as a valet, and who two years later married a dressmaker called Ellen Pennifold. They'd go on to have eight children, including Percy. At the time this young man of mixed heritage volunteered to go and fight for the empire, he was working as an electrician. We know that he was five feet six inches tall, and was described as a man of 'ordinary physique and intelligence'.

Historians are never too certain what to call the conflict

that began when Queen Victoria was still on the throne in October 1899 and ended in May 1902, well over a year after her death. Was this conflict the 'Boer War', the 'second Boer War' or the 'South African War'? They're more certain that it wasn't a 'good war',[1] and that Britain's role was soaked in blood and controversy, including the use of concentration camps. The war seemed to cap an era of Victorian imperialism, which saw Britain greedily covet access to and control over the newly discovered diamond and gold mines in the two independent Boer states, the Southern African Republic and the Orange Free State. The war was politically divisive even at the time, with so-called 'jingos' like Joseph Chamberlain on one side, and pro-Boer anti-imperialists, such as David Lloyd George, on the other.

In any event, Clifford's military career was brief. He was shot in the right arm and left foot, after the train that he was travelling on was ambushed in July 1901. He was sent to hospital to recover, but his wounds were deemed serious enough for him to be declared medically unfit for any further military service and so he was invalided out of the army.[2]

On his return to England Clifford tried his hand as a cab driver. However, perhaps because of the residual pain from his injuries, he left this work and attempted to become a bookkeeper. That too seems to have fallen through, and Clifford found himself serving a prison sentence for 'brothel keeping'. A brothel was at this time defined as a place where more than one woman practised prostitution or was suspected of doing so. This was a rather loose description and one which painted a very different picture from the large and organised brothels that W. T. Stead had conjured up in 'The Maiden Tribute of

Modern Babylon', with the pimps and madams intent on the exploitation of young girls. And, as the historian Professor Julia Laite has argued, the looseness of the definition of what constituted a brothel resulted in many women being made homeless, and the 'crucial safety networks between women in the sex industry, built on shared accommodation and mutual support, were eroded'.[3]

Clifford lived initially with a woman called Susan Hughes. They had a baby together, although the child – a boy – died in infancy. It was Susan who introduced Clifford to Maud Walton, who was eight years his junior and had a minor criminal record. There's some suggestion that Maud's family – specifically her mother and her sister – may have been involved in selling sexual services and that Maud also occasionally worked as a prostitute. Clifford and Maud married in 1911, and while they did seem to love one another their relationship was rocky and characterised by arguments and separations. Clifford was jealous and suspicious of Maud and at times ashamed of her. By 1913, they had separated and were living apart.

At the beginning of April 1914, Clifford and Maud appear to have been trying to arrange some sort of reconciliation, deciding to spend a long weekend together in Brighton. Clifford bought two return train tickets and organised lodgings near the station, on North Road. Maud also had a new dress to wear for the occasion. On one of the evenings they were in Brighton they visited a friend of Clifford's, where they all enjoyed a drink. On return to their lodgings Clifford told the boarding-house owners that he and his wife were having 'a jovial time', and then asked for tea to be brought up to their room in the morning. This was duly delivered and left outside the door. Maud called out 'thank you' from behind the door, although the tea was still there around noon. Two loud bangs were also heard at noon, although the boarding-house owner initially put this down to a car backfiring on the road. Eventually the owners went into the room and found the couple lying on the bed, each with a bullet wound to the head. Maud was dead, but Clifford was still conscious.

He was taken to the Royal Sussex County Hospital and was in a coma for ten days, with the bullet lodged in his skull.

The Brighton Police arrested him for Maud's murder. In court, Clifford presented a defence of insanity. He claimed to have been driven mad with shame by rumours that his wife had been with other men, and a letter that was found in their room, addressed to Maud's mother Augusta Walton, stated:

I am on the verge of distraction. I have found out that Maud is playing with three men, besides myself. That must not happen. She has told the most awful lies about everything. Bury us together. I have no regrets because I have lived my life. You must show this to the coroner.

This defence wasn't accepted and, of course, we only have Clifford's word that Maud was behaving in this way – claims that were vehemently denied by her mother. In fact, Mrs Walton argued that it was Clifford who had been acting as Maud's pimp and that he'd coerced her into sex work to provide him with an income. Clifford was hanged on 11 August 1914, by which time Britain was at war once again.

*

I've spent a little time outlining the details of Percy Clifford's murder of his wife Maud as it raises several issues that are of interest, as well as posing a few criminological questions. Was this murder premeditated, for example, and therefore the trip to Brighton had been carefully planned by Clifford so as to carry out the murder? If that was the case, why buy two return train tickets? Should we view this as an example of what we'd now call 'murder-suicide'? Or as a form of 'family annihilation' – disappointed by how his relationship has turned out, Clifford attempts to manage his feelings by annihilating what he saw as the source of the disappointment that he felt not just about his family but about his life more generally.

This case particularly highlights matters related to masculinity and race – two themes that run throughout the book. Clifford was of mixed heritage and had married a white woman. This was something that was repeatedly mentioned in press accounts of the trial and used as a form of 'othering' him and his 'dangerous sexuality', at a time when there were still widespread fears about black men and 'white slavery'.[4] Clifford was also executed and was therefore one of the fifty-six ethnic minority men hanged in Britain in the twentieth century. This equates to 5 per cent of those who received the death penalty, at a time when less than 1 per cent of the British population were from ethnic minorities.

Clifford's story therefore throws some light on the experience of being black or mixed heritage in the Victorian and Edwardian era, long before the 'Windrush generation' of black immigrants started to arrive in Britain after the end of the Second World War. He had fought in the 'white man's war' in South Africa, although we simply have no evidence why

Clifford wanted to do so, or even if he viewed the conflict in this way. However, it's interesting that this wartime service on behalf of the state, which had seen him wounded in action, wasn't enough to ensure clemency after he'd been sentenced to death.

The second issue that Clifford's story illustrates relates to masculinity and how that was expected to be performed. Having previously been convicted of keeping a brothel, this looks like evidence that not only challenged the expectation of what men did to earn money, but also of monogamy and what it meant to be married. There were dangers here for Maud. Simply by marrying, a woman's legal existence was surrendered under the common-law doctrine of coverture – literally, 'to be hidden' – to the legal personality of her husband. A married woman couldn't sue or be sued unless her husband was also party to the suit; she couldn't sign a contract unless her husband joined her; nor could she make a valid will unless her husband agreed to its contents.

A husband also assumed legal rights over his wife's property, as well as any property that she subsequently inherited. Even a wife's personal possessions – including all her clothing and any money that she might have saved or earned – passed entirely to her husband. Furthermore, a woman's body was held to belong to her husband, and it was only in 1891 that a High Court ruling denied a husband the right to imprison his wife in pursuit of his conjugal rights. The husband decided where the couple should live, often taking his new bride away from her family and friends, how their children should be brought up and virtually every other aspect of their relationship. Most men saw nothing wrong with these 'rights', even if John Stuart Mill thought that this was one of 'the chief hindrances to human improvement'.

Clifford himself might be seen as having been 'living off' his wife – 'poncing' – rather than earning his own income. If Maud was indeed also selling sexual services for herself, she was also denying her husband access to the money she made – money that was legally his, and which might have been a motive for the murder. By refusing to allow herself and her earnings to be controlled by Clifford, Maud was asserting her independence and her ability to manage her own affairs. Had he bought the two return train tickets because he expected to have persuaded, or coerced, Maud to start working for him again? Whatever the truth of the matter, given that work defined what it meant to be 'respectable' and served to shape gender roles, Clifford can be seen to have failed: he was disreputable both as a man and as a provider; and his wife – whether she was selling sexual services or not – was behaving in ways that challenged the legal expectations of her role in relation to her husband.

One final criminological truism is confirmed by this case: husbands have throughout modern British history killed their wives, as the next sequence of murders is going to demonstrate all too tragically.

*

When George Joseph Smith proposed marriage to Edith Pegler in July 1908, he was already a convicted bigamist and fraudster. Edith was charmed by his proposal but would soon discover that her new fiancé roamed around the country, ostensibly on business, and he asked her to only communicate with him through the Woolwich Equitable Building Society.

Smith was always restless and didn't want to stay for too long in the same town or city. Edith dutifully moved with him from one place to another – from Bristol to Bedford, then to Luton, Southend-on-Sea, Croydon, Walthamstow, Tunbridge Wells and Bath. After they'd set up home, Smith would once more leave Edith by herself and go off again. On his return, Smith would entertain Edith with stories of his money-making schemes. He claimed that he bought and sold Chinese figurines, oil paintings and jewellery, and then pumped the profits into property. Sometimes he would bring her clothes, and warned her that baths were dangerous for women, especially ones with weak hearts.

When Edith was eventually cross-examined at her husband's trial in June 1915 for the murder of three 'wives' – the true source of his income – she denied having any knowledge of these other women. And, when she was asked, almost incredulously, 'You went back to him when he asked you to go back?' she simply replied, 'Yes.'

Edith's straightforward response reflects the legal and social position of women at the turn of the twentieth century. The Married Women's Property Acts of 1870 and 1882 had made a small attempt to redress the balance, but women were still denied the right to vote, they couldn't join most professions and they had very limited access to higher education, all of which left them under pressure to 'marry well'.[5] The average wage for a working-class single woman was well below subsistence level. Legal rules, social convention and the dominant economic structure conspired to force women into marriage and then ensured that they'd be entirely dependent upon their husbands. In 1871 nearly 90 per cent of women between the ages of forty-five and forty-nine were or had been married. So, Edith Pegler remained with Smith because she'd no other option in a hierarchical culture that was dominated by men – some of whom turned the 'civil death' that came with marriage into actual mortality. Power and privilege still rested firmly with men, half a century after John Stuart Mill had called for 'perfect equality'.

Smith had a few tricks up his sleeve to keep the real nature of his business secret from Edith. He used several aliases, at various times calling himself 'George Love', 'George Rose', 'Henry Williams', 'Charles Oliver James' and 'John Lloyd'. His geographic transience had an instrumental purpose as moving from town to town helped him avoid detection. These relocations never amounted to more than a few hundred miles, but just by crossing a county boundary, and therefore moving into a different police force area, Smith was able to leave behind the murders which had been committed when he was using a false name.

Bigamy was central to how Smith trapped women and was a tactic that he'd developed over time. For example, he legally married Beatrice Thornhill in Leicester in January 1898, but less than a year later he married an unidentified 'Miss' in London. Thereafter he spent two years in prison, prior to marrying Edith Pegler in Bristol in 1908. At least that marriage was legal (by then, Smith had divorced Beatrice Thornhill, although we don't know what happened to 'Miss'), and he'd remain officially married to Edith for the rest of his life. Nevertheless, on 17 September 1914 Smith married Alice Reavil, a domestic servant whom he'd met in Bournemouth only nine days previously. Alice's story, which she told at

Smith's trial,[6] graphically demonstrates the speed with which he worked, what he hoped to gain and how devastated his victims were on discovering his fraud – if they survived.

> On 7 or 8 September I was in the gardens on the front, sitting on a seat, when a man came and spoke to me ... We had some conversation, in which he said he admired my figure. After an hour's conversation, in which he informed me he was an artist, and had £2 per week from some land in Canada, he made an appointment for 6 p.m. the same evening. I met him as arranged; he did not tell me where he was staying; I never knew. Next day I met him as arranged, and he then told me his name was 'Charles Oliver James'. He said he had been to Canada and his agents sent him money. He also said he understood I had some money. I met him every evening ... after the third or fourth day of our acquaintance he asked me to marry him, and I consented, and he said he would put his money with mine and he would open an antique shop ... he asked how much money I had, and I said about £70 odd, and some furniture, including a piano. He asked me to sell them, and I decided to ... We went to the registry office and were married by special licence.

It's worth pausing here to assess Smith's methods in more detail, and to reflect on the wider significance of what Alice described. Note the lies that Smith told – starting with his name, but also his claims that he had a regular income, that he was an artist and that he had entrepreneurial ambitions. An antique shop must have seemed aspirational to Alice, as would stories of Canada and the agents who sent Smith his fictitious weekly income. However, all the talk of money was designed merely to get Alice to reveal details of her own savings and property. It was just a few days before Smith turned the conversation to marriage. He was what we'd now call 'love bombing'. The speed with which the proposal was accepted surely reflects the importance of marriage for a woman locked in a hierarchical, paternal culture. Nor did Alice hesitate to sell her piano and other possessions, because being married was far more important than mere belongings. Having sold everything she owned, she raised just £14 – the equivalent of about £1,000 today.

Alice continued her story with details of what happened after she married Smith:

We ... went to 8 Hafer Road, Battersea Rise [in London] where he had taken two furnished rooms ... on the way he showed me a lot of bank notes, and he asked me for my £14 to put in the bank with his. I gave it to him. When we got to our lodgings ... he produced a post office withdrawal form for me to fill up to draw all my money from the bank. I filled it up, and added, 'with interest to close account', and we went out together to post it ... he put it in the box. All my clothing was at this address, and was kept in four boxes ... On 21 September we went to the post office, Lavender Hill, to obtain the money ... he told me to ask for all £1 notes, but they gave me four £10 notes and two £5 notes, and the remainder in £1 notes and cash. In all I received £76 6s and some coppers. He picked up the notes and the cash – the odd six shillings. I never saw the notes again.

Alice explained that they returned to their lodgings and paid the bill with a view to moving on to new premises the following day. Smith also arranged for their newly packed assets to be taken to a locker in Clapham station. At Smith's trial, Alice related what happened the following morning:

On 22 September we left the house . . . we got on a tramcar, and on the way he spoke of Halifax, Nova Scotia, and asked me if I would like to go. He took some penny fares, and we got off at some gardens. We walked through the gardens, and on getting to the other end he said he was going to the lavatory, and asked me to wait. I did so and waited about an hour. He did not return, so I returned to 8 Hafer Road, and found the attached telegram waiting for me. [It read, 'Wait home for letter. Next post – James.']

The letter was clearly designed to stop Alice going to the police. Obviously, she would have feared that something had happened to Smith, but the letter eased her concerns and, more importantly, gave him the opportunity to escape. While Alice waited for the post, Smith travelled to Clapham Station and removed all of their possessions. He then returned to Edith Pegler in Bristol, where he gave his ever-loyal wife Alice's trousseau.

Alice sadly concluded her evidence:

The result of my meeting with [the] prisoner was that I was left with only a few shillings and the clothes I was actually wearing. What he had taken consisted of the whole of my life's savings.

However, she must soon have realised she was lucky. She could easily have been murdered, as she had met Smith in the middle of his killing cycle. By that stage he'd already claimed the lives of two women – Bessie Mundy and Alice Burnham – and shortly after running out on Alice he would murder a third, called Margaret Lofty.

*

Smith married Bessie Mundy on 26 August 1910 and killed her in July 1912. Of the three murders he committed, this first one is perhaps the most tragic, because it reveals something of the desperation of women in Bessie's position in Edwardian England. She was thirty-three in 1910, living comfortably in Weymouth on the proceeds of some £2,500 left in trust for her by her father, who'd been a bank manager. Bessie received her income from the trustees, headed by her uncle, who sent her eight pounds a week. Smith, styling himself Henry Williams, told Bessie that he was a thirty-five-year-old bachelor and a picture restorer. Interestingly, Smith regularly presented himself as a painter, or as involved in the art world in some capacity. He might have thought this afforded him some cachet, or perhaps he concluded that it allowed him to breach normal social conventions so he could swiftly become intimate with his intended victim. It certainly worked in this case, as Smith quickly gained Bessie's confidence, and they married soon after their first meeting. On their wedding day he instructed a local solicitor called Wilkinson (who would give evidence at the trial) to request a copy of the trust's papers from the Mundys' family solicitor. However, the trust had been set up well and Smith apparently couldn't find a way to get his hands on his new wife's inheritance. Consequently, he had to make do with what Bessie had in the bank – about £150. Just over two weeks after their marriage, he absconded from Weymouth. It would be almost two years before Bessie met her husband again.

In a remarkable coincidence, they were both in Weston-Super-Mare in spring 1912. Bessie was staying at a local boarding house called Norwood House, which was owned by a friend of her aunt, Mrs Sarah Tuckett. On 14 March Bessie went out to buy some flowers and en route she spotted her missing husband looking out to sea. Of course, an alternative reading is that this meeting was no coincidence. Smith might have devised a way to access Bessie's trust fund, then found out where she was staying and travelled there to be 'discovered' by her. Whatever the truth, he had some explaining to do about why he'd left Weymouth – an abandonment that must have caused Bessie severe embarrassment. The reunited couple visited a local solicitor, with the wonderful name of Wadsworth Burrow Lillington, of Baker and Company, on the day of their chance meeting. Years later, Lillington provided some details of Smith's smooth talking at the trial:

> He began by informing me that he had been for some time seeking his wife, and that he had that day casually met her in the street. He then explained to me the circumstances in which he alleged he had left his wife in Weymouth. He said that he believed at the time, although it had subsequently proved to be incorrect, that he had contracted a contagious disease, that he feared to communicate it to his wife, and that therefore he thought it better that he should leave her.

It's impossible to say whether Bessie believed this story to be true, or if she merely wanted to believe it, but she was sufficiently convinced to take him back, in spite of the obvious implication in Smith's statement that at the time of their marriage he'd contracted a venereal disease. Having made his confession, Smith asked Lillington to write to Bessie's uncle in the hope of establishing better relations between them, and the solicitor duly did so.

At the trial, Lillington was asked to describe Bessie's demeanour during this meeting. He replied that she was in the 'assenting manner':

> I should say that she had very little indeed to say, except that she did reply to any question that I put to her. I think she volunteered the statement that she had forgiven the past.

Bessie's 'assenting manner', her reluctance to speak unless spoken to and her forgiving nature were all esteemed qualities of the idealised wife in early twentieth-century Britain. They're also perfectly consistent with the doctrine of coverture – Bessie's (supposed) husband had certain rights over her that were upheld by the law of the land. The fact that they went to a solicitor on the day of their apparently coincidental meeting suggests that Smith was fully aware of these rights, and it explains why Lillington did very little to challenge such an incredible story.

Of course, Bessie could have behaved differently. She didn't have to give Smith the benefit of the doubt. But as a middle-class woman schooled in the mores of Edwardian culture, she had to try to make her marriage work, even though that marriage was to a man she hadn't seen for nearly two years. Bessie's landlady, however, was much less forgiving of Smith: Mrs Tuckett was far from impressed by him, his return, or any explanation that he offered. She also telegraphed Bessie's aunt to inform her of what had happened. Reading between the lines, she'd clearly tried to stop Bessie leaving with Smith. Mrs Tuckett and Smith seem to have had an argument, and Smith had then used it as a pretext to move on. Bessie said, 'I suppose I may go with my husband,' to which Mrs Tuckett had reluctantly replied, 'I cannot hold you back, you are thirty.'

Mrs Tuckett never saw Bessie again, although Smith wrote to her the following day. In his letter he mentioned the 'heated argument' that had taken place, and said that, 'for the sake of peace', he and Bessie had left. The letter continued:

> All I propose to state at present beside that which has already been stated by Bessie and myself before the solicitors that it is useless *as the law stands* [emphasis added], and in view of all the circumstances, together with the affinity existing between my wife and self, for any person to try and part us, and dangerous to try and do us harm or to try and do us harm or endeavour to make our lives miserable ... Bessie shall soon have a settled, comfortable home and be happy with me. I trust there are many, many years of happiness before us.

Here again we detect Smith's familiarity with the law; he knew how it protected him as a husband. There are also some obvious threats, which indicate that Smith was dangerous as well as educated.

The couple moved to Herne Bay in Kent, on the other side of the country, where Smith took further legal advice about Bessie's trust fund. Counsel's opinion was sent to him on 2 July 1912. It suggested that if mutual wills were made – each favouring the other – then Bessie's fund would come to Smith if she died, and he survived her. This amounted to Bessie's death warrant. A mere five days after the wills were drawn up, on 13 July, Bessie was found drowned in her bath. By the end of the year Smith was in possession of all of her estate.

Smith would kill two more 'wives': Alice Burnham, whom he married on 4 November 1913 and who was dead just over five weeks later; and Margaret Lofty, whom he married on 17 December 1914 and murdered the following day. As is obvious from this timeline, the frequency of Smith's crimes increased as he became a more competent murderer – a trend that can be found with most serial killers. The time between 'marriage' and murder also decreased markedly: Bessie was killed after nearly two years, Alice survived for only five weeks and Margaret was murdered within a few days of her wedding. This shouldn't be taken as evidence that Smith preferred Alice to Margaret but simply indicates that he needed more time to extract money from her family.

Alice was twenty-five years old when she married Smith. She lived in Aston Clinton in Buckinghamshire, where her father Charles was a fruit grower. A stout but healthy woman, she worked as a nurse. Her family didn't like Smith, although no precise reason is given for their hostility in the trial papers, which merely state that Charles thought Smith was 'evil' and didn't like his behaviour. As a result of the family's opposition, Smith and Alice travelled to Southsea, and they were married in Portsmouth register office. This time, Smith used his own name on the marriage certificate. The day before the wedding he'd insured Alice's life for five hundred pounds – although the relevant paperwork was not completed until 4 December – and four days after that she made a will in favour of her husband. Smith also started to demand money from the Burnham family.

Charles had given Alice a promissory note for a hundred pounds, to be paid on her marriage, and Smith now set out to obtain this money. However, Charles didn't give in easily, so Smith wrote to his new father-in-law complaining of his 'obdurateness, contempt and remorse' and asking 'what earthly right have you to scorn your daughter in these ways?' It seems that Charles had previously written to Alice to suggest that Smith shouldn't be given access to the promissory note. But Smith was having none of it: 'It is mentioned in the letter Alice received on the 11th instant that as I have an income – the £100 and interest should stand over. A more foolish and illegal action I have never heard. The money is payable on demand, failing which I will take the matter up myself without further delay.'

Nevertheless, Charles still delayed giving Smith any money, which infuriated his son-in-law. He also made enquiries into Smith's background, approaching a Mr Redhead of Horwood and James Solicitors to see if he could establish anything about Smith's past. Having got wind of this, Smith wrote to Charles on 24 November, sarcastically claiming: 'my mother was a Buss horse, my father a Cab-driver, my sister a rough-rider over the arctic regions – my brothers were all gallant sailors on a steamroller'. Three days later he wrote again, this time with more menace: 'I do not know your next move but take my advice and be careful.'

Meanwhile, Alice had written to her father to ask him to release the money as promised. Charles finally relented, perhaps because of Alice's request but more likely because Smith had the law on his side and would surely win any court case brought on the matter. In his evidence at Smith's trial, Charles explained: '[on the] advice of my solicitor I drew up a cheque for the money which I owed to my daughter'. This was cashed on 1 December 1913. Eleven days later, Alice was found dead in her bathtub in Blackpool, where the pair had moved from Southsea.

His final victim was thirty-eight-year-old Margaret Lofty, who married Smith just over a year later in Bath. On their marriage certificate Smith used the name 'John Lloyd' and claimed he was a land agent. Margaret's father was the Reverend Fitzroy Fuller Lofty, who had died in 1892, leaving a widow, a son and two other daughters. She worked as a companion to elderly ladies in cathedral cities but clearly aspired to a better life through marriage. However, she had been disappointed in love the year before she met Smith, when she discovered that the man she was courting already had a wife.

Perhaps this goes some way towards explaining Margaret's eagerness to engage with Smith. She seems to have guessed that her mother and sisters wouldn't have approved of him, so they married clandestinely. By the time of the ceremony, Smith had already persuaded Margaret to take out a life assurance policy with the Yorkshire Insurance Company in Bristol for the sum of seven hundred pounds.

The newly married couple immediately left Bath for

London, where Smith had booked rooms in Highgate. The next morning Margaret visited a firm of solicitors in Islington to make her will, in which she bequeathed everything to her new husband. Later she withdrew all of her savings from the Muswell Hill post office. That evening she took a bath.

Death by drowning in their baths of three brides in as many years produced sympathetic notices in various regional newspapers. However, the relatives and friends of Smith's first victim – as well as Sir Arthur Conan Doyle – were suspicious of the supposedly grieving husband, and they took their concerns to the police. Smith's money-making scheme began to unravel as several forces finally put two and two together, and he was eventually arrested on 1 February 1915. The more sensational press noted that he seemed to possess 'mysterious powers' and at his trial 'women thronged round him in the dock ... at the Old Bailey the police had special instructions to make it as difficult as possible for women to be present'. He was executed seven months later at HMP Maidstone.

The voluminous descriptions of Smith and his *modus operandi* paint a picture of personal responsibility, centring on the 'mysterious powers' he supposedly used to seduce women. However, Smith is merely a grotesque reflection of late Victorian and Edwardian British culture. These 'mysterious powers' weren't unique to him, but commonly enshrined in the law, custom and practice of the times. To achieve his ends, Smith had been obliged to deal with male lawyers, insurance and estate agents, bankers and a host of other professionals. Yet none of these highly educated men thought that his actions and demands were unusual or suspicious. Wadsworth Burrow Lillington, for example, carried out his client's instructions to the letter, despite the fantastic nature of the story he'd just been told. Moreover, Smith himself was fully aware of his legal rights in relation to his wives' property, and he wasted no opportunity to inform others of those rights if the situation demanded it – as it had with Charles Burnham.

Smith's 'mysterious powers', which is of course another form of 'othering', were simply the ruthless exercise of authority based on gender and marital status. Most single women, especially those past the normal 'marrying age', couldn't afford to ignore the attentions of a suitor, no matter how recently they'd met, nor how obsessively interested he seemed to be in her finances. It could be argued it was exactly what was expected of a soon-to-be husband at this time.

*

Precisely how these three women came to be drowned in their baths was a matter of speculation for several years. The record of Smith's trial states simply that he'd used 'certain means' to drown them, and no elaboration is offered. Perhaps it was feared that publishing details of how he'd come to kill might have encouraged others to commit what we'd now call 'copycat' crimes. However, the authorities knew only too well how Smith had managed to drown these women without leaving any tell-tale bruising which, at first, made it appear as if they'd died as a result of a tragic accident. This understanding was established through a series of experiments undertaken in early 1915 by the forensic pathologist Bernard Spilsbury and Detective Inspector Arthur Neil.

Spilsbury, the 'father of forensics', was the Home Office's legendary pathologist. He first came to prominence in 1910, with his work demonstrating that Dr Hawley Crippen had indeed murdered his wife Cora and then buried her remains in the cellar of their house prior to fleeing across the Atlantic with his lover. Even though the remains didn't include a head, limbs or bones, Spilsbury proved that they nonetheless bore the mark of an ovariectomy scar that linked them to Cora.[7] It was enough to convict Crippen. Almost singlehandedly Spilsbury invented the role of expert witness and, like a real-life Sherlock Holmes, seemed able to crack the most intractable cases by transporting forensic science 'from the mortuary to the front page',[8] convincing juries that he'd not only worked out 'who dunnit' but also how.

In Smith's case, using a nurse in a bathing suit as their guinea pig, Spilsbury and Neil discovered that if they pulled her ankles in the air while she was sitting in the bath, her head would quickly slip under the water and she couldn't move. This meant that she wouldn't be able to thrash about, which might have left some tell-tale marks on her hands or arms. The rush of water resulted in vagal inhibition, and it was this which caused their sudden deaths – the vagus nerve runs from the brain through the face and thorax and into the abdomen. This experiment was so 'successful' that it took several minutes of artificial respiration before Neil and Spilsbury were able to revive the poor nurse.

The British public's continuing fascination with forensic science – from long-running drama shows like *Silent Witness* to the many and varied documentaries focusing on forensic teams – more than likely has its roots in the work of Spilsbury which came to public notice during this era.

*

There are a number of other legacies from this period, and from the Boer War specifically, that continue over our time frame. These would include the creation of the popular reputation of Winston Churchill, who covered the war as a correspondent for the *Morning Post* and in which role he was captured and imprisoned by the Boers, eventually to escape in controversial circumstances. Churchill and his ongoing place in the British imagination, which would be cemented during the Second World War, was fashioned at this time when new heroes were being created to carry the story of Britain. So too the founding of the Union of South Africa in 1910 – essentially a white union, which excluded black people from power and was a self-governing dominion of the British Empire – seemed to reflect more generally a prevailing attitude towards Britain's colonies and the people who lived there. Closer to home, we can see what might be called an Edwardian 'social imperialism', which saw the creation of the Boy Scout movement and ushered in reforms aimed at improving the lot of the conscripts and volunteers who'd fought in the war. It did this by creating a favourable political climate so as to introduce free school meals, maternity benefits and health insurance. Today we might describe this as 'levelling up'.

Even the horrors of the concentration camps used by the British during the Second Boer War, and which had been castigated in the press by the Quaker Emily Hobhouse, seemed to have little discernible effect on liberal consciences. The government set up the Fawcett Commission to investigate the claims, although Hobhouse was roundly criticised at the time for daring to suggest that the British could behave with anything but civility.[9]

The idea of British fair play and reasonableness rather than

cruelty and sadism is of course one of our foundational narratives – a story that we like to tell about ourselves, and how
the British Empire was administered. As recently as 2020, a
YouGov poll showed that more than 30 per cent of those sur-
veyed were 'proud' of what the British Empire had achieved
and only 19 per cent were 'ashamed'.[10] In the end, the Fawcett
Commission concluded that Hobhouse had indeed been
telling the truth. That did not prevent the then Conservative
MP Jacob Rees-Mogg remarking on BBC 1's *Question Time*
in February 2019 that Boer families had been put in concentration camps for their 'own protection', as opposed to being
part of a deliberate policy of weakening the Boers' resolve to
fight. He also suggested that the mortality rate in the camps
was comparable to that in Glasgow at the time.

Of course, British armies were able to spend time in Africa,
the West Indies and Asia only after it had become possible to
stop the spread of a variety of tropical diseases, such as ma-
laria. These medical and scientific advancements could also
be used to help indigenous populations, and in all of this we
see the moral justification for empire being advanced. As one
academic has put it, 'It implied that scientific insights could
be redeployed to promote superior health, hygiene and sani-
tation among colonial subjects. Empire was therefore seen as
a benevolent, selfless project.'[11] We still like to think that our
empire was peaceful and compassionate – 'the white man's
burden'; it brought 'civilisation' to places which had been 'wild
and unruly'; it made healthy those people who'd once been
sick. Perhaps Percy Clifford, a working-class Briton of mixed
heritage, believed in that foundational myth too.

*

Myths abhor nuance and thrive on dividing things up into black and white, good and evil; they're sensitive to even the mildest of criticisms. Developments associated with DNA, for example, are usually viewed as an uncomplicated success story in the fight against crime, but is that fair, or just another myth which has become attached to forensic science in general and 'DNA fingerprinting' specifically?

DNA fingerprinting has been used by the state to justify the establishment of the UK National DNA Database (NDNAD), which was set up in 1995 and is now one of the largest and oldest DNA databases in the world, holding more than seven million profiles. There have been various controversies concerning the NDNAD, but of particular interest here is that by 2007, 40 per cent of black men had their DNA profile on the database, compared to just 13 per cent of Asian men and 9 per cent of white men.[12] Two years later the government's own Human Genetics Commission acknowledged that 'the profiles of over three quarters of young black men between the ages of 18 and 35 are recorded'.[13] This is always justified on the basis of fighting crime, but what evidence is there to back this up?

A 2019 analysis of the effectiveness of NDNAD produced some startling results. For all crimes recorded in England and Wales in 2015–16, DNA was linked to outcome in only 0.3 per cent of cases, and this low rate had remained unchanged since the database was created twenty years earlier. Even for cases involving rape and murder DNA has a relatively minor role to play. In recorded rape cases just 0.6 per cent had a DNA hit linked to their outcome, with slightly higher results related to all homicides recorded, at 8.4 per cent of cases. Yet even in these cases the police already had a prime suspect. The authors of the research concluded that 'DNA is still, for the most part, insignificant as a crime-solving tool'.[14]

Despite criminological evidence to the contrary, this myth of DNA's vital importance in the fight against crime remains persistent, and is reinforced by TV programmes, films and books. It's a myth that therefore must perform some cultural function, although what that might be is far from clear. Perhaps it simply serves to reassure the public that crime doesn't pay, that the police will eventually arrest the offender and that, no matter what, at the end of the day science will allow good to triumph over evil. We have to hope that it does. However, let's not forget that it was the worried family of Bessie Mundy who raised their concerns with the police about George Smith, and the brave testimony of Alice Reavil which ensured his conviction, rather than the early forensic science and experiments of Bernard Spilsbury.

CHAPTER THREE

Case Four

The Murder of Percy Thompson, 1922

To all those who lead monotonous lives, in the
hope that they may experience at second-hand
the delights and dangers of adventure.

AGATHA CHRISTIE,
dedication to *The Secret Adversary* (1922)

Agatha Christie's debut novel, *The Mysterious Affair at Styles*, written in 1916 at the height of the First World War, was the result of a bet with her sister. The book had a somewhat tortuous publication history, rejected by six publishers before finally being picked up by the Bodley Head and published in 1921. Christie would go on to write another sixty-five detective novels and fourteen short-story collections, as well as more than twenty plays. She's now rightly regarded as one of the world's most successful writers. *The Mysterious Affair at Styles* introduced the Belgian detective Hercule

Poirot to the reading public, and *Curtain: Poirot's Last Case* was Christie's final book, released in September 1975. When Christie died in January 1976, theatre lights in London's West End reportedly dimmed on news of her passing.

Christie specialised in writing 'clue puzzle' novels which offered enough hints for the reader to solve the case for themselves – a style which can be detected in the current vogue for 'cosy' crime writing.[1] She was particularly associated with the 'Golden Age' of crime fiction between the wars, along with several other celebrated female writers such as Dorothy L. Sayers, Margery Allingham, Patricia Wentworth and Ngaio Marsh. It remains one of those curious ironies that women still disproportionately produce and consume crime writing, even though its contents usually involve lethal violence against their own gender.[2] That aside, in 2022 British readers bought one hundred crime books and thrillers a minute, amounting to 12 per cent of all book purchases that year.[3]

Christie's second novel, *The Secret Adversary*, was published in 1922 – the same year as T. S. Eliot's *The Waste Land* and James Joyce's *Ulysses*, two central works of the modernist movement – and is of particular interest to this chapter's murder case. At its core, the book is a simple and jingoistic spy thriller, with some very naive political views. The narrative is concerned with identifying and then stopping the mysterious 'Mr Brown', who is intent on doing damage to the British state. It also has about it a touch of modernism and, above all, two central characters who throw some light on a couple who would be convicted of murder in December 1922 and executed the following year. Let's meet Tommy and Tuppence.

*

Lieutenant Thomas Beresford had been wounded twice fighting in the First World War and, having been discharged from the army, was job-hunting. It wasn't going well and, as he says early in the novel, 'What good am I? What do I know about business?' Tommy is of course not only a shortening of Thomas but also a term in popular usage at that time to describe ordinary soldiers.[4] Tommy is therefore as much an everyman as a character in his own right. We don't even get a description of him until halfway through the novel, and when we do he's referred to as 'one of those young Englishmen not distinguished by any special intellectual ability, but who are emphatically at their best in what is known as a "tight space"'. The temptation is to see Tommy as a symbolic character, even if he's also one of the two protagonists. However, we do learn that he has 'a pleasantly ugly face', slicked-back red hair, looks like a 'gentleman', a 'sportsman', and that his brown suit is 'perilously near the end of its tether'.

Tuppence – as in having only two pennies to rub together – is Prudence Cowley, the fifth daughter of Archdeacon Cowley of Little Missendell in Suffolk. Tuppence doesn't really get on with her father, although she is 'awfully fond of him'. She worries him, as 'he has that delightful early Victorian view that short skirts and smoking are immoral. You can imagine what a thorn in the flesh I am to him!' She wears her black hair in a bob but, like Tommy, we find out more about her through the choices that she makes, rather than physical descriptions. A character called Julius P. Hersheimmer, an American industrialist trying to track down his cousin, remarks to Tuppence, for example, that he'd always thought that 'English girls were just a mite moss-grown. Old fashioned and sweet, you know, but scared to move around without a footman or maiden aunt. I guess I'm a bit behind the times!' Tuppence isn't like those English girls, but is charismatic and impulsive, a 'flapper' – a member of the subculture of Western women in the 1920s prepared to flout Victorian convention in what they wore and how they behaved.

Tuppence and Tommy have known each other since childhood and, at the start of the novel, decide to set up a business together called The Young Adventurers. They're described as 'an essentially modern-looking couple', or as they've recently been described, 'Bright Young Things on a budget'.[5] Money, as much as tracking down the mysterious Mr Brown, is one of the central preoccupations of the narrative. Tommy and Tuppence are short of funds and are so poor that they have to share the bill at the local Lyons Corner House, which also identifies them as willing to break the social conventions of the day. Where money is concerned, Tuppence recognises that 'marriage is my best chance. I made up my mind to marry money when I was quite young. Any thinking girl would! I am not sentimental, you know.' She says that she 'loves money' and, returning to that theme later in the novel, repeats that she does intend to marry 'if I can find someone rich enough to make it worth my while'. She directs these comments to Hersheimmer, the American millionaire, who clearly does have money, although she'll later reject him in favour of Tommy.

Choosing Tommy over Hersheimmer has much more lasting significance within the book than finding the elusive quarry, although that is worthy of comment. It transpires that Mr Brown is none other than – and with a book that has been adapted several times for the screen and is now over a hundred years old, I hardly think we need a 'spoiler alert' – Sir James Peel Edgerton, KC, one of the most prominent lawyers in the country, and widely seen as a future prime minister. This is of interest as Christie has a habit of using characters who are part of a community, rather than strangers as her villains. Among her Golden Age contemporaries, she is the least likely to 'other' the various rogues, scoundrels and murderers in her work. Edgerton even has a special interest in criminology, writes letters to Tommy and Tuppence to throw them off the scent and keeps a book in which he describes his crimes. In it, Edgerton notes:

> It is madness to keep this book. I know that. It is documentary evidence against me. But I have never shrunk from taking risks. And I feel an urgent need for self-expression ... The book will only be taken from my dead body ...

This need for self-expression is of course a modernist motif, although in the novel Edgerton's book is given to Scotland Yard for safe keeping and, we're assured, will 'never be publicly exhibited': 'Sir James's long association with the law would make it undesirable.' The adjective 'undesirable' which finishes this sentence is doing a great deal of heavy lifting but might be excused as a form of English understatement for what is simply a cover-up.

So, in summary, in Tommy and Tuppence we've two characters in their twenties who are seeking the delights and dangers of adventure. As a 'modern couple' – even on a budget – they don't want to lead monotonous lives, although at the start of the novel their lack of funds affords them few opportunities to do otherwise. Tuppence acknowledges that marriage would solve her precarious financial situation, but she'll eventually opt for love rather than the cash of an American millionaire. And, at the end of their adventure, they discover that they've been fighting a villain at the very heart of the British establishment, who keeps a diary about his various crimes and misdemeanours that's so explosive it needs to be kept secret and out of circulation. These themes are worth bearing in mind when we consider our real murder case, which also has about it the whiff of a literary imagination.

*

In the very early hours of 4 October 1922, Percy and Edith Thompson were making their way back to their home at 49 Kensington Gardens in Ilford.[6] Edith and Percy, who was three years older than his wife, had been married in January 1916, and whether by choice or otherwise they'd no children, which for some would prompt questions about whether their marriage was a happy one. It's also likely that Percy knew that Edith had been having an affair for the last sixteen months with a merchant seaman called Freddy Bywaters, who'd briefly lived with them in Kensington Gardens and whom Edith had known since childhood. Bywaters had gone on holiday with the couple to the Isle of Wight in June 1921, ostensibly to accompany Edith's sister Avis. Shortly afterwards, Bywaters and Edith, who was eight years older than her lover, began a sexual relationship. This would result in Percy and Bywaters coming to blows and, unsurprisingly, the young man was asked to leave the house. Thereafter the relationship between Edith and Bywaters was conducted mostly from afar by letter, postcard and telegram, given that Bywaters was usually at sea, and therefore life – or so it must have seemed to Percy – could carry on as much as it had always done.

On the evening of 3 October 1922 Percy and Edith, in the company of Edith's aunt and uncle, had gone to the Criterion Theatre in Piccadilly Circus in London to see a Ben Travers farce called *The Dippers*. Edith loved the theatre, music and fashion. Even though she was only in her late twenties she'd become a very successful professional woman, at a time when only one in three married women worked. Many of the letters that were sent to her from Bywaters were addressed to her place of work at Carlton & Prior, a wholesale milliner near Aldersgate station, where Edith worked as chief buyer. Edith earned more money than Percy, although, as the law demanded, it was his name on the deeds of the house in Ilford, which they had bought in 1920 for £250. Like many young women of her age at this time, Edith smoked, drank in bars, wore her hair in a modern style, gambled on horses and was happy to flirt with men. She also read a great deal, was interested in drama and thought that housework was 'drudgery'. In short, Edith was a savvy young woman who, as one of her more recent biographers has described her, 'was having it all'.[7] The temptation here is to suggest that 'having it all' can also be seen as referring to having both a husband and what today would be called a 'toyboy'.

This latter, somewhat cheap observation is simply meant to suggest that at a time when newspapers were commenting on 'our spare girls' – there were more young women than men as a result of the war – Edith's circumstances would've evoked jealousy among her peers, as much as she would have been seen as 'a new type of woman'. She would've been viewed as threatening the moral status quo and, in that sense, she was just like Tuppence, who didn't really get on well with her father because of his 'early Victorian' views, and was a 'thorn in the flesh' to him. Edith was to prove to be a thorn in the flesh for British sensibilities too, and not just for fictional elderly clerics.

Kensington Gardens was a twenty-minute walk from Ilford station. We know that at about midnight Edith and Percy left the station by the York Road entrance, and then crossed over to Belgrave Road. Near the junction of Endsleigh Gardens and Belgrave Road, someone roughly pushed Edith away from Percy, and she fell slightly dazed to the pavement. There followed a short but ferocious attack on Percy, who was stabbed repeatedly by his assailant. As might be expected with this type of blitz attack, there were cuts all over his body, including a number to his left side below the ribs, and three severe stab wounds to his neck. One of these penetrated the floor of his mouth, and another severed the carotid artery. Percy quickly fell against a wall and slid down to the ground with a 'pitiful groan'. He was dead, and his blue suit would later be described as having a 'zigzag of cuts'.[8] The area was covered in blood and one witness, John Webster, remembered Edith screaming, 'Oh don't! Oh don't!' as she ran towards where her husband had fallen, and as his assailant fled the scene. When Edith was asked by a number of people who came to her assistance what had happened, she replied: 'Oh don't ask me, I don't know,' but even accepting that she might have been in shock, this wasn't true. She had recognised Bywaters immediately from the clothes that he was wearing.

Events thereafter moved very quickly, with one thing leading to another. Bywaters was arrested on the evening of 4 October, and it was soon established that he had links to the Thompsons – especially Edith. Detectives then went to Bywaters's mother Lillian's house and his mother, who'd warned her son about his relationship with Edith, allowed the police to search his bedroom. There they uncovered a cache of letters that Edith had written to him while he was at sea. The police found even more letters on his ship. These letters would become the basis of the case against Edith, who was duly charged with murder and appeared before Stratford Police Court on 6 October. She was then remanded to HMP Holloway.

The trial began at the Old Bailey on 6 December. Edith, against the advice of her barrister, insisted on taking the stand, and tried to explain away passages in the letters that had been admitted in evidence. These seemed to indicate that she'd attempted to poison Percy and had actively conspired in the events which led to his murder. To put it bluntly, she didn't make a good witness. The trial was over just five days later, with both found guilty of murder. Their appeals failed, as did demands for clemency, and so Bywaters was hanged at HMP Pentonville and Edith at HMP Holloway on 9 January 1923. From that moment onwards, their case became a cause célèbre, with it suggested that Edith had been 'hanged for committing adultery'.

The letters that Edith wrote to Bywaters were central to the guilty verdict. Over time, a lively game of textual analysis – worthy of Agatha Christie herself – has developed among competing historians, trying to ameliorate what Edith expressed in writing and render it wholly irrelevant or, at the very least, legally inadmissible. The case is thus usually discussed from a perspective in which Edith and, to a lesser extent Bywaters, are already seen as being the victims of a miscarriage of justice; that the legal proceedings were 'gendered' and therefore hostile to the childless Edith, with the trial judge coming in for particular opprobrium; and that, paradoxically, Edith should be viewed as both an extraordinary and an ordinary woman, who hadn't really committed murder at all.

Who gets lost in this historiographical process is poor Percy – the murder victim – who was subjected to an horrific knife attack and lost his life when he was just thirty-two. His role in the process of reclaiming Edith gets reduced to a subtle form of 'victim blaming'. He's the dull and uninspiring anchor that kept Edith chained to a loveless and unfulfilling marriage, and who was prepared to use violence once he'd found out about his wife's affair.[9] This serves to reverse what happened to the three main participants: Percy is either rendered invisible or even partly culpable, rather than the victim of a murder; Bywaters, and especially Edith, are seen as being victims and deserving of our sympathies, as opposed to the perpetrators of a dreadful crime in which a man lost his life, and who therefore warranted being punished.

The most recent and important contributions about the case come from Professor René Weis, a Shakespearean scholar who teaches at University College London; Professor William Twining, also attached to UCL, an expert in jurisprudence, proof and legal method; and Laura Thompson, probably the most perceptive of all the biographers of Agatha Christie.

Weis is the author of the campaigning *Criminal Justice: The True Story of Edith Thompson* and did much to bring the story of Edith and Bywaters to contemporary audiences. Twining's contribution is to offer a 'Wigmorean analysis', arguing that, from an evidentiary perspective, none of Edith's letters indicate a conspiracy to murder. He argues that there was no planning behind the attack on Percy; his murder was not the conclusion of a fantasy that Edith might have had; and nor did she incite Bywaters to commit the murder. Above all, according to Twining, there is a 'broken chain' of evidence. There's no connection between Edith's behaviour and what Bywaters does – at one or more points the chain between what she wrote and what would eventually happen to Percy was broken.

Thompson's *Rex v Edith Thompson: A Tale of Two Murders*, published in 2018, is the most recent contribution about the murder. It's a lively and much more balanced account of what happened, especially the role of Edith (who Weis tends to sanctify) in that it recognises how flawed she was as a character. Thompson concludes that Edith was 'guilty of something, but nothing that was the business of the law'.[10]

Not all of the letters that Edith wrote to Bywaters were submitted in evidence, but of those that were, perhaps the most important and damning phrases – as far as the prosecution was concerned – that she used included:

21 November 1921: yesterday I met a woman who had lost 3 husbands ... and some people I know can't lose one.

December [1921]: I had the wrong porridge today, but I don't suppose it will matter, I don't seem to care much either way.

You'll probably say I'm careless and I admit I am, but I don't care – do you?

2 January 1922: Darlint [*sic*], I've surrendered to him unconditionally now – do you understand me? I think it is the best way to disarm any suspicion[.]

10 February 1922: About 2am. He woke me up and asked for water as he felt ill ... I told Avis about the incident only I told her as if it frightened and worried me as I thought perhaps it might be useful at some future time that I had told somebody.

22 February 1922: Darlingest boy, the thing I am going to do for both of us will it ever – at all, make any difference between us, darlint, do you understand what I mean.

1 April 1922: ... he puts great stress on the fact of the tea tasting bitter 'as if something had been put in it' he says.

24 April 1922: I used the 'light bulb' three times but the third time – he found a piece – so I've given up – until you come home.

1 May 1922: I don't think we're failures in other things and we mustn't be in this. We mustn't give up as we said. No, we shall have to wait if we fail again[.] You said it was enough for an elephant. Perhaps it was. But you don't allow for the taste making only a small quantity to be taken[.] I was buoyed up with the hope of the 'light bulb' and I used a lot[.] I suppose

as you say he's not normal. I know I shall never get him to take a sufficient quantity of anything bitter[.] You tell me not to leave finger marks on the box – do you know I did not think of the box but I did think of the glass or cup or whatever was used. I wish I wish oh I wish I could do something.

18 May 1922: It must be remembered that digitalis is a cumulative poison[.] I'd like you to read 'Bella Donna' first you learn something from it to help us.

13 June 1922: ... he was on the ottoman at the foot of the bed and said he was dying and wanted to – he had another heart attack – thro [*sic*] me. Darlint I had to laugh because *I knew* it couldn't be a heart attack.

14 June 1922: ... how can you get ptomaine poisoning from a tin of salmon?

4 July 1922: Why aren't you sending me something ... If I don't mind the risk why should you? Have you studied 'Bichloride of Mercury'[?]

23 August 1922: The attacks continue so I am told of course I know differently – but I say nothing & laugh all to myself right deep down inside[.]

20 September 1922: Yes, darlint you are jealous of him – but I want you to be – he has the right by law to all that you have the right to by nature and love – yes darlint be jealous, so much that you will do something desperate.

2 October 1922: darlint – do something tomorrow night will you? Don't forget what we talked [about] in the Tea Room, I'll risk and try if you will[.]

All of this seems shocking and deplorable, but do these extracts really prove her guilt?

*

Criminologists are often asked to consider the letters that have been written by perpetrators, or those who are suspected of having committed a crime.[11] They use different analytical methods, including something known as a 'criminological autopsy'.[12] This is a version of a psychological autopsy, which is a procedure that seeks to reconstruct a suicidal death through reading letters or documents left by the person who's taken their own life, as well as interviewing surviving family members or friends.[13] Clearly there are difficulties in reading historical texts and trying to make some sense of them in the present. However, it has been suggested that 'the past has left images of itself in literary texts, images comparable to those which are imprinted by light on a photosensitive plate. The future alone possesses developers active enough to scan such surfaces perfectly.'[14] I rather like the self-confidence here but would suggest that any such scanning and reading can only ever be partial and incomplete, rather than fixed and definitive.

There's no doubt that Edith does mention poisoning Percy in some of the letters that she wrote to Bywaters. There's specific mention of bichloride of mercury, digitalis – which would cause cardiac arrhythmia – and ptomaine poisoning, and she discusses how she'd put glass in her husband's food via the 'light-bulb method'. She also reports a conversation where Percy said he was worried his tea tasted 'bitter', as if something 'had been put in it', and mocks his fear of having a heart attack. On the other hand, we know conclusively that when Sir Bernard Spilsbury, whom we encountered trying to discover why so many new brides drowned in their baths, conducted an autopsy on Percy, none of his organs showed any signs of poison.

It's also possible to read passages related to how she'd taken 'the wrong porridge' as evidence that she had been trying to take something so as to induce miscarriage, having fallen pregnant with Bywaters's child, although perhaps because it would've made her appear unsympathetic, she didn't present this defence in court. Several different interpretations and readings have been advanced by Weis, Twining and Thompson for other seemingly incriminating passages. For example, in the very last letter that she sent to Bywaters, dated 2 October 1922, 'do something tomorrow night will you? Don't forget what we talked [about] in the Tea Room, I'll risk and try if you will' can be explained as Edith encouraging Bywaters to take her sister Avis out, rather than kill Percy. The 'I'll risk and try if you will' in that context is merely an allusion to giving up on their relationship while risking being constantly reminded of the love they once had if Bywaters does start dating Avis.

What emerges from a more criminological reading of the letters is that they're a mixture of fantasy and reality, and that what's imagined by Edith bleeds seamlessly into what she believes to be true, or at least wants to believe to be the truth. This analysis would also note that the more innocent readings of the letters – some of which I've alluded to above – were not accepted by the jury, and nor do the exculpatory attempts that we see particularly in Weis consider how these letters were interpreted by Bywaters. Edith might have been transmitting, but it was Bywaters who was receiving.

One way to think about this is to imagine that the corpus of Edith's letters performs the same function as a social media account would today. The letters, including those that weren't entered in evidence, but which talk about Edith's love of the cinema, books, theatre, dance, fashion, horse racing and so forth, present a version of herself that she wants to be consumed by others, or in this case by Bywaters. They're an idealised version of herself, in much the same way that online profiles today only offer a view of the self that we want others to see. As my colleague, criminologist Professor Elizabeth Yardley, has argued, 'the self is increasingly performed on and through networked media, an array of resources that enable us to narrate, represent and maintain ourselves as social actors'.[15] That's what we can see happening in the letters Edith writes: they're the way that she narrates, represents and attempts to maintain who it is that she wants to be, and who it is that she wants to be with. Indeed, research about how contemporary social networking sites (SNSs) operate suggests that most people use them to maintain existing relationships rather than form new ones. They're a way to engage with those who are already friends.[16] Thought of in this way, we can view Edith's letters, and how Bywaters reacted to them, by considering new research into the role that SNSs in general, and Facebook in particular, play in homicide.

With Elizabeth, I started to research a phenomenon called 'Facebook murder'.[17] In short, how was this SNS used by those who'd go on to commit murder? It soon became clear that hostility was exacerbated by all SNSs through a process of 'online disinhibition' which, in turn, is a by-product of the social clues that would occur during offline, face-to-face communication being filtered out. This could be aggravated by 'asynchronicity' – there were delays between sending a message and receiving a response, which allowed someone's train of thought to progress and their anger to mount. And, of course, just as Edith's letters could be stored away in a box on Bywaters's ship or at his mother's house, SNSs create 'data permanence' – you can revisit a post or a message at a time of your choosing, perhaps many months after it had originally been posted. You can ruminate over its meaning, twisting and turning what might have been an innocent comment into something much more provocative and confrontational; something that demanded you take action.

There is merit in thinking about Edith's letters to Bywaters like this, and therefore using the research about Facebook murder to inform our understanding of why he'd attack and kill Percy. After all, just like an online post, Edith's letters to him were kept and stored – they were a permanent record of what she'd written to him and, in this way, he could deliberate over their meaning at a time of his choosing, irrespective of when they'd originally been sent. And Bywaters and Edith could not meet regularly and talk face to face, as he was at sea for almost all of their relationship. Laura Thompson comments that it's 'almost shocking how seldom the couple actually met', and calculates that they'd been in each other's company for only a few weeks over the course of their relationship, which had lasted for more than sixty weeks.[18] There's therefore an absence of the normal social clues that might have allowed Bywaters to better interpret what Edith had written, and which therefore contributed to his disinhibition, despite the asynchronicity of when the letter had actually been sent and how this might have made him feel at that time, or later. This is one way of challenging Twining's 'broken chain' of evidence argument.

Within our Facebook murder research, we discovered there were six different types of murderers who used this SNS. We described them as: Reactors; Informers; Antagonists; Fantasists; Predators; and Imposters. A Reactor, for example, 'reacts to content posted on the SNS by attacking the victim offline. This may be immediately after viewing the content that makes them angry, or there may be a time delay in which they revisit the content and ruminate over its meaning.' This type of killer was usually associated with murders that had a context of sexual intimacy, jealousy and revenge. As for the Fantasist, this was someone who used the SNS to 'perform or indulge in a fantasy. For Fantasists, the line between fantasy and reality has become increasingly blurred and the homicide may be a way of maintaining the fantasy or preventing others from discovering the deception.'

From this perspective it seems obvious that Bywaters can be described as a Reactor, while Edith was using her letters as a Fantasist. However, the legal question remains: does that mean that Edith deserved what she got? Even by the judicial standards of 1922–23 she shouldn't have been hanged, and both Weis and Thompson provide excellent analyses of the social and cultural circumstances that saw Edith sent to the gallows. However, it's also obvious that she was nonetheless culpable in Percy's death. Without the letters that she wrote to Bywaters outlining her attempts to poison her husband so that she could be free from him, he would have lived and no doubt she would've remained in an unhappy marriage for the rest of her life. Without those letters Bywaters would never have murdered Percy and – who can tell – he might even have courted and then married Avis. Edith is culpable because there was so much more going on within the totality of this relationship than simple adultery. It might also be possible to suggest that they were engaging in a *folie à deux* – literally a madness shared by two – and that Edith's delusional fantasies were gradually accepted and then murderously acted on by Bywaters.

*

Agatha Christie wanted her readers to experience vicariously 'the delights and dangers of adventure' through the actions of childhood friends Tommy and Tuppence. Edith had also known Bywaters from childhood, but while she might have wanted to marry him that was not to be – there was no happy ending in that respect, as there would be for Tommy and Tuppence in the denouement of *The Secret Adversary*. However, both couples existed only on paper. Their different adventures were created by Christie's prose and by Edith's letters, even allowing for the very few weeks when she and Bywaters were together and could conduct their relationship in person. Neither couple was authentic – the literary creations Tommy and Tuppence most obviously so, but there's a sense that Edith and Bywaters were also only authentic on the page, as they too had been created by a woman's imagination. And while the adventures in *The Secret Adversary* involved

Tommy and Tuppence fighting an establishment figure in the guise of Sir James Peel Edgerton, KC, a prominent defence barrister, Edith and Bywaters seemed to have to take on the whole of the legal and criminal justice system by themselves, with sadly predictable results.

Both Edith and Tuppence had two men in their lives. Tuppence had Tommy, but also Julius P. Hersheimmer. Edith had married Percy, but she longed for Bywaters. Both had to choose, and even if Edith's choice was more difficult, as divorce in the 1920s was very rare, she could still have decided to leave Percy and start her life again with Bywaters. She didn't make that choice, but instead wrote letters to her lover in which she suggested that she was trying to poison her husband. Tuppence, the daughter of a cleric, also had a choice – dependable but poor Tommy, or the fabulously rich Julius. She chose Tommy over wealth, and that choice seems symbolic.[19] Tuppence wanted gentility and good taste, rather than vulgar wealth; she chose an English gentleman, albeit one who couldn't find a job, rather than an American titan of capitalism. It might be stretching the symbolism too far, but in her choice is there not a moral lesson, both for other women who read the novel and also about Britain's future? What Christie seems to be suggesting is that we should stick with reliable, childhood friends, no matter the shiny temptations that lie elsewhere.

CHAPTER FOUR

Case Five

The Murder of Helen Priestly, 1934

Lacking Aberdeen, Scotland would not be so
securely balanced. This is a city, which to mix my
metaphor, nails down the map of Scotland in the
north-east with the hard metal of the Scottish
character.

H. V. MORTON, *In Search of Scotland* (1929)

Sometimes a 'grain of sand' can be found in an image, although I doubt if these particular photographs had been
viewed by more than a handful of people for over half a century. They'd probably still be gathering dust in the files of the
former Grampian Police for another fifty years had Aberdeen
not established the Granite Noir Crime Writing Festival in
2017, which aimed to 'explain the darkness within and around
us'. For the 2018 festival, the writer Diarmid Mogg published a
number of historic crime-scene photographs taken within the

city, from a collection that he curated at a local gallery.[1] These included several sharp black-and-white photographs taken by the police on 21 April 1934 of an impressive granite tenement located at 61 Urquhart Road.

A tenement is a stone-built block of flats on several storeys, served by a common stairway. Now usually associated with Glasgow and slums, tenements were in fact popular with working *and* middle-class tenants, architecturally attractive if simple and robust, and constructed to offer protection from the vagaries of the Scottish weather. Some did indeed become what might be termed a 'slum', but they also had solidity, neighbourliness and a sense of community.

The photographs published by Mogg presented a short series of interior and external views of the tenement, but it was the first photograph that caught my attention – clearly taken from across the street, revealing the building's front elevation. This tenement is on four storeys, and it's clear from the windows that there are two flats on each floor. Two things stand out. First, outside on the pavement are several delivery bicycles, which undoubtedly belonged to the butcher John Lyon, who had a shop on the ground floor of the adjoining tenement. The fact that they were unattended suggests something about the implicit trust that comes with living communally and how, over time, you slowly become aware of other tenants' foibles and idiosyncrasies, likes and irritations; who was reliable, trustworthy or, on the other hand, best to avoid.

Second, while most of the residents had opened their curtains to welcome the day, two had not. The blinds are drawn on the window of the ground-floor flat on the right-hand side of the building, and also on the windows of the flat immediately above. It would soon transpire why the residents of these two flats didn't want anyone to look inside. One housed the killer of a little girl called Helen Priestly, and the other her distraught parents. Communal living might engender trust, but sometimes petty tensions and disputes could spiral disastrously and catastrophically out of control – as photographs taken inside the tenement would show.

In this chapter I use Helen's murder to discuss a range of social, economic and cultural issues about the 1920s and 1930s so as to see that world in a tragedy that happened within a solid, grey tenement in Aberdeen. However, before considering the murder, let's zoom out and set the scene more broadly.

*

The 1920s and 1930s are often described, somewhat dismissively, as the 'inter-war years'; a period of borrowed time until the inescapable happens and Britain is at war once again. This rich and lively period in our history – an age when radio, photography and the cinema had all become popular – tends to be summed up by a few set-piece events and images. One famous set of images involves the huge crowds that attended the first FA Cup Final at Wembley in 1923, controlled by mounted police, including an officer on a white horse. Other iconic moments include scenes of the General Strike, which brought the country to a standstill between 4 and 12 May 1926, and the abdication of King Edward VIII in December 1936, with the former king addressing the nation on the BBC, in a speech recorded at Windsor Castle.

The former Labour MP Roy Hattersley chose another image 'to represent the hard reality of Britain between the wars':

The one picture of life in inter-war Britain which is most deeply impressed on the collective memory illustrates the abiding tragedy of men without work . . . it is the march that set out for London on 5 October 1936 which is embedded in the national memory. It called itself, and came to be known as, the 'Jarrow Crusade'.[2]

The town of Jarrow, on the banks of the River Tyne, was dominated by Palmer's Shipbuilding and Iron Company. With the closure of the yard, unemployment soared. Two hundred men, led by the mayor and lady mayoress of Jarrow for the first leg of their journey, were chosen to carry a petition to London. They marched with blue-and-white banners, accompanied by a mouth-organ band and their local MP – the legendary Ellen Wilkinson. However, at the end of their journey of nearly three hundred miles it's difficult to be certain what they'd achieved, and Hattersley's suggestion that the marchers had 'deeply impressed' the collective memory seems, almost ninety years on, generous at best.

Mass unemployment was a major issue at this time, not just in Britain but throughout the industrial world, as traditional industries such as coal mining, steel and shipbuilding declined. The numbers of miners, for example, fell from over one million in 1920 to 675,000 in 1938, and by the mid-1920s nine out of ten miners in Northumberland, Durham and South Wales had been laid off.[3] There was genuine hardship in parts of Britain, with many people paying exorbitant rents for second-rate housing, barely surviving on a substandard diet. Yet to characterise the period only from this viewpoint ignores another truth. The majority of those who lived through the 1920s and 1930s became better paid, were better dressed, lived in better houses, an increasing number drove motor cars, took paid holidays, watched and attended sports events, went to the cinema, listened to the BBC, and generally enjoyed higher standards of living. This was a time which saw the growth of a professional middle class and, in England at least, the development of new, lighter industries that would keep the majority in work. The country became culturally more homogenous, so that the aspirations of one group were largely identical, or at least sympathetic to those of another. Perhaps that's why the Jarrow Crusade was fronted by the mayor and mayoress and along the way the marchers were provided with food, accommodation and clothing, not only by local trade unions but also by churches and ordinary members of the public. A service in support of the marchers was held in Ripon Cathedral – some seventy miles south of Jarrow. Ellen Wilkinson, Jarrow's Labour MP who joined the marchers, wrote a book about the events, published in 1939. *The Town That was Murdered* remains one of the most excoriating accounts of the effects that unbridled capitalism can have on working-class communities.

What emerges from a fresh look at this period is that people seemed to matter to the state in ways they hadn't before. The state was therefore interested in what had happened to Helen Priestly inside the ground-floor flat of a tenement in Urquhart Road, Aberdeen. She mattered, as did her parents. The right to vote had been extended; initiatives were taken to improve the lives of ordinary people with regard to their health, housing and benefits; and the state formally accepted its responsibility for both the care of the elderly and the education of the young.[4] This was no communist revolution – no matter what some people might have feared[5] – but a slow, social democratic evolution, and one which allows us, from today's vantage point, to glimpse in its wake the beginnings of the development of a modern, rather than an imperial, Britain.[6]

The Representation of the People Act of 1918 trebled the electorate to over twenty-one million people by giving the vote to every man over the age of twenty-one and to women over thirty who owned property. The extension of the vote to some 8.5 million women has often been viewed as a 'reward' for their efforts on the home front during the war, although there are a variety of other reasons for their enfranchisement. Most obviously it appeased moderate suffragists, who might otherwise have supported the type of direct action employed by the suffragettes before the war. Women didn't receive the vote on the same terms as men for another ten years, when the Representation of the People Act of 1928 allowed all women over the age of twenty-one to vote and which added an extra five million names to the electoral register. So, by 1928, women were viewed politically, legally and socially in a very different way to how they'd been perceived in the Edwardian period, when they had been subsumed by the legal personalities of their husbands and were drowned in their baths.

Between 1919 and 1922 Lloyd George's coalition government built more than two hundred thousand 'homes fit for heroes' and the Addison Housing Act of 1919 stimulated house-building by offering subsidies to local authorities to invest in construction projects aimed at housing working-class families. In 1914 only 1 per cent of the population rented council accommodation, but by the outbreak of the Second World War this figure had increased to 14 per cent. Over four million homes were built between 1914 and 1939, and by the outbreak of war almost one family in every three was living in a home that had been built after 1918, almost all of which were wired for electricity. Even after the Addison Housing Act was repealed in 1921, the principle of offering subsidies to local authorities to build affordable homes was enshrined in a further five Acts passed between 1923 and 1935.

Better housing contributed to improved health, and a Ministry for Health was created in 1919. Several public health acts were passed during this period, and by 1936 nineteen million wage-earners were covered by National Health Insurance provisions, which saw those protected receive a small cash pay-out when they were sick and enabled them to consult a doctor and receive treatment without charge. The Holidays and Pay Act of 1938 increased the number of people who were entitled to a week's paid holiday, and a significant number would spend their break at one of the two hundred holiday camps that began to spring up along the coastline of Britain, and which could now be reached by a growing number of families able to buy and then drive the many new cars being produced.[7] For those who stayed at home, there were now over four thousand cinemas, and weekly attendance at the 'pictures' was over twenty million. By 1939 some thirty-four million people had access to a radio and over eight million licence holders were able to tune in to the BBC, as well as follow events in the twenty million newspapers sold each day. In 1930, circulation for the *Daily Express* and the *Daily Mail* had approached two million, and by 1934 the *Daily Mirror* reinvented itself as a tabloid with crime a staple feature.[8]

*

We can see the influence of these trends in the literature of the period. Reading newspapers and taking holidays by the sea, for example, were central to the narrative in Graham Greene's 1938 novel, *Brighton Rock*. In this classic English *noir* thriller, the murder of the journalist Charles 'Fred' Hale of the fictional *Daily Messenger* is set against the backdrop of a bank holiday in the seaside resort of Brighton. In the narrative, Brighton is shown to have two faces. Not only the glitz and apparent glamour of the tourist industry, with ice creams and day-trippers, but also organised crime hiding behind that façade, which is dominated by poverty, razor gangs and villains, including the protagonist, a teenager called Pinkie Brown.[9] Greene was confident that the setting of *Brighton Rock* would appeal to his readers because taking trips to the sea for relaxation had already become widespread. We might also note a resonance with how Percy Clifford came to murder his wife Maud in lodgings in North Road in Brighton in 1914.

The action in *Brighton Rock* centred on a murder and the city's criminal underbelly. However, the period was characterised by a relative lack of crime in general and murder specifically to the extent that this was described as the 'English miracle' – the country's rising population wasn't matched by an increasing crime rate. Nor were there any active serial killers that we know of between December 1914, when George Smith murdered his final victim, Margaret Lofty, and August 1943, when Reg Christie started his killing spree by murdering Ruth Fuerst at 10 Rillington Place in Notting Hill. This is even more remarkable when compared with the number of serial killers who were active in Germany over the same period, when a dozen instances were recorded.

These included the so-called 'Vampire of Düsseldorf', Peter Kürten, who was charged with nine murders in 1931; Fritz Haarmann, who murdered twenty-four male sex workers in Hanover between 1919 and 1924; and Bruno Lüdke, who may have murdered as many as fifty-one people over a fifteen-year period that began in 1928.[10]

There are reasons to be sceptical about this 'English miracle' (which would include figures for Wales). If we look at homicide figures for England and Wales, for example, which cover the offences of murder, manslaughter and infanticide, there does seem to be a drop between 1900 and 1910 and in the 1920s and 1930s. The rate of homicides per million of the population was 9.6 in the first decade of the twentieth century but had gone down to 7.5 per million of the population in the 1930s. In fact, it wouldn't reach the level of the 1900–10 figures until the 1970s.[11]

This does seem to be miraculous, and gave rise to a perception that murder wasn't a problem because the English were so civilised. Sir John Moylan, for example, the Receiver for the Metropolitan Police, assured the public in 1926 that out of a population of eight million in the city there had only been 'sixteen murders, the work of fourteen persons, of whom eight committed suicide, and in only one case ... was the murderer undiscovered'.[12]

At first glance, the official figures seem to support Moylan's rosy conclusion. Between 1880, when the office of the Director of Public Prosecutions was created, and 1966, immediately after the death penalty was abolished, the average number of murders recorded each year in England and Wales was 150. Between 1900 and 1909 there were 1,500 murders recorded – an average of exactly 150, and the same average was recorded for 1923 and 1924. In only five of the 104 years between 1862 and 1966 were there fewer than 120 murders recorded or more than 179 – thus neatly creating an average of 150. In 1972 the Home Office stopped publishing separate figures for murder.

This wasn't really a miracle at all but, as the economic historian Howard Taylor has argued, a statistical sleight of hand.[13] Taylor has shown that the figures had been doctored to create a 'public illusion' and that the actual rate of murder had been suppressed. He suggested that the Treasury's unwillingness to fund prosecutions – which meant that local rate-payers would have had to meet as much as half of the costs – had kept numbers artificially low. The local police screened allegations and reports of crimes, and this 'gatekeeping role' dictated the number and range of offences that got prosecuted. Murder trials were expensive, and so it wasn't in everyone's interests to have too many prosecutions.

This could be taken to suggest that the absence of active serial killers between the wars was merely the result of a failure of the police to record murder accurately, and so save on the expense. That's possible, but even if the police hadn't been willing to label a death as suspicious and investigate it as a potential murder, a recently emergent and voracious popular press would have been only too delighted to take up the cause. Murder always creates great public interest and, gruesome as it may be, an active serial killer remains good for the circulation figures – as was shown in 1888.

There's some evidence to support this conclusion from a cursory glance at the newspapers themselves, for in the 1930s their columns were filled with stories of murder. One which has some resonance with what I've been describing was the 'Brighton Trunk Murder' of June 1934. A cloakroom attendant at Brighton station noticed a strange aroma emanating from a trunk that had been deposited. The attendant opened it and discovered the torso of a young woman. The following day the remainder of her body was discovered at King's Cross station in London, and for the very first time this led to a public appeal in England to identify the victim. This generated reports of the disappearance of Violet Kay, a dancer in Brighton. The police interviewed her lover – a man called Tony Mancini – and then they searched the lodgings that the pair shared in 52 Kemp Street. They found Violet's body in a trunk in the cellar, and so charged Mancini with her murder, although he was later acquitted. Sadly, this also meant that the police still had no idea about the identity of the body that had been discovered in the trunks at Brighton and King's Cross stations. In 1976 Mancini – by then in his sixties – confessed to the *News of the World* that he had indeed murdered Violet.

This period did also see improvements in policing and forensic science – something that we will encounter shortly with the Aberdeen murder – but it's unlikely that the relative lack of murder, and especially serial murder, can simply be explained by these developments. What does seem to have kept the murder rate low, even accepting Taylor's analysis, was the sheer scale of state initiatives and the willingness of successive governments to intervene and improve people's lives. People mattered in Britain in ways that they did not in the Weimar Republic, and especially in Hitler's Germany. Most obviously in the Third Reich the lives of Jews, gay people, the elderly, gypsies and the mentally ill were seen as irrelevant to the state's future and therefore a drain on resources. From there it was but a short step to concentration camps and eventual extermination.

Compare all of that with what was happening in Britain, which was in the throes of creating an 'inclusive society', where every citizen was viewed as important to the development of the nation. Not only that, but the ties that bound one Briton to another were becoming all-encompassing. Literature, newspapers, cinema and the BBC were all helping to create a sense of what it meant to be British, and that in turn fostered an awareness that other Britons – people just like you and me – were important too. The government took the lead by extending state protection to those groups that had previously been forced to manage as best they could by themselves, or with help from their immediate family. Now they were viewed as having something to offer and so became more appreciated and, in turn, less vulnerable. That's important, for being valued has always been a good defence against murder and especially serial murder – or, at the very least, would ensure that your disappearance would get reported to the police, the first link in the chain that leads to justice.

Having set the broader context, let's now travel up to Scotland to visit the Granite City.

*

Scotland rarely features in histories of modern Britain. Even Professor David Edgerton's otherwise excellent *The Rise and Fall of the British Nation: A Twentieth-Century History* has only seven entries for Scotland in more than seven hundred pages of text. One commentator has bemoaned the fact that 'the political history of Scotland between the wars ... has been almost entirely wiped out of the story of modern Britain'.[14] If Scotland is considered, it's usually through a passing reference to some set-piece event, especially those associated with the 'Red Clydesiders' – people like James Maxton, John Maclean, John Wheatley and David Kirkwood – and the threat of revolution in Glasgow. This disparate group of trade unionists, Christian socialists and Independent Labour Party supporters, some of whom were Marxists, have become historic, heroic bogeymen, and given an influence far out of proportion to what they actually did, or even threatened to do.[15] They were, on the whole, reformists rather than revolutionaries, gradualists rather than insurrectionists, and at the time of their political emergence Scotland was – and remains – an avowedly capitalist country, resolutely democratic, although characterised by profound inequality. Even 'fiery' James Maxton's famous quip as he boarded the train from Glasgow to take up his seat in the Commons that there was 'no need to hurry – it'll all belong to the people when we come back' was made in the context of winning a democratic election, rather than blowing up the Houses of Parliament.

The 1920s and 1930s remain politically important to Scotland and 1922 was a pivotal year when Labour became a genuine political force north of the border, returning twenty-nine MPs to Parliament and capturing over 30 per cent of the popular vote in the general election. The Scottish National Party (SNP) was founded in 1934 when the National Party of Scotland and the Scottish Party amalgamated. In passing it's also worth noting that the general election of 1922 saw the election of Edwin Scrymgeour as MP for Dundee – the only member of the Scottish Prohibition Party ever to be elected to the Commons – ousting Winston Churchill, the sitting MP, who of course wasn't noted for his temperance.

The inter-war years weren't kind to Scotland, especially in comparison to other parts of Britain, even if some of the broader cultural developments that I've described reached north of the border. There were nearly 140 cinemas in Glasgow alone by the 1930s; there was a radio in 40 per cent of Scottish homes; and Scotland could boast a newspaper readership as voracious as anywhere in the world.[16] However, while the economy of England diversified, Scotland still seemed wedded to the heavy industry that had made her a world leader in several fields prior to 1914. In 1913, for example, more ships were built on the Clyde than the tonnage produced in either Germany or the USA.[17] However, by 1933 seven out of ten ship workers were out of work. More than a quarter of the Scottish workforce was unemployed at this time – a larger proportion than in the rest of the United Kingdom and, perhaps unsurprisingly, there was a great deal of emigration so that the population of Scotland fell between 1921 and 1931.[18] As Professor Tom Devine has put it, echoing a number of earlier Scottish historians, 'the industrial structure of Scotland seemed to ossify. In 1939 it was not significantly different from the manufacturing it inherited from Victorian and Edwardian times.'[19]

These developments, or lack of them, had a variety of knock-on effects, from a slower emergence of a consumer culture to a generalised fear that Scotland's best days were in the past. The nation seemed to lose its self-confidence. Its higher rates of unemployment, overcrowding – with a greater proportion of the population living in only one room than in other parts of the United Kingdom[20] – and poorer health outcomes marked Scotland out not only as less willing, or able, to transform its economic base, but also as somewhere that was being left behind. This is perhaps most memorably captured by Simone de Beauvoir in her autobiography *Force of Circumstance*, written about her travels with Jean-Paul Sartre immediately after the end of the Second World War. She reflects on their trip to Scotland that 'Scottish austerity was too much for us. It was very difficult to find rooms, and impossible to work in them: no table and no desk lamp' – so much so that 'our hearts sank at the grimness of the towns'.[21]

Something that de Beauvoir's rather depressing observation captures is the fact that Scotland was a heavily urbanised culture, despite all the wild, romantic tales that have been written about the Highlands. By 1951 two-thirds of the Scottish population lived in towns of more than five thousand people, and even at the start of the twentieth century Scotland was one of the most urbanised countries in the world. The Scottish journalist and novelist George Blake, writing in *The Heart of Scotland*, published in 1934, thought that 'Scotland is grossly over weighted with cities'.[22] Glasgow, for example, was one of the greatest cities of the world at this time – 'the Second City of the Empire' – and, given its setting and beauty, Edinburgh was 'the Athens of the North'. However, any discussion of Scottish urban centres often starts and ends with Glasgow and Edinburgh, although there remain other important cities, and two of the most significant – Dundee[23] and Aberdeen – rarely get the attention they deserve, even in Scottish textbooks.

Aberdeen is situated on the north-east coast and is

sometimes known as the Granite City or, more recently, 'the Houston of Europe', a nod to the city's role in the North Sea oil industry. Granite is a stone local to the north-east and was once considered as being too hard to use for construction and decoration. However, from the 1830s onwards steam-powered technology revolutionised the use of granite, and Aberdeen soon found itself architecturally transformed and reconstructed, as old buildings were destroyed and new roads laid to make way for commercial expansions and development. With the construction of Union Street, still one of the most impressive boulevards in all of northern Europe, Aberdeen acquired a 'new town', just like Edinburgh, to accommodate a growing number of businesses and the professional classes who owned them.[24]

These changes weren't to everyone's tastes. The Aberdonian architect and historian James Fenton Wyness wrote in anger about the city's architectural heritage being destroyed so that 'nothing remains in Exchequer Row, the Green, the Netherkirkgate, Schoolhill, Broad Street and the Gallowgate, once the finest streets in Scotland'.[25] Wyness, by all accounts an opinionated and touchy man,[26] also thought that Aberdeen was a 'City with so much to say, yet says so little. A City whose roots lie deep in a rich and colourful past; whose story is that of Scotland and whose contribution to the nation's work and worth has been considerable. Yet Aberdeen is reserved, reluctant, one might say, to "put her goods in the window".'[27] The sense that Aberdeen is a city populated by those who are silent and uncommunicative, reserved and reluctant, has been picked up repeatedly over the years by a number of commentators and visitors to the city. Edwin Muir, for example, on his Scottish journey in the mid-1930s, commented on the 'reserve' that he detected in this part of Scotland,[28] and from this same period George Blake thought that Aberdeen's 'racial psychology' set it apart. By this he seems to have meant what he considered to be 'that queer element of Northern reserve', so 'Aberdeen does not readily give the stranger the impression of either warmth or ease. The ostensible mood is quite definitively chilly.'[29] Writing slightly earlier, H. V. Morton observed 'here was a city built of the hardest known stone' – a substance that had entered the souls of people who lived there – and where life was characterised by 'struggle and determination'. As for how Aberdonians communicated with one another, he told a story of a trip that he made to the local fish market:

> The most mysterious commercial transaction I have ever witnessed. The auctioneers appear with little books. A crowd of buyers follows. There is no shouting, no gesticulation; they might in fact be performing a burial service in some unknown tongue. I defy a stranger to discover unaided what passes between auctioneer and buyer in Aberdeen fish market.[30]

Mystery and silence, reserve and reluctance, no shouting or gesticulation and the failure of the killer to put 'her goods in the window' would also characterise the murder of eight-year-old Helen Priestly in a tenement in the city by her downstairs neighbour Jeannie Donald.

*

On the face of it, this seems like an appalling but relatively simple murder to explain, although in my account I've chosen

113

to exercise some self-censorship. I've only included details which are necessary to explain what happened and how this influenced the course of the investigation and trial but, even so, some of the material remains distressing.[31]

Helen Priestly, who lived on the second floor of 61 Urquhart Street with her parents Agnes and John, had been sent to fetch a loaf of bread from the local Co-Op by her mother around lunchtime on 21 April 1934. Seemingly she didn't return from her errand and was never seen alive again. A local nine-year-old boy called Dick Sutton claimed that he'd watched Helen being dragged onto a tram by a middle-aged man wearing a dark overcoat. The police released a description of both Helen and the man described by Dick, and this was used as the basis of public appeals for information on the radio and at cinemas in the city – setting a precedent that would become commonplace. A frantic and widespread search involving hundreds of people, which didn't end until the early hours of the next morning, would prove fruitless. Then at around five o'clock on the morning of 22 April, Alexander Parker, a neighbour of the Priestlys, was about to start searching again when he noticed a distinct blue hessian bag with a faded Canadian export stamp propped up against a wall that led to a shared toilet on the ground floor of the tenement. The bag hadn't been there the night before. Alexander peered inside the sack and discovered Helen's body.

It was quickly established that the little girl had been strangled. There were also bruises on her thighs, and other internal injuries suggested that she had been raped – presumably by the man seen dragging her onto a tram. However, when Dick Sutton was re-interviewed by the police, the boy admitted that he was mistaken, and that he hadn't seen Helen and the man in an overcoat at all. Whether this was a genuine error, or he'd just wanted some vicarious attention is unrecorded, but it meant that the police had been pursuing an unreliable lead. It wasn't a stranger who'd murdered Helen, but a culprit much closer to home.

House-to-house enquiries soon established that the Priestlys didn't get on with their downstairs neighbours, Jeannie and Alexander Donald. The Donalds had a seven-year-old daughter, also called Jeannie, who went to the same school as Helen. There were suggestions that Helen had hit Jeannie in the past. This is difficult to prove definitively, and even if we could, is there a childhood that isn't patterned with falling out with peers and neighbours? What's clear is that even though both little girls were musical, they rarely socialised. Helen played the piano – one had been bought for her as a birthday present – and she took lessons from a teacher who would come to the flat. Jeannie, meanwhile, was a talented dancer, and her mother would make dresses for her to wear at her performances. On the night that most of Aberdeen was out looking for Helen, the Donalds were attending one of Jeannie's recitals.

It emerged at trial that there'd been a 'feud' between the Priestlys and the Donalds for four years, although according to the Priestlys, 'it had all started over such trivial, piffling matters' that they couldn't remember the origin of the bad blood between the two families. This forgetfulness, which is of course another form of silence, shouldn't necessarily be taken at face value. Quite apart from the rumours that Helen had bullied Jeannie, it was suggested that she was constantly harassing Mrs Donald by knocking at their door and then running away. It was said that Mrs Donald could often be seen 'scowling' at Helen when she was playing in the street, and that Helen had called her 'coconut'. This is perhaps a reference to her hairstyle, or that she was perceived as being 'nuts' – that she had mental health problems.[32] It's hard to see how the Priestlys wouldn't have been aware of these tensions, although this does begin to creep into the territory of 'victim blaming'. Helen herself has sometimes been described by commentators as 'little' – implying her vulnerability and innocence – 'a wee bit quiet, but she was a confident girl' but, on the other hand, 'a rather unpleasant child, rude, naughty and impertinent' and 'precocious'.

Whatever the truth about Helen, and whether these incidents involving her should be seen as 'piffling' and 'trivial', there was still the matter of the rape. That obviously threw suspicion onto Alexander Donald. However, he worked as a barber in the city and had several witnesses who could place him in the barbershop at the time when Helen disappeared. It was thereafter established that Helen hadn't been raped, and that her injuries had in all likelihood been made manually. This is an example of what we would now call 'staging' behaviour – a deliberate attempt by the offender to manipulate the crime scene, or the circumstances surrounding the commission of the crime, so as to deflect the police's attention away from their guilt. Leaving Helen's body so near to the tenement either implies that it was impossible to move her further away, or that her killer was acting irrationally. I would suggest that the former hypothesis gets us closer to the truth.

Local intelligence about the feud and Jeannie's central part in it meant that suspicion now fell on her. She was quickly arrested and charged. Several pieces of evidence pointed in her direction. The blue hessian bag, for example, was only used by one Aberdeen bakery, and the owner was able to explain that he'd given such a bag to a local woman, who was quickly identified as Jeannie Donald. The bread that was found in the Donalds' flat was of a different brand from that which they normally used and was undoubtedly the bread that Helen had been sent to fetch.

A number of fledgling forensic scientific techniques also seemed to point to Jeannie's guilt. Key to all of this was John Glaister, Jr, Professor of Forensic Medicine at the University of Glasgow, who made specific studies of human and animal hair, and who has become a legendary figure in Scottish forensic medicine. He stated that hairs found on Helen's corpse and in the blue sack matched Jeannie Donald's hair. We would now describe this as pseudoscience, or even worse as 'junk science', as this practice – at a time long before the discovery of DNA – was based on disproven claims that an individual's hair could be reliably matched to them based on visual analysis. In reality microscopic analysis of hair is virtually worthless as a means of identifying someone.[33]

In any event Jeannie denied it all, and was to plead not guilty at her trial, held on Monday 16 July 1934 in Edinburgh High Court. Her defence was based entirely on discrediting the Crown's case and, in particular, that it would've been impossible for Jeannie to have raped Helen. However, three pathologists gave evidence for the Crown confirming that Helen hadn't in fact been raped, as the crime was understood at that time. The Crown called several other forensic witnesses and also used the crime-scene photographs taken by the police to support their prosecution. They suggested a sequence of events which in effect was accepted as a motive. They proposed that Jeannie, having grown tired of Helen's knocking on her door and being cheeky towards her, had hidden and waited until she returned from running her errand. Jeannie had then surprised Helen, who had an underlying thyroid problem, and this encounter had caused her to faint from the shock. Fearing that she'd killed her, Jeannie took the little girl into their flat and stored her inert body in a cupboard under the sink, before she was able to transfer it to the baker's sack, which she later left outside the tenement. The 'rape' was intended to suggest that Helen had been killed by a man, and it was alleged that Helen may have awoken from her fainting fit when this was taking place. Helen had attempted to scream, and so Jeannie had put her hand over the girl's mouth, which caused Helen to choke on her own vomit. Jeannie herself didn't give evidence, and nor was an alibi offered on her behalf – indeed she never discussed with her own legal advisors what had happened. No witnesses were called for the defence.

The jury took just eighteen minutes to find Jeannie Donald guilty of murder, and a clearly distraught judge then sentenced her to hang. This sentence was commuted to life imprisonment the following month – very few women were hanged in Scotland in the 1930s – and Jeannie spent the remainder of her custody in the women's prison in Duke Street in Glasgow. Prison officials described her as 'the finest prisoner they had ever had, quiet and well-behaved'.[34] She was granted parole ten years later, in 1944, to care for Alexander, who by that time was dying of cancer, and when the country was once again at war. Jeannie lived the rest of her life at liberty under an assumed name and died in 1976, at the age of eighty-one. She never discussed why she'd murdered Helen, not even with her own family. Like a good Aberdonian, Jeannie had a 'proud self-sufficiency'; she was impassive and unmoving – except when she cried out, having been found guilty – and strange and silent. These characteristics governed her life before the murder and equally typified what we know about her existence after her release. There was no shouting and gesticulation; no attempt to put her 'goods in the window'.

*

Let's try to make sense of this awful murder and consider whether the narrative presented by the Crown still stands up and, more broadly, put this murder in the context of the time. To do this we need to take seriously the dispute between the Priestlys and the Donalds, as this seems to be the key to unlock the silences that surround what happened. These silences have over time become embedded within a narrative that also wants to present 61 Urquhart Road as a tenement that's 'imposing but dilapidated' or, more bluntly, as a slum. The words 'tenement' and 'slum' now seem to go together; they've become synonyms and therefore interchangeable. One commentator has even described the flats in Urquhart Road as 'providing squalid and cramped living conditions for the working-class folk who were resigned to living out their lives in the oppressive surroundings'.[35] This seems like another form of victim blaming, as if these circumstances were almost chosen by the inhabitants; it denies their agency and so they become 'resigned' to live in the tenement.

It's here that the crime-scene photographs can again come

to our assistance. Thanks to the police photographer, we've internal views of the Donalds' flat and therefore a good way to assess if it deserved to be characterised as 'squalid' or 'cramped'. As far as squalid is concerned, it's obvious that the flat was clean and tidy. Mr Donald's suits hang on the kitchen door, and there's crisp, laundered white linen hanging from the pulley – a drying rack attached to the ceiling. Beneath the window is a sink, and below that a pair of cupboards. There's a basket, bucket and box of Lux in the cupboard on the right-hand side. Lux was the soap powder which undoubtedly was used to wash the shirts hanging on the pulley. It was said that this is where Helen's body was first stored after she'd been brought into the flat, before being transferred to the baker's sack and left outside in the close, where it was found by Alexander Parker the following morning. There's even a photograph of the sack, still containing the dead girl's body.

While it would be unfair to criticise the flat as being squalid, it was cramped. While the Priestlys had three rooms, the Donalds lived all of their domestic life in two. We see in a photograph a kitchen table and a few chairs dominating the main room, and a curtained alcove behind which the entire family would sleep. Mr Donald slept closest to the wall, with Jeannie in the middle, and then Mrs Donald on the outside. There would have been little or no privacy. This does raise the question as to whether Jeannie could have done all that she was convicted of without someone else being aware of what had happened. Would it really have been possible for her to have hidden Helen's body under the kitchen sink, keep it there, then bundle her into the baker's sack and take it outside without either her daughter or her husband noticing?

We also need to frame our understanding of the murder more generally within the context of tenement life in the 1930s. The most detailed account of this time comes from Ralph Glasser, a psychologist who was brought up on the third floor of a tenement in Warwick Street in the heart of the Gorbals area of Glasgow and won a scholarship to study at Oxford before the outbreak of the Second World War.[36] He was happy to put his 'goods in the window'. Glasser describes in broad and vivid detail both the communality and lack of privacy, and the many problems associated with this type of housing. He also describes how life was organised inside the tenement block by the people who lived there. He remembered that 'every foot of space was taken up by beds, mattresses on the floor, a few bare wooden chairs [and] a battered kitchen table'. As for the communality, Glasser recalls, for example, that the people in his tenement 'pooled resources' to give a family called the Varnetts 'a farewell tea' and, despite their relative poverty, how an 'unfamiliar luxury' characterised the event. On that 'special day every possible surface on our staircase, inside and outside the flats, had been scrubbed with carbolic soap'.

This event can be contrasted with what the tenement was like on a normal day. Glasser explains how Warwick Street was a place of 'grime and poverty, or rather various levels of poverty and, in retrospect, an incongruous clinging to gentility, Dickensian social attitudes and prejudices'. As such, 'respectable was an important word. Certain ways of behaving, using bad language, a girl wearing a blouse or dress too close-fitting, or in other ways too revealing or suggestive, staying out after ten at night, were not respectable.' He was at pains to point out that parents instilled in their children 'the standard prohibitions'. He did also acknowledge that violence 'was intertwined with everyday life' and that its 'inescapable rough edge, logical, cathartic' had to be accepted 'like the rain and cold'. Most important of all, violence was 'seldom random' but represented 'the working out of long-running feuds, passing quarrels, [and] drunken sessions of insult'.[37]

Instead of thinking about life in a tenement as being chaotic, unruly and anarchic, we should instead see how living there was patterned by communality, the desire for respectability, the 'clinging to gentility' and therefore how there were 'certain ways of behaving'. From this perspective there'd be some significance in the fact that the Priestlys had a piano, and a teacher who would come to the flat to give Helen her lessons. And, at the very least, Helen's playing would have created some distracting noise for the downstairs neighbours – the Donalds. Likewise, Helen's constant knocking at the door and then running away, which I find hard to believe wasn't discussed by the Donalds and the Priestlys, and calling Jeannie 'coconut' took on a significance that transcended name-calling and a childish game. These were not, in other words, 'trifling' or 'piffling' matters. Rather, over four years, these behaviours would have become symbolic of a persistent failure to acknowledge the respectability and gentility of the Donalds. As they would have seen it, they'd lost face within the tenement not only collectively as a family but also by how Jeannie as an individual had been humiliated as a woman, and as a mother.

Jeannie needed to respond to that situation, and I wonder to what extent her attack on Helen was 'cathartic' and 'logical' in the way that Glasser describes. Jeannie must have felt dishonoured, ashamed and self-conscious, and by murdering Helen she regained a recognition of the self that she felt that she'd lost with every childish knock at her door and overheard piano lesson, and whenever Helen called her 'coconut'. It's these minutiae of the everyday, which are so often lost to history, that create the rhythms and patterns that govern people's lives, and which can sadly sometimes lead to murder. In fact, this conforms to the circumstances in which many murders occur, whether in our past or today. Murder, in my experience, is often prompted by a desire to regain a self-esteem that's perceived by the murderer as having been stolen by their victim. Sometimes calling names, as much as sticks and stones, really can break bones – in a tenement flat as much as anywhere else.

CHAPTER FIVE

Cases Six and Seven

*The Murder of Rachel Dubinski, 1941,
and the Murders Committed by Gordon
Cummins – 'The Blackout Ripper'*

Aspects of life here – civility, courtesy, coziness –
have always bound Britons to their country . . .
They are part of the British myth, along with
lovely countryside, dogs and horses, rose gardens,
the Armada, the Battle of Britain.

R. W. APPLE,
New York Times, 9 October 1985

E very country has an origin myth – the story that it likes
to tell about its creation to explain who the people who
live there 'are'. Over time, these myths influence that nation's
responses to problems and crises, and guide how it will relate
to other nations. These origin myths might also help its

inhabitants to recognise something about themselves and, in turn, what sorts of compromises and accommodations they might have to make. Of course, these myths can be true, or almost true, but all too often, because their function is to simplify and suppress, they can also be deceptive. Sometimes they're simply lies.[1]

Nations – all nations – embed their origin myths not only in art, music, folklore, poetry, literature, public buildings, bank notes, stamps and statues, but also within state propaganda and even within their constitution. In explaining why, for example, the thirteen American colonies went to war against Great Britain in 1776, the preamble to the Declaration of Independence boldly states that 'We hold these truths to be self-evident, that all men are created equal, that they are endowed by their Creator with certain unalienable Rights, that among these are Life, Liberty and the pursuit of Happiness.' These powerful words are still seen to reflect American democracy and values. It's less regularly mentioned that the man who wrote them – Thomas Jefferson, who would become the third president of the United States of America – owned over six hundred enslaved people during his lifetime, which was the most of any American president.[2]

British history is even more messy, chaotic and eccentric than that of America. Our own origin myths are complicated by the fact that 'Britain' accommodates other nations and so, for example, while the Spanish Armada, referred to by the American journalist R. W. 'Johnny' Apple at the start of the chapter, does have some relevance for the story of the English and what they think about themselves, as would the Battle of Trafalgar, it doesn't necessarily have any meaning for the

Irish, Scots or Welsh. The Scots, for example, don't sing songs about Trafalgar or the failure of the Spanish Armada but about the Battle of Bannockburn – an English defeat.[3] On the other hand, in locating the 'British myth' within the Battle of Britain, Apple seems to be on safer ground and could almost have been channelling Winston Churchill himself, who told the Commons in June 1940 that 'I expect the Battle of Britain is about to begin' and:

> Upon this battle depends the survival of Christian civilisation. Upon it depends our own British life, and the long continuity of our institutions and our Empire. The whole fury and might of the enemy must very soon be turned on us. Hitler knows that he will have to break us in this island or lose the war.[4]

The Battle of Britain took place between 10 July and 31 October 1940, mostly over southern England, overlapping with the Blitz – the period of intense night air raids especially but not exclusively on London. Combined with the earlier evacuation of the British Expeditionary Force from Dunkirk between 27 May and 4 June 1940, we have the three cornerstones on which the modern British origin myth has been built.[5]

Here I'm using the term 'myth' to denote a symbolic narrative that might only sketchily relate to real events. It's the symbolism that's crucial. For example, the phrases and ideas attached to the Battle of Britain tell a story of a British David – isolated and alone – standing up against a Nazi Goliath. As the historian Alan Allport has put it, the British emerge from this type of myth-making almost as characters from Tolkien's *The Lord of the Rings*. They're hobbits, he suggests, or Shire folk; they are naïve, peaceful and unworldly – at least until they are riled. However, 'the British people who fought and defeated Hitler from 1939 to 1945 were not nearly as innocent as hobbits. Nor as unprepared for the viciousness of total war. Not anything like as nice.'[6]

*

The Battle of Britain myth involves heroes triumphing over evil, despite facing overwhelming odds. It's the story of 'the few' – those plucky and fearless British pilots, often very young men, defending the country against the battle-hardened, experienced and 'show-off' Luftwaffe, who seemed to have limitless resources to fall back on.

There are elements which are true within this narrative. Of the 2,937 RAF men who flew in the Battle of Britain, most were under the age of twenty-six. However, far from the image of dogfights in the sky, with Spitfires shooting down Messerschmitts, only about 15 per cent of fighter pilots ever shot down another aircraft. Nor was the RAF particularly out-gunned by the Luftwaffe. By September 1940, for example, the Germans had only 735 single-engine fighters ready for duty; they were losing more planes than the British and replacing the aircraft that they had lost at a much slower rate – their monthly fighter production was only 30 per cent of Britain's.[7] It should also be remembered that the British had another advantage in that they were fighting over home territory, and therefore should a pilot be shot down – and survived – he would have been able to get help, rather than be treated as an enemy combatant.

The idea of the RAF pilots being 'the few', which often becomes more generally associated with a sense that Britain was isolated and fighting the war alone, also underplays the role of pilots from defeated European nations and those of the British Empire. There were some six hundred pilots who were non-British, but more generally a lack of acknowledgement about the role played by soldiers, sailors and airmen from the Empire has come to pattern these myths. Britain could hardly paint itself as a nation of Shire folk – just eager to be left in peace – if it also acknowledged that it had managed to conquer and still controlled almost 20 per cent of the world's land surface. One way of maintaining a sense that Britain was isolated was therefore to marginalise the role of the Empire in supporting Britain during the war, from the provision of manpower and equipment to supplying goods and services, and instead create an inward-looking narrative that emphasised self-reliance, stoicism and standing alone.

None of this is meant to denigrate or disparage what happened during the Battle of Britain, when clearly great courage and sacrifice was shown by many of those involved. I'm not trying to create a 'reverse myth' – and both Dunkirk and the Battle of Britain were crucial in eventually ensuring victory over Germany. However, it's also clear that they've been co-opted to symbolise the national character and are summoned to explain what it means to be British whenever the occasion demands: peaceful, perhaps even naive, innocent and civilised but, when provoked, able to stand up to a bully with grit and determination, despite the iniquitousness of the contest. That myth might have made sense at the time, but can it really be sustained now?

'The Blitz' is derived from *Blitzkrieg* – the German word meaning 'lightning war'. It took place between September 1940 and May 1941, and while it was largely concentrated on London, the German air force also bombed other British cities, particularly Portsmouth, Southampton, Bristol, Cardiff, Birmingham, Coventry, Liverpool, Glasgow and Belfast. It was supposedly a time when people united in the face of adversity, and where the shared characteristics of a national personality surfaced. And then, through later re-telling, these features became absolute and immutable. This myth has been dramatically characterised as having:

> A great script: a small gang of fiercely independent people refuse to cave in to the bad guys. The bad guys decide to punish the wilful defiance in an appalling show of might. Despite the hardships, the small gang becomes more tightly bound, laughs in the face of terror, takes everything the forces of evil can dish out and sends them packing. A simple story, but full of drama, full of powerful images and, for the British, scripted a long time before 1940.[8]

The Blitz saw eight months of mainly night-time bombing by the Luftwaffe, during which nearly 70 per cent of all British civilian deaths and injuries during the war occurred. From September to November 1940 there were six air raids a week on the capital, resulting in at least ten thousand deaths. High-profile landmarks such as St Paul's Cathedral, Buckingham Palace and the Royal Courts of Justice were bombed, although the real focus of the raids was often the city's East End. However, it's important not to overestimate the lethal damage caused by the Blitz. While there was a 1 in 272 chance of being killed during an air raid, more Londoners died of TB that year than from German bombs. Clearly there was also damage to infrastructure and changes to how people had to live their lives – blackouts, most obviously – but there was no mass panic among the population.[9]

The Blitz has come to embody defiance in the face of adversity and a collective spirit that 'we are all in it together'[10] – transcending class and self-interest in a collective, communal show of solidarity. But when we consider the crimes committed during this time – including murder – this element of the myth quickly unravels. Crime in London was widespread. The war provided opportunities for two serial killers to begin their respective killing cycles and gave more 'ordinary' murderers opportunities too; and the blackout even gave its name to one particularly notorious spree killer. However, before describing these murders, let's consider London's wartime underworld, which effortlessly reveals that behind every myth there's a more nuanced, harsher reality.

*

Billy Hill liked to describe himself as the boss of Britain's underworld.[11] Born in London in 1911, he had twenty siblings, several of whom were also offenders. Hill describes in his autobiography[12] how he'd been a thief 'for as long as I could remember'. He served his first sentence aged fourteen, describing borstal as 'the finest finishing school for criminals any underworld could wish for', and was in and out of jails fifteen times before deciding to go straight.

Hill's speciality was 'thieving' and his gang, who were based in Camden and known as the 'Heavy Mob', became particularly adept at blowing up safes. If the occasion demanded, Hill would also use physical violence and liked to carve a V for victory sign on his victims' faces but insisted that this was only done as a last resort. His big opportunity to move up the criminal hierarchy came as a result of the war. When war was declared in 1939 the Sabinis – the Italian gang who controlled most of the crime in the city – were soon interned on the Isle of Man as foreign nationals.[13] This left London to be fought over by two rival gangs: Hill's Heavy Mob and a gang organised by five brothers called Black. The Blacks, based in Islington, initially had an advantage but, bit by bit, the Heavy Mob took control of the city and Hill, through his network of connections to Manchester, Birmingham and Glasgow, was thereafter able to establish what would now be described as a national organised crime group.

Hill characterises his offending life at this time as 'those were the roaring days, those war-time days in London. Money was easy, the villains were well loaded with dough, and we were all busy.' He insists that 'lots of people profited through the war' and suggested that this state of affairs was mainly the result of 'the shortage of police manpower' and so 'we were able to do just as we wanted'. Hill describes how:

All I had to do was to take a stroll round the West End and I was literally besieged by people wanting to buy almost anything from a pair of nylon stockings to a fresh salmon or shoulder of good smoked bacon. We were loaded with bent tom [jewellery], which we usually got rid of as soon as we could. But we also had furs, rolls of cloth suiting, shoes, textiles, whisky, rolls of silk, tea, sugar and foodstuffs, even rare spices which fetched a fortune from the Soho café proprietors who needed that sort of thing.

He said that someone should 'write a treatise on Britain's war-time black market. It was the most fantastic side of civil life in war-time – make no mistake.' In these 'halcyon days' Hill claims to have been earning £400 a week, even as he was waiting for his call-up papers (which don't ever seem to have arrived) and that he had 'money to burn. And, brother, was there some blaze.'

Hill clearly benefited from the black market, but he also committed other types of crimes. In fact, he saw the black market merely as 'bread and butter money'. The shortage of the police and the realities of the blackout provided significant opportunities. As he put it, 'the real profits always came from good screwing jobs' such as robberies and thefts, and he and his gang went as far as hiring a hearse to carry their loot so as to avoid suspicion, given how people had become used to seeing these vehicles on the streets. The gang staged a series of jewellery robberies in the West End of London, including a raid on Carrington's in Regent Street, which netted Hill £6,000. However, not everyone was this criminally sophisticated and Hill thought that 'every Tom, Dick and Harry had turned to crime', which was perhaps an allusion to the amount of looting taking place. Finally, ever the criminal entrepreneur, Hill also made money out of deserters, who 'all needed bent ration books and identity cards. They all needed money and friendship to manage to exist.'

Hill's colourful dramatisation of his crimes provides an alternative and rarely considered account of what life was like in London during the war. Of course, all autobiography tends to exaggerate as the author wants to present himself as special and extraordinary. However, it's possible to corroborate some of Hill's claims using official sources The official recorded crime statistics for England and Wales saw a 57 per cent increase between 1939 and 1945, and there was a corresponding rise in the number of people receiving a criminal conviction, which went up by 54 per cent. Court records also show that by 1945 there'd been more than 114,000 prosecutions for black market activity, and looting was so rife that in November 1940 it featured in twenty of the fifty-six cases heard at the Old Bailey.[14]

One gang of looters, called the 'bomb-chasers', often wore official ARP (Air Raid Precautions) helmets and arm bands as disguises and drove what appeared to be an ambulance – they were so convincing that members of the public often helped them. The private papers of the Reverend John Markham, rector of St Peter's Walworth in south-east London, who had responsibilities for training ARP wardens, are particularly enlightening on this aspect of criminal activity. He describes how he had to make 'discreet inquiries' about one man who volunteered 'and found out that he was a burglar and that his van was full of tools.' This man would drive to business premises that had been hit by a bomb 'and dive into the ruins to find the safe. His only concern with us was that he wanted the cover of a warden's badge as an identity card.' The Reverend Markham, with some exasperation, described how he was loath to leave the possessions of people who'd been killed in an air raid even for a few hours or 'they would be gone'.[15]

Hill's autobiography is even more interesting about the

idea that people pulled together during the Blitz – something which is exposed when he attempts to justify his criminal enterprises. This justification might be termed a 'class analysis'. For example, he observes that 'no one can deny that even during our worst rationing periods the rich people with available cash could get what they wanted', as opposed to 'the workers' who had to go without. He also noted that 'if you had the chance to walk into any of our posher hotels in any city during the war, you could see the rich gorging to their hearts' content'. As far as Hill saw things, in what was already an iniquitous situation he might as well make a profit out of those who could afford his services. He went further in his analysis and implicated the state. He observed that what he'd learned about Sir Francis Drake and Sir Walter Raleigh at school was that they had been 'gangsters – weren't they nicking something that didn't belong to them? Only because it was on behalf of their government that made it legal.' He used this as an explanation for 'nicking a bit of fruit from the stalls in Seaton Street market near where I lived'. As for empire, Hill believed that 'as far as I can see, the British Empire, and all empires for that matter, were all nicked in the first place'.

There's evidence to support some of what Hill describes from one remarkable source – Mary Churchill, the prime minister's youngest child. Mary was born in 1922, and her papers offer a wonderful insight into the life of a young, privileged woman at the height of the Blitz. She's been described as pretty and spirited, but also somewhat naive, which comes across in some of her writing. Armed with a £5 weekly allowance from her parents, Mary enjoyed all that London had to offer, and noted that 'despite the blackout, theatres were full, there were plenty of nightclubs for late dancing after restaurants closed, and many people still gave dinner parties'.[16] Two of her favourite places to go – after she had dined at the Savoy Hotel – were the Players' Theatre near Covent Garden and the 400 Club, the 'night-time headquarters of Society' located in Leicester Square. These experiences would obviously be outside the pockets of working-class Londoners.

A sad echo of what Hill describes also emerges when Mary remembers the bombing of the Café de Paris, a nightclub located on Coventry Street in Piccadilly. On 8 March 1941 two bombs fell down a ventilation shaft into the basement ballroom and exploded in front of the stage where Ken 'Snakehips' Johnson was performing with his band. Thirty-four people were killed, including Snakehips, who was decapitated, and eighty were injured. Mary and a group of friends had been on their way to the Café de Paris, but found their way blocked and had to go elsewhere. When they eventually realised what had happened, Mary wrote, it made things feel 'real – many fatal & serious casualties. They were laughing and dancing just like us. They are gone now in a moment from all we know to the vast, infinite unknown.' Tom Shaughnessy, one of her group, thought that they should all just carry on with their revelries, and so they did until the early hours of the morning. Mary later reflected that 'I am a little shocked that we headed off to find somewhere else to twirl whatever was left of the night away'.[17]

What Mary and her friends perhaps didn't know was that looters immediately descended on the Café de Paris and rummaged through the coats and handbags of the dead and dying to remove their watches and jewellery. Some went even

135

further. An eyewitness, Ballard Berkeley, remembered that 'one hears a lot about bravery during the war, but there were also some very nasty people ... these people slipped in pretty quickly [after the explosion] and it was full of people – firemen, wardens, police – so it was very easy to cut off a finger here [to take a ring] or steal a necklace, and it did happen'.[18]

The truth is, whatever myths we may tell ourselves about the Blitz spirit, many people were out for themselves. Of course, the looters at the Café de Paris were stealing from those who'd been killed by German bombs, but home-grown British murderers could also use the opportunities that war provided to kill and try to evade detection too.

*

The relative absence of police, and blackout conditions at night, provided not only the cover of darkness for a prospective killer, but also lessened the chances of their being caught. And, as with looters, they could use the uniforms of those who were legitimately expected to be out in the streets to hide evil intentions and create a sense of trust in those whom they targeted. The serial killer Reg Christie, for example, actually became a War Reserve constable (even though he already had a criminal record) and was zealous in enforcing blackout conditions in the neighbourhood around Rillington Place in Notting Hill, where he and his wife Ethel lived. He oozed authority in his uniform and tin hat, and so enjoyed the power that came with this role that he was known locally as 'the Himmler of Rillington Place'. His role also allowed him access to people and places that he might not otherwise have had, and it's likely that this was how he met and gained the trust of his first victim, Ruth Fuerst, whom he murdered in August 1943 after they'd had a brief affair. Christie then buried Ruth in the back garden of 10 Rillington Place, prior to Ethel returning from Sheffield, where she'd been staying with relatives.[19]

Ethel Christie, who would also be murdered, was just one of a mass movement of people in and out of the city. By the end of September 1939, the population of Greater London had shrunk by 1.4 million from a pre-war total of 8.6 million.[20] Some of these people, especially children, were formally evacuated, while many simply moved to avoid the bombs and then, like Ethel, returned as the raids over the city became less frequent. Others wanted to avoid being called up. John George Haigh, another London-based serial killer, known more popularly as the 'Acid Bath Murderer', killed his first victim, William McSwann, in September 1944. To cover up his disappearance Haigh explained to William's parents, Donald and Amy, that their son had wanted to avoid military service and so was hiding in Scotland until the war ended. He forged several letters in William's handwriting, explaining that he was indeed in Scotland, and sent them to the McSwanns to maintain the pretence. At the end of the war, when William would have been expected to reappear, Haigh simply killed Amy and Donald too. So, between 1943 and 1949 – when Haigh was arrested, convicted and then executed – there were two active serial killers operating in London, both using the disruption of war and its aftermath to cover their tracks.[21]

Haigh used acid to destroy the bodies of his victims and then poured the messy human sludge down the drains, although later, when he had access to factory premises, he refined this technique. Other murderers simply used the reality that, after an air raid, dead bodies were often found in the bombed-out debris of ruined buildings. Who'd be able to tell if the person had been killed by the falling bombs, or had met their end by more sinister means? And even if there were suspicions about what might have happened, would the authorities be able to identify the victim if the body was sufficiently mutilated? We should also remember that with scores of people dying every day, the will to pursue a murder investigation was undermined, as it generated other fears. Quite apart from discouraging the idea that people were united and all pulling together as a result of having a common enemy, murder also implied that the formal agents of law and order might not be able to cope or keep the civilian population safe.[22]

*

We know surprisingly little about Rachel Dubinski, except that she came from a traditional Jewish background and had four sisters – Polly, Mary, Florence and Hannah – and a brother called Nathan. We know that she married Harry Dobkin at Bethnal Green Synagogue on 5 September 1920 and that their marriage was arranged by a shadkhan, a Jewish marriage broker. It wasn't a happy union. Harry was later asked at his trial, 'Were you fond of your wife?' to which he replied 'No, sir,' and when questioned as to when this state of affairs had started, he answered rather tartly, 'The day I got married.' The couple parted ways after six weeks, although by that stage Rachel was pregnant and would later give birth to a son called Stanley. The couple were legally separated after three months, and Rachel secured a maintenance order against Harry for £1 per week, although he rarely paid. As a result, he was sent to prison on several occasions, and even though the maintenance order was subsequently reduced to ten shillings per week, he'd still end up back in prison for non-payment and was only released in October 1940, some five months before Rachel disappeared.

Almost everything else about Rachel's life is rather sketchy. We've now uncovered her date of birth – 7 August 1892 – but when her sister Polly was first questioned about this she wasn't sure, apart from agreeing that when she disappeared Rachel was in her forties. Nor did she really know Rachel's natural hair colour, or her height. She was, however, in possession of a solitary black-and-white photograph that had been taken of her sister in the 1930s, when she'd been visiting a holiday camp. Polly had then had this holiday snap enlarged by a professional photographer. A somewhat waspish commentator from the time suggested that in the photograph Rachel looked like 'a rather wan, damp, dispirited personality, but she'd somehow contrived to twist her features into a watery smile'.[23] That's uncharitable, and perhaps if she was dispirited it might've been because she had to spend so much of her time chasing Harry for money. There were also allegations that Harry had assaulted her in the past, although the charges brought against him were subsequently dismissed. Polly later suggested that Rachel had been so badly hurt during one such assault that she'd ended up in hospital. She'd even visited Rachel at St Clement's Hospital in Bow but was distressed when she discovered that this was an asylum, and so she had Rachel discharged. Finally, we also know that Rachel liked to visit a medium with the glamorous name of Madam Nerva, although this rather chic title was undermined by the fact that the medium's first name appears to have been Hilda. Perhaps these visits imply that Rachel wanted something more in her life; that she had dreams and ambitions which kept being thwarted and so she was eager to know when her luck might change.

Compared with this lack of information, we know much more about the day that Rachel disappeared. On 11 April 1941 she met Harry at a café in Kingsland Road in Shoreditch, near to where he lived. Exactly why she wanted to see her long-estranged husband is a matter of conjecture, although he seems to have still owed her money. By then Stanley was nineteen years old and so he could hardly be described as a child. Rachel was wearing a fawn tweed jacket, a blue woollen jumper, navy blue skirt, black shoes and a brown hat. They had a cup of tea together and then, according to Harry, had parted on good terms. He watched as Rachel caught the number 22 bus, which would've taken her back to her mother's house in Bethnal Green. That was about 6.30 p.m., and then Harry claimed he'd gone off to buy a pair of trousers.

Rachel never made it to her mother's and was reported as missing the following day by Polly. She obviously shared with the police her suspicions about Harry, his short but turbulent marriage to her sister and how he'd been in prison on several occasions. It was four days before the police got round to interviewing Harry, who was working as a fire watcher for a firm of solicitors located on Kennington Lane. The police would have known that there had been a fire two days earlier in the cellar of Vauxhall Baptist Church in Kennington Lane, near to where Harry worked, even though there'd been no air raids that night. The police searched the solicitors' premises and questioned Harry at some length. They seem to have reasoned that it was unlikely that he would've killed his ex-wife after twenty years, and, in any event, Harry had no history of violence on his record. Rachel was just one of those women who, for various reasons, disappeared during the war, and may have had mental health issues. Perhaps, they thought, she'd taken her own life. In essence, as one historian has put it, they were both dismissed as 'pathetic characters' – an ex-wife with mental health problems and a rather hapless, feckless husband.[24]

Nothing more was known about Rachel until some bones were discovered by workmen clearing up the debris of damaged buildings in Kennington Lane on 17 July 1942. Parts of a skeleton were found, with a few pieces of flesh still attached, under a flagstone in a cellar of the Baptist church. Initially it was thought that the remains must have belonged to an air-raid victim and they were taken to the mortuary at St George's Hospital. The coroner, Hervey Wyatt, then asked Dr Keith Simpson – lecturer in forensic medicine at Guy's Hospital – to perform a routine post-mortem on these 'bits of old air-raid casualty'. Three months later Harry would be charged with Rachel's murder.

All the uncertainty and confusion about Rachel's life and circumstances, and specifically what had happened to her after she left her former husband to supposedly catch the bus home, would be transformed through Simpson's investigation. Where there had once been ambiguity and doubt, now there was order and certainty. We might still not know that much more about Rachel's life, but Simpson seemed to be able to allay the public's fears that anonymous bodies and bones would ultimately be identified, and that wrongdoing would be punished by the state.

We have two good, if somewhat contradictory, sources about Simpson's investigation: his own memoir, *Forty Years of Murder*, published in 1978; and that of his somewhat eccentric secretary Molly Lefebure, *Evidence for the Crown: Experiences of a Pathologist's Secretary*, published in 1959.[25] Lefebure remembers Simpson taking possession of the 'bits' and saying to her, 'Well, the probability is that she's no more than an air-raid victim, but even so she will provide me with a very interesting essay in reconstruction; some entertaining spare-time work.' Perhaps because this reduces Rachel to a form of gruesome lab entertainment and rather detracts from his reputation, Simpson's account, published twenty years later, is far more professional and claims that he knew immediately that Rachel had been a murder victim. Of course, by the time his memoir was published Simpson was something of a celebrity and, having read his former secretary's book, wanted to enhance his part in what became known as the 'Dobkin Case'. However, at the time he was accorded a relatively secondary role by the police, who already had suspicions through their knowledge of their earlier interviews with Harry about the disappearance of his ex-wife.

There were two distinct features to Simpson's investigation. First, he had to discover how the victim had died and then, second, could the victim be identified? The skeleton had been found neatly buried under a slab of stone, as opposed to in a bomb crater, and this suggested that the cause of death hadn't been the result of a bomb blast. He also noted that the head and limbs had been cut cleanly through and that the lower limbs and lower jaw were missing. The tissue had been stripped from the skull, except for a small patch at the back, which had brown and grey hairs still attached. The body had been burned in several places. Slaked lime was also found sprinkled on and around the corpse, and this had killed any maggots which might have eaten all the flesh. As a result, there was still tissue preserved on the throat and the womb. Finally, Simpson also found a dried blood clot in the larynx, which was bruised and which indicated to him pressure had been exerted when the victim was still alive. Simpson concluded that death was the result of strangulation.[26]

Simpson used a number of forensic techniques to form an impression of who this victim might have been by calculating height and hair colour, although we need to remember that the police were aware that Rachel Dobkin had disappeared. He also had Mary Newman, head of the Photography Department at Guy's Hospital, replicate a photographic technique that had been used in Scotland several years earlier, in the Buck Ruxton murder case.[27] This involved superimposing the holiday snap taken of Rachel onto a photograph of the skull that had been found. As Simpson later noted, 'the portrait fitted the skull like a mask'. Dental records were also used to confirm that the victim was indeed Rachel Dobkin. In total, Simpson concluded that he could establish twenty-four points of identification between Rachel and the remains that had been found in the cellar of the church. Harry was duly charged with his ex-wife's murder, and the jury took just twenty minutes to find him guilty at his trial at the Old Bailey on 17 November 1942. He was executed at HMP Wandsworth on 27 January 1943, and both Simpson and Molly Lefebure were in the prison to perform his post-mortem. As Simpson was later to say, it was the case 'that every young pathologist dreams of' and Lefebure's conclusion was much the same – it was 'the case of a lifetime'.

The 'Dobkin Case' might have made Simpson's reputation, and it was certainly a cause célèbre in the newspapers at the time, but it's hard to escape the conclusion that Rachel has become rather lost in the process. 'Dobkin' might just as easily apply to Harry as it does to Rachel (which is why I've used their first names throughout the chapter). In fact, because of his trial, we know considerably more about him than his ex-wife. Poor Rachel has become a footnote in the history of forensic science; a bundle of bones and some flesh to be reconstructed by a brilliant man; and a painful reminder that husbands – and ex-husbands – all too often kill their wives. The desire of the authorities to use the case to suggest that killers would get punished and that the police were up to the job also undermines the reality that the police were overstretched and that many killers often got away with murder for exactly the reasons that I've outlined. Although he too would be caught, and more quickly than Harry Dobkin, all of this becomes even more dramatically exposed in the case of Gordon Cummins – the 'Blackout Ripper' – whose four victims have become almost as anonymous as Rachel Dobkin.

*

The crimes of Gordon Cummins have been described as 'rarely told' or simply as 'forgotten'.[28] That's inaccurate, as there have been a number of books about the 'Blackout Ripper' or the 'Wartime Ripper', as well as book chapters, and several true crime documentaries and podcasts about the six-day period in February 1942, when he killed four women in London and attempted to kill two others.[29] A great deal of this coverage centres on his ghastly, sadistic activities and his use of a range of domestic items to cut and slash, insert and defile – sometimes while he was in the act of killing, but also after his victim had died.

Cummins never admitted his guilt and said nothing substantive when he was interviewed by a prison psychiatrist while awaiting trial. That means we're left with several questions as to why this seemingly feckless but happily married man, who appears to have been socialised in other aspects of his life, would have wanted to engage in this type of extreme and sexualised behaviour. There are a few clues. He pretended to be from a titled family – his acquaintances teasingly called him 'the Duke' or 'the Count' – which suggests that he lived in a fantasy world. He was often offending when he was drunk, or at least when he'd been drinking heavily. However, perhaps we should simply see his attacks, murders and sexual sadism as a bizarre, situational and personal reaction to war. The blackout, and the fact that he wore his RAF uniform when offending, simply created for him the conditions in which these personal demons could be expressed and which therefore allowed him to attack and murder.

Whatever might have motivated Cummins, there's still the depressing reality of the four women that he killed, and at least two others whom he assaulted. It is these women, rather than Cummins, who've been forgotten and it's their stories that are rarely told. When they are remembered, they've often been characterised as 'prostitutes', which is simply untrue in at least one case, and what should it matter if the others did at times sell sexual services? Like Rachel Dobkin they've become the basis on which to discuss the success of forensic pathology, or the police's investigation.

Cummins was eventually convicted and hanged for the murder of Evelyn Oatley, who was killed on 10 February 1942 in her flat in Soho. Evelyn, who sometimes used the name Leta Ward, was the wife of a poultry farmer from Lancashire, but had come to London in 1936 in the hope of getting stage work. Her husband would often visit and had recently stayed with her for a week – only returning north on 3 February. Evelyn worked in various nightclubs as a hostess, having given up her hopes of becoming a star like her idol Gracie Fields, and occasionally sold sexual services.

Evelyn was Cummins's second victim, but he was charged with her murder as there was good forensic evidence in the shape of numerous fingerprints which connected him to the crime scene. His first victim, where the forensic evidence was much weaker, was forty-one-year-old Evelyn Hamilton, a pharmacist whose body was discovered in a street-level air-raid shelter in Marylebone on the morning of 9 February. It was clear from her injuries that Evelyn had put up a ferocious fight and this might have deterred Cummins from engaging in any sexual assault or post-mortem mutilation. Evelyn, an independent woman in a professional job, had recently re-signed from a position in Hornchurch in Essex, and was only in London prior to catching a train to take her up to a new role in a chemist's shop in Grimsby.

Cummins's third and fourth murder victims were Margaret Florence Lowe and Doris Jouannet. Margaret was a single mother with a fifteen-year-old daughter called Barbara, whom she was putting through a private school in Southend-on-Sea. Barbara would visit her mother at the weekends and the pair would go off together to visit various

London landmarks. One of the ways that Margaret paid for her daughter's school fees was by selling sexual services. She was murdered in her flat in Marylebone on 11 February, although her body lay undiscovered for a further two days until Barbara came to visit. Doris was murdered on the evening of 12 February in the two-roomed ground-floor flat in Bayswater that she shared with her French husband Henri, who had fallen on hard times and was working in a hotel. She only occasionally sold sexual services when she 'needed a few extra shillings', bringing her clients back while Henri was out. Doris's body had been horribly mutilated, although it was established that the cause of her death was strangulation.

In between the murders of Margaret and Doris, on 12 February Cummins had attacked Catherine Mulcahy, a sex worker who was able to escape serious injury through summoning the help of a neighbour, and then the following evening he assaulted a young married woman called Margaret Heywood. After they had shared a drink, he pushed Margaret into a doorway near Piccadilly Circus and started to strangle her. She lost consciousness but was saved when Cummins fled the scene having been disturbed by a delivery boy called John Shine. In his haste Cummins left behind his RAF-issue gas mask and haversack, and the former had his service number printed inside. When he realised his mistake, he stole another airman's gas mask and haversack in an effort to deflect the blame, but after a six-day spree of murder and assault he was finally apprehended. He was executed at HMP Wandsworth on 25 June 1942.

*

The crimes that Billy Hill, his Heavy Mob and others committed during the Blitz undermine the myth that everyone was 'pulling together' against a common enemy. A surprising number of people were simply out for themselves. Those committed by Cummins are also a dramatic reminder that women could face dangers from those who were wearing a British uniform, as much as they might be bombed by the Luftwaffe. The blackout and the relative absence of policing offered opportunities for many who wanted to rob, loot, rape and murder, among them those who might never have previously considered that they'd be capable of doing so. It's hard to escape the conclusion that for every Harry Dobkin who was apprehended, many more like him seem to have evaded justice. Even Cummins was only caught because he was spiralling out of control and taking greater risks. How many more women might he have murdered if John Shine hadn't interrupted him, forcing him to leave incriminating evidence behind? War might have shone a light on the best and the bravest, but we've too easily forgotten that it also allowed others to flourish in the shadows.

CHAPTER SIX

Case Eight

The Murder of Kelso Cochrane, 1959

If Labour win the next general election – which
I doubt – then Britain might just as well fold
itself up and disappear quietly into the bottom of
the sea.

JOHN GEORGE HAIGH, the 'Acid Bath Murderer',
in a letter to his parents written from the
condemned cell at HMP Wandsworth, 1949

The murder at the heart of this chapter is the racist killing of Kelso Cochrane, a thirty-two-year-old carpenter, on 17 May 1959 in Notting Hill, west London. It happened while he was walking home from hospital, where he'd been having his broken thumb re-plastered. Originally from Antigua, Kelso was not the first, and nor would he be the last, black person murdered because of the colour of their skin. In fact, his death offers a tragic foretaste of the murder of the black teenager Stephen Lawrence over thirty years later.

As far as we know, Kelso was the first black person murdered in Britain since 1945 although, as discussed, given the ability of the state to suppress the actual numbers of murders in any given year it's entirely possible that other black people had been murdered before 1959. Kelso's murder is significant because it both looks forwards to post-war issues which would become more pressing, such as immigration and how to integrate those who come to Britain to make it their home, and backwards to the end of the Second World War and how that conflict shaped events after 1945. That shaping took a surprising direction in the first general election that was called – just two months after the conclusion of the war in Europe.

*

The general election of 5 July 1945 saw a landslide victory for the Labour Party, led by Clement Attlee. Sir Winston Churchill, the country's inspirational wartime leader, was trounced at the ballot box and, contrary to John George Haigh's prediction quoted at the start of the chapter, Attlee would also go on to win the next general election too, albeit with a much-reduced majority of just five seats. By then Haigh had been executed. Haigh, like many of the serial killers that I've interviewed, was a bit of a snob and complained bitterly in the letters that he wrote to his parents of post-war Britain being governed by 'uncouth colliery and railway clerks'.

Britain was indeed transformed between 1945 and Kelso's murder fourteen years later, even if the city in which he was killed was still scarred by the German bombing campaign and unexploded bombs continued to be discovered. As recently as 2018, the Ministry of Defence explained that it had to make safe about sixty Second World War bombs every year through controlled explosions.[1] However, most importantly for our history, the National Health Service was set up in 1948 and a variety of industries – coal, steel and the railways, and utilities such as gas and electricity – were nationalised. The establishment of the 'welfare state', the foundations for which had been laid in 1942 by a ground-breaking report by William Beveridge, aimed at abolishing the 'five giants' – want, disease, squalor, ignorance and idleness – is rightly regarded as one of the most significant developments in British history.

As the 1940s gave way to the 1950s, traditional accounts have concentrated on describing several set-piece events including the Suez Crisis, the Cold War, the existential threat posed to civilisation by the atom bomb and seemingly equally threatening developments in popular culture, especially those associated with young people. What drives much of this type of narrative is an attempt to understand whether or not Britain was in decline as a global player. Such discussions often harness a famous quote from prime minister Harold Macmillan in 1957: 'Let us be frank about it: most of our people have never had it so good.'[2] This period was seen not just as a time of greater prosperity but also when people, especially working-class people, were better educated and lived for longer, although within a Britain that seemed to wield less power and influence on the world stage.

Politically, this is characterised as a time dominated by 'consensus'. This rather underplays how the Labour government broke with economic orthodoxy and instead embraced the progressive liberal economics of John Maynard Keynes.

However, the social welfarism that came to direct the policies of the 1940s and 1950s was accepted by all major political parties. This type of state support can be traced back to the early decades of the twentieth century and especially to the inter-war years when, as I've suggested, 'people mattered', although this was expanded further and then fully embedded after 1945.

Consensus literally means a generally agreed position or opinion, and suggests that everyone was pulling in the same direction. This might have been the case within the political process, as Labour and the Conservatives accepted and then adopted much of the same broad governmental agenda when they were in office. However, there were several populist tensions within the country. Race was and continues to remain one such tension.

The politics of law and order are an instructive way to open up this post-war period. This era was the beginning of 'English exceptionalism' – when the criminal justice policies of England and Wales (and to a lesser extent Scotland) took a very different direction from those of our European neighbours. This exceptionalism continues to this day and therefore can be seen to help to define what modern Britain is. The first major piece of legislation about criminal justice after the war was the Criminal Justice Act of 1948 which abolished penal servitude, whipping and hard labour; the Prison Rules – introduced in 1949 – asserted that prison existed to help prisoners lead a 'good and useful life'; the Prison Act of 1952 laid the foundations for our current arrangements within prisons; the much-praised 1959 white paper, Penal Practice in a Changing Society, attempted to bring the penal system in line with post-war social arrangements; and HMP Grendon, which opened in 1962, is still the only British prison to operate wholly as a therapeutic community.

However, what really happened after the war to create this 'English exceptionalism' is that our prison population started to grow in ever greater numbers – and which for a time included someone suspected of Kelso's murder. Far from the rosy view suggested by notions of prisons offering a 'good and useful life' for inmates and the establishment of HMP Grendon, penal regimes became harder and much less tolerant.[3] The 1948 Criminal Justice Act, for example, also introduced detention centres – new institutions for young people who, according to James Chuter Ede, Labour's Home Secretary, were 'a type of offender to whom it appears necessary to give a short but sharp reminder that he is getting into ways that will inevitably land him in disaster'.[4] These views were the origins of the 'short, sharp, shock' of Margaret Thatcher's Conservative government in the 1980s. As for the numbers of people being sent inside, the average daily prison population in 1938 was just over eleven thousand men and women but ten years later had increased to about twenty thousand and by 1958 it was over twenty-five thousand. And, except for a small drop in numbers in the early 1990s, the prison population has continued to grow inexorably over our time frame.[5]

It might be possible to locate the origins of exceptionalism in Britain and Europe's differing experiences of war. Mainland Europe seemed to want to make sense of and then come to terms with having lived under the jackboot of Nazi occupation, and therefore saw a common bond with those whom it subsequently imprisoned. For example, the entire Law Faculty of the University of Oslo had been incarcerated during the Nazi collaborationist regime of Vidkun Quisling, and when they were subsequently released wrote the most liberal penal code to be adopted within all of Europe. The maximum penalty in Norway for *any* crime became twenty-one years – a term that remains to this day.[6] Britain, on the other hand, saw itself as 'standing alone', having to remain defiant in the face of the threat of invasion, as well as dealing with the realities of the crime wave during the Blitz, and therefore had much less sympathy with those who committed crime. We happily locked criminals up and saw no common cultural bond between the offender and those who were law-abiding. This makes the murder of Kelso, and especially the failure of the police to bring his killer to justice, all the more troubling.

*

We know much more about Kelso's murder in the early hours of 17 May 1959, and the failed police investigation to find his killer, than we do about his life.[7] We do know he was born in 1926, in the small Antiguan village of Johnson's Point, and that he had several siblings and half-siblings, including four brothers: Stanley, Eustace, Fitz and Malcolm. Stanley remembers Kelso working with their father – also called Stanley – in his carpentry workshop and that their father had built the Cochrane home. It would be at his father's side that Kelso would learn his own carpentry skills, although he also harboured dreams of becoming a lawyer. We know that when he was nineteen Kelso moved to Dominica, where he worked as a carpenter, but, for whatever reason, he returned to Antigua three years later. He moved to Florida in 1949, briefly joined the US Army and then married a woman from South Carolina with the marvellous name of Kansas Green. They had a daughter, whom they named Josephine, and the couple left Florida for New York, where they seem to have been supported by one of Kelso's uncles, who was a lawyer. Their marriage didn't work out and there were allegations of domestic abuse. This has never been proven but the marriage was obviously unhappy and ended in divorce. In February 1954 Kelso's American visa expired and so he was deported back to Antigua. Neither Dominica nor the USA, the army or becoming a husband and father had provided Kelso with the platform on which to build his life. However, he was still a young man and clearly restless. This time, as a British citizen he wanted to try his luck in the 'mother country', and his brother Stanley loaned him the money for his passage across the Atlantic. Kelso boarded a French liner called *Colombie* in Guadeloupe, listed his occupation as a carpenter and gave his proposed address as Liverpool. He arrived in Plymouth on 4 September 1954, but instead of Liverpool headed for London.

Five years later, we know that Kelso was living in a rented room at 11 Bevington Road, situated at the northern end of Portobello Road in Notting Hill, west London. This was a district where many Caribbean immigrants settled, and the area of Colville in particular became known as 'Brown Town'. In the weeks before his murder Kelso's girlfriend, Olivia Ellington, a trainee nurse from Jamaica, moved into his bedsit and friends later suggested that she and Kelso had talked about getting married. At this time Kelso was working as a carpenter, earning £15 per week and was described as 'quiet and hard-working'. He was tall and athletic, a smart dresser and he loved jazz – especially Ella Fitzgerald. On the Wednesday before his murder Kelso had broken his left thumb at work, and this resulted in him having to wear a plaster cast. On Saturday 16 May he and Olivia had done some shopping and then met up with Kelso's younger brother Malcolm, who was living in Stoke Newington. After Malcolm left Bevington Road, Kelso and Olivia had gone to Hyde Park to visit Speakers' Corner, then returned home later in the evening.

The pain in Kelso's thumb prevented him from getting to sleep and so he decided to go to Paddington General Hospital on Harrow Road. He was seen by Dr James Givans, who prescribed strong painkillers, and the doctor remembered that Kelso had been 'pleasant, smiling and sober'. These details would later become important in correcting some local rumours. Kelso seems to have left the hospital just before midnight and begun the walk home – he didn't have money for a taxi.

As he approached the junction of Southam Street and Golborne Road a gang of five or six white youths surrounded him. There was shouting, pushing and shoving, and it would've been difficult for Kelso to have defended himself as not only was he outnumbered, he also had one of his arms in plaster – perhaps it was this obvious vulnerability which had encouraged the youths to attack him in the first place. A few seconds later he was lying on the ground outside the Bagwash Laundry, just yards away from a police phone box which linked directly to Harrow Road police station. Kelso had been stabbed through the heart, although he didn't die there in the street. He was taken by taxi to St Charles' Hospital, about half a mile away, by Horatio Lewis and Ken Steele, two passers-by who'd witnessed the fight. At about half past midnight they arrived at the hospital, where Dr Mohammed Seddiq and a nurse attended to Kelso. Fifteen minutes later, he was pronounced dead.

By then, Detective Sergeant Sidney Coomber and Detective Constable Frank Buchan were at the hospital, and it was Coomber who informed Horatio and Ken of Kelso's death. Dr Donald Teare, the Home Office pathologist, would later conduct the post-mortem and declared that Kelso had died from a wound made by a 'very sharp, stiletto-type knife driven in horizontally, entering through the fifth rib, penetrating two inches, deep into the main chamber of the heart, thereby causing severe haemorrhaging'. It was a wound, observed Dr Teare, that had been 'delivered with unusual velocity' and which required 'considerable force'. No trace of alcohol was found in Kelso's blood during the post-mortem.

Meanwhile, some time between two and three in the morning at the *Sunday Express*, a junior reporter called Frank Draper received an anonymous tip-off that 'three white youths had stabbed a darkie [*sic*] named Cochrane on Golborne Road, Notting Hill'. The front page of the paper's 4 a.m. edition led with the headline 'Murder in Notting Hill'. We don't know who it was that had provided this information.

*

Who murdered Kelso and why was no one ever charged and convicted of the crime? The first question is much easier to answer than the second, as there's little doubt that we know the identity of Kelso's killer. It was described as an 'open secret' at the time, and the murderer has since been named in a book and several newspapers.[8] Of course, in the 1950s policing and forensic science still relied on witness testimony, the harvesting of local intelligence, blood typing, matching fibres found on the victim to clothes worn by the suspect and finding the murder weapon, but even in the absence of DNA fingerprinting and all the developments in forensic science more generally, there was still an excellent chance of bringing charges in the case.

There were several witnesses who saw Kelso being killed: Horatio Lewis, Ken Steele, George Isaacs – who drove the taxi to St Charles' Hospital – as well as a young woman called Joy Okine and her mother, who observed the attack from the first-floor window of their flat on the corner of Golborne Road. The police were at the crime scene within hours of the murder taking place, and quite quickly several staff were assigned to the case. At the height of the investigation there were twenty-four officers working on Kelso's murder, divided into three teams, each with a specific task: conducting house-to-house enquiries; interviewing local youths who were in the area at the time and who had a criminal record; and, finally, searching for the murder weapon, which was known to be a stiletto-type knife, five to six inches long. These teams were under the over-all command of Detective Superintendent Ian Forbes-Leith.

Forbes-Leith is an interesting character. Known as 'the pride of Hendon', he'd joined the Metropolitan Police in 1936 under the Trenchard Scheme. Hendon Police College, de-scribed as a 'police Sandhurst', had been established by Lord Trenchard, who became Commissioner of the Metropolitan Police in 1931, and the Trenchard Scheme was his attempt to introduce an 'officer class' into what was seen at the time as an 'artisan service'. The scheme was resented by many within the Metropolitan Police and policing more generally, partly because it was seen to limit the promotion prospects of those who were recruited in traditional ways. Sir Robert Mark, for example, who would himself become Metropolitan Police Commissioner in 1972, was a grammar-school boy who didn't go to Hendon, but had instead joined the Manchester Police in 1937. He'd later describe in his autobiography how policing has 'nothing to do with the creation of a socially acceptable status designed to equate the police with the armed forces'.[9] On the other hand, the public-school educated Forbes-Leith comfortably conformed to the stereotype of the new breed of police officer that Trenchard had encouraged. He had impeccable manners, was conscious of the clothes he wore, and was rarely photographed without a bowler hat and smoking a pipe. He quickly rose up the ranks and in 1955, at the age of thirty-eight, became the youngest detective superintendent ever appointed by the Metropolitan Police. Promotion to an even higher level seemed guaranteed.

The police arrested and interviewed several people, but two youths in particular were suspected of having been involved in the murder and so were kept in police custody for over forty-eight hours. Pat Digby was a twenty-year-old painter and decorator who had previously been employed as a steward in the merchant navy, and his twenty-four-year-old friend Shoggy Breagan worked as a labourer. On the night that Kelso was murdered they'd both been at a party at Ma O'Brien's house in 18 Southam Street, although they initially told the police that they'd never left the party. Police visited their homes and removed articles of clothing, and both eventually admitted that they had indeed been in the street when Kelso was killed. They'd left the party after all but, they claimed, it must have been after Kelso had been attacked as they saw Horatio and Ken offering him help. Digby admitted that he had blood on his clothes but explained that this was because he and Shoggy had been fighting. Shoggy was arrested separately, after Digby, but they'd had every chance to corroborate their stories about the night in question, as they were placed in adjoining cells at Harrow Road police station. As for how the blood had got onto Digby's clothes, many years later Shoggy admitted that it wasn't true that they'd been fighting, although there's very little that he said that can be relied upon. Shoggy had been arrested on several occasions in the past, and just nine days before Kelso was murdered he'd been released from HMP Maidstone, where he'd been serving a three-year sentence for grievous bodily harm – he'd participated in an attack on three black men in Paddington.

Pat Digby is believed to have been Kelso's murderer. He confessed to his friends at the time and later to his stepdaughter, who constantly challenged him about what he'd done. It's this local intelligence which has led to the identity of Kelso's killer being described as 'the worst-kept secret in Notting Hill'. It's also been suggested that Digby hid the murder weapon – which was never found – under the floorboards of his mother's house in Wilsham Street. Pat Digby died of ischaemic heart disease in December 2007, and so it's impossible to test whether his confession at the time, and what he said thereafter, could be used as the basis on which to bring a murder charge.

If all of this is accurate, the next question that logically flows is why were charges never brought in 1959? Can the answer be, as one commentator has put it, 'the will to convict just wasn't there [and] that it was considered best to let it lie'.[10] 'It' is, of course, a reference to Kelso's murder, but who was it that considered this to be the best course of action, or rather inaction? To understand whether this evaluation of the case is credible, we need to go back to the race riots that took place in Notting Hill the year before Kelso was killed.

*

The Notting Hill riots began on the August bank holiday weekend of 1958 and continued until Wednesday 3 September. No one was killed, but these were the largest, most sustained peacetime street disturbances since the end of the war, which, coupled with trouble that had broken out in Nottingham the week before, created a widespread sense of panic and alarm. At their height the riots involved perhaps no more than five hundred people, but street disturbances continued in the area every night and eventually led to 140 arrests by the Metropolitan Police. Those who were arrested *and* charged (seventy-two white men and thirty-six black men) were indicted on such offences as grievous bodily harm, affray and possessing offensive weapons.

However, these were not the first 'race' riots. After the First World War, for example, there had been racial tensions focused on black seamen living in Glasgow, Liverpool and Cardiff. In June 1919 white men in Cardiff formed lynch mobs to attack black sailors and four people were killed, while in Liverpool seven hundred black people were locked up in a local jail to protect them from attack. After the Second World War there had been antisemitic rioting in several Lancashire towns during the economic depression of 1947.

In other words, there's a history of minority groups being used as scapegoats for various social, cultural and economic problems long before 1958. Sadly, this has continued in more recent times. After the fatal stabbing of three young girls, and the attempted murder of eight other children and two adults at a Taylor Swift-themed dance class in Southport, Merseyside in July 2024, for example, a torrent of misinformation and false claims by right-wing extremists led to racist street violence in the town and then riots in other parts of England and Northern Ireland. These false claims suggested that Axel Muganwa Rudakubana, the man later convicted of these offences, was an asylum seeker, recently arrived in England from Syria, and Muslim. In fact, Rudakubana was born in Cardiff, although by the time of the attack he was living close to Southport, in the village of Banks with his parents – both of whom are Christians who had emigrated from Rwanda. Neighbours described the family as being 'heavily involved' in the local church. While it is difficult to ascertain a precise motive for his behaviour, it would appear that Rudakubana had mental health issues, was autistic and had a fascination for violence, especially mass murder.[11] Even so, these tragic murders were used by far-right influencers, especially on social media, to push an anti-immigrant and xenophobic agenda, despite the fact there was no evidence to support their claims. No one is quite certain who it was that first spread these rumours, or how they took hold in some communities to such a degree that they prompted people to riot.

There have been various explanations for the origin of the Notting Hill riots. Sometimes the cause is seen to be located within social problems such as poor housing, overcrowding and unemployment, or economic distress more generally. As was discussed when considering the crimes committed by Reg Christie, the Notting Hill of the 1940s, 50s and 60s was very different from the Notting Hill that people have now become familiar with through the eponymous Hollywood movie. On other occasions, the cause of the riots is rooted in specific interracial tensions, which have tended to become focused on black men in relationships with white women. The assault of Majbritt Morrison, a Swedish woman living in the area, and who had a Jamaican husband, is often wrongly cited as the spark for the riots, and while this wasn't the cause of what happened it's clear that there were attacks on interracial couples on the streets of Notting Hill. Finally, the riots have sometimes been explained as simply a form of lawlessness, which has often been attached to young people, or youth sub-cultures and especially the so-called 'Teds' or 'Teddy Boys'.[12]

All of these factors probably did create the context within which the riots took place, but they're not in themselves, or even when taken together, the cause of the riots. The most persuasive explanation comes from the historian Christopher Hilliard, who has carefully analysed and then mapped all of the arrest data collected by the police.[13] Hilliard is able to show that for every black man arrested (although not necessarily charged) there were three whites detained, but that these white rioters didn't actually live in the area, unlike those who were black. In other words, the white rioters weren't living cheek by jowl with black neighbours at all. Most of the white men arrested were also in work, as opposed to being unem-ployed, and so they hadn't lost their job to a black immigrant willing, for example, to work for less pay – a trope which is often cited. All of this suggests that the cause of the riots wasn't whites living in tense proximity to black people and thereafter competing for scarce housing stock, jobs or lovers. Something else was going on, and Hilliard argues convincingly that the riots were an attempt to defend status, to take back 'territory', a 'way of asserting working-class traditions'. The cause of the riots was, for him, a need to 'claim public space for white people'.

This recent interpretation is also borne out in the comments and behaviour of a number of right-wing – and sometimes extremely right-wing – politicians of the time. Sir Oswald Mosley, the former leader of the British Union of Fascists, for example, wanted to use the riots as the platform on which to build his bid to win the Kensington North parliamentary constituency, which encompassed Notting Hill and Ladbroke Grove, for his Union Movement. Other fascist groups were also active in Notting Hill before and in the aftermath of the riots, such as Colin Jordan's White Defence League. Mosley was banned from speaking in council halls and therefore happily took to the streets to conduct his rallies and promote the need to 'keep Britain white'. He favoured repatriation of black immigrants. It's significant that Mosley conducted one of his first outdoor meetings in July 1959, on the corner of Southam Street and Golborne Road, where Kelso had been murdered. The site was carefully chosen to evoke a narrative that white residents had 'had enough' and so decided to 'fight back'. And while Mosley was roundly defeated at the polls – he received only 8 per cent of the vote, compared with the Labour incumbent who received nearly 43 per cent – he set a template for other, more mainstream politicians to copy.

In 1964, for example, Peter Griffiths, won the West Midlands constituency of Smethwick for the Conservatives from the sitting Labour MP (against the national trend) by using openly racist and anti-immigrant rhetoric. His campaign's unofficial slogan was 'If you want a nigger neighbour, vote Labour'. However, perhaps the most infamous use of racism and anti-immigrant sentiment came in the Conservative politician Enoch Powell's 'Rivers of Blood' speech in April 1968. Powell spent several minutes of his talk outlining the plight of an elderly woman in his Wolverhampton constituency who rented out rooms in her house. She had, Powell claimed, been living in 'a respectable street' but with an influx of Caribbean neighbours, 'one house after another [had been] taken over'. The quiet street, he argued, had therefore become a place of 'noise and confusion' and so she'd become 'afraid to go out'. When she did go to the shops, she felt intimidated by the black children who 'followed her'. Just like Mosley, Powell was implying that a community of whiteness was being 'threatened' by immigrants of another colour and that the battlegrounds for the future direction of the country were to be the streets.

At the time of Kelso's murder in 1959, the Conservative government, led by Harold Macmillan, was acutely aware of the riots that had taken place the year before and the sense this had created that Britain was becoming 'overrun' with immigrants. He was also aware the riots had damaged the country's reputation abroad, both within the Commonwealth and more widely. What had happened in the Notting Hill riots seemed to echo the racist violence of the American South, and an open letter sent to the prime minister within twenty-four hours of Kelso's murder by the Committee of African Organizations stated that what had happened to Kelso 'rivals what we have seen at Little Rock or the recent lynching of Mr M. C. Parker of Poplarville, Mississippi'.[14] Nor did the government need to be reminded about how the riots could be harnessed for political purposes, even if Jordan and Mosley would go on to be defeated.

Given all of this, it's not really so surprising that the institutional will to find and convict Kelso's murderer might have been lacking. A conviction would also have meant the killer would've received the death penalty, with all the potential that this could create to keep racial tensions high. Far better, from this cynical perspective, to have the murder presented as a form of random lawlessness, rather than a targeted attack based on the colour of Kelso's skin. Within forty-eight hours of taking over the investigation, Forbes-Leith declared that 'the stabbing has absolutely nothing to do with racial conflict – the motive could have been robbery', and an unnamed senior officer at Scotland Yard told the *Daily Mirror* that what had happened was the work of a 'group of about six anti-law white teenagers who had only one motive in view – robbery'.[15] From other reporting at the time, it's clear that this group of six included Digby.

*

I've described how the identity of Kelso's murderer was an 'open secret' and 'the worst-kept secret in Notting Hill'. I've also suggested that the government of the day might not have wanted to uncover the killer from fear that this would inflame racial tensions. I use the word *might* here because much as I'd prefer to deal in certitude, that's not been possible for several reasons. First, and most important, the official files related to

Kelso's murder remain closed until January 2054 and, seemingly, according to the police, the case remains 'open' and so they refused to release their files to Kelso's family.[16] That makes it impossible to be definitive about what the police were thinking, assess the evidence they'd gathered and know who they thought was the likely suspect. We can't at this time fully consider why they didn't bring charges against Pat Digby but instead let him go. This racist murder therefore cannot be thoroughly investigated until after the files are made public and their secrets revealed. But let's ask the obvious question – whose interests does this secrecy serve?

Nor should we ignore the anonymous tip-off to Frank Draper at the *Sunday Express* describing Kelso's murder, or the unidentified source at Scotland Yard who said that the murder was an act of lawlessness rather than racism. Again, we're left dealing with conjecture and I have to draw conclusions on the basis of incomplete information. Might Ian Forbes-Leith, the police's 'high flyer', the youngest ever detective superintendent, have been the source of the tip-off? He adamantly denied this at the time but was never again promoted and resigned from the police a few years later. It's hard to resist the temptation that it was known that he'd tipped off the press and that his card had been marked.

Neither historians nor criminologists like to deal in inference or speculation, but it's impossible to offer certainty or fact when the secrecy that surrounds police investigations – even those from nearly seventy years ago – remain closed to any form of public scrutiny. So too the informal culture of journalism, where sources are always protected and remain secret, and where money can be exchanged in return for information, also makes it almost impossible to be definitive and to deal in truth. Of course, the administration of government itself can also hide behind secrecy – in the guise of the national interest. Clearly there will be times when this is legitimate, especially when the country is at war, or there are fears that sensitive material essential to the running of the state might fall into the wrong hands. But who is it that defines who those wrong hands belong to, or for how long materials retain their sensitivity? Our next chapter will again deal with this type of official secrecy and also more informal clandestine cultures that develop as a way of offering protection.

However, let's end this chapter by thinking about one of the legacies of Kelso's murder – the Notting Hill Carnival. This joyous street celebration found its current form in the 1960s, but had its roots in the circumstances surrounding Kelso's death, although it was already taking shape before his murder. Organised by a Trinidadian journalist called Claudia Jones, a 'Caribbean Carnival' was held indoors at St Pancras Town Hall in 1959 – largely to celebrate black culture – and had as its slogan 'a people's art is the genesis of their freedom'. In 1966, the first outdoor festival took place in and through the streets of Notting Hill, and surely there's no better way of expressing your identity and that of your community than bringing music, dance and costume to the street – to a public space – in a positive and inclusive way. Finally, in 2009, the site of Kelso's murder was recognised with the erection of a blue plaque. On it are these words: 'His death outraged and unified the community, leading to the lasting cosmopolitan tradition in North Kensington'.

CHAPTER SEVEN

Cases Nine and Ten

*The Murders of William Elliott, 1960
and George Stobbs, 1961, and the
Murder of Rita Ellis, 1967*

Secrecy, being an instrument of conspiracy, ought
never to be the system of a regular government.

JEREMY BENTHAM,
Essay on Political Tactics (1791)

This chapter is concerned with the much mythologised
'swinging sixties' but uses the murders of three people –
two of whom were killed by the same man – to also discuss
secrecy in many of its guises. From sexual interests that had
to be kept hidden so as to conform to cultural norms, to the
secrets that are still being kept by the state and its agents. I
want to explore why Britain is so obsessed with secrecy – an
obsession that seems to have taken even greater hold in the

169

last few decades – and outline how this makes it difficult to hold the state accountable. The official files on both murder cases I've chosen remain closed to public scrutiny and, even if the culprit in the first of these two cases has been apprehended, crucial details about the murders that he committed and the police investigation that followed continue to be hidden from public view. The second murder case is unsolved. Why should that be?

However, let's begin with the secrecy that accompanies trying to express love when it is prohibited by law. The irony here is of course that for many people the 1960s were *not* characterised by sexual revolution and 'letting it all hang out'. For many people – whether gay or straight – the supposed freedom and decadence of the era simply passed them by. Even those who might have wanted to embrace a sexual revolution found that it was safer to keep their interests to themselves. And for some, this enforced status quo could cost them everything – including their lives.

*

On 9 August 1967 the playwright Joe Orton was bludgeoned to death by his lover Kenneth Halliwell in the flat they shared at 25 Noel Road in Islington, London. Halliwell struck Joe nine times over the head with a hammer and then killed himself by taking an overdose of Nembutal. Their bodies were discovered the following morning by a chauffeur sent by the movie director Richard Lester, who wanted to discuss filming options with Joe who, earlier in the year, had written a script for the Beatles' third film, which he'd called *Up Against It*.[1] Halliwell left a suicide note in which he suggested that the murder could be explained by what Joe had written in his diaries – 'especially the latter part'. However, the last diary entry is for 1 August 1967 and so it has always been presumed that some of the pages had been torn out.

The pages that remain are filled with vivid stories of Joe's covert sexual encounters with other gay men at a time when homosexuality was not only illegal but also viewed by many as a psychiatric illness. A few months before his murder, for example, on 4 March 1967, he describes how 'the little pissoir under the bridge [on Holloway Road] had become a scene of frenzied saturnalia'. This 'sexual debauchery' in a public lavatory took place while 'two feet away the citizens of Holloway moved about their business'. In July 1967 he describes meeting a 'very stupid looking' young man in another public toilet who suggested that they should go to the park where, he said, 'I'll shag you.'[2]

The Sexual Offences Act 1967, which received Royal Assent on 27 July 1967, legalised homosexual acts in England and Wales on condition that they were consensual and in private between two men who were twenty-one years old or above. This legislation followed hard on the heels of other legislative changes and various social and cultural developments that have come to characterise the period. The Murder Act (the Abolition of the Death Penalty), for example, was passed in 1965 with the last executions in England and Wales taking place in August of the previous year, and in Scotland in 1963;[3] the Beatles spearheaded a 'British invasion' of the global music charts and in their wake seemed to make all things British fashionable; *Dr No* – the first James Bond movie, starring Sean Connery, was released in 1962, with Bond quickly becoming the world's favourite spy; the NHS Family Planning

Act of 1967 made oral contraception widely available; Mini cars and mini skirts became omnipresent; and England won the World Cup at Wembley in July 1966, defeating Germany in extra time.

These disparate events and triumphs give a flavour of the transformations and optimism of this era, even if many changes had roots in earlier periods of our history. Their ubiquity in popular memory and historical accounts have made the 1960s one of our most fictive and fanciful decades. Yet the reality is that for many people optimism did not replace pessimism, and life continued much as it had always done.[4] Nonetheless, the 1960s are usually seen as a time of change and cultural revolution, largely prompted by young people and made discernible by a new openness about sex and sexuality. This is perhaps summed up by Philip Larkin's poem 'Annus Mirabilis', written in 1967. Larkin famously and satirically wrote that 'sexual intercourse began in nineteen sixty-three', between the lifting of the ban on D. H. Lawrence's *Lady Chatterley's Lover* in November 1960 and the release of 'the Beatles' first LP'.[5]

Joe Orton never benefited from the changes in legislation related to homosexuality. While his diaries offer a remarkable insight into how gay men managed to meet and express their sexuality at a time when they had to keep these preferences secret -- even to the extent of having their own language[6] -- most gay men kept their sexuality hidden and this in turn made them vulnerable to blackmail, homophobic attacks and, in extreme cases, murder.

Homophobia – a pathological hatred of gay men that's based on a perception that homosexuality disrupts 'natural law' – was never far from the surface in Britain. Homosexuality may have become legal in limited circumstances in 1967, but homophobia didn't just disappear overnight. In fact, one academic has described it as 'perhaps the last acceptable prejudice'.[7] This persistent homophobia, and a corresponding need for gay men to keep their sexual identity secret, sets the context for two horrendous murders committed by a former soldier in the British army called Michael Copeland, just as the sixties were supposedly starting to swing.

*

William Elliott was a balding, bespectacled sixty-year-old estate clerk at a teacher training college who lived with his two sisters – Sarah and Martha – in Haddon Road in Bakewell, Derbyshire.[8] He drove an iconic Isetta car which, because of its egg shape and small, rather odd windows was known as a 'bubble car'. It was perhaps the only thing that people noticed about William who, unlike Joe Orton, kept himself and especially his sexuality well hidden. Friends would later describe him as quiet, generous, polite and reserved.

What these friends perhaps didn't appreciate was that just a short drive away from Bakewell were a number of pubs in the market town of Chesterfield, such as the Three Horse Shoes, the Spread Eagle and the Queen's Head, where William could go and meet other men with similar interests. And, close to these pubs, were the Markham Road public toilets, which performed much the same function as the 'little pissoir' frequented by Joe Orton on the Holloway Road. It's impossible to know exactly how many men used these toilets for this purpose. However, following William's murder in June 1960, the police interviewed 'more than eight hundred males who admitted taking part in such practices'. By then, a second gay – or, perhaps more accurately, bisexual – man called George Stobbs had been killed in similar circumstances in March 1961. The police noted that 'the social standing of an individual does not form a barrier between homosexuals' and that 'complete strangers will get together without hesitation to some isolated spot to commit indecent acts together'.[9]

We glimpse both homophobia and incredulity in these observations, almost as if the police were exploring a new world. What's more surprising is that the man who made them, Ernest Bradshaw, the future Detective Chief Superintendent of Derbyshire Constabulary, wasn't speaking in 1960 or at the height of the investigation but writing in an extraordinary article published in the *Police Journal* in 1977 – a decade after the Sexual Offences Act and more than fifteen years after the murders. Bradshaw, who was transferred to Chesterfield as detective inspector in December 1959, offers a very detailed picture of an investigation that was to last for almost five years before bringing the suspect to trial. It also outlines his own bizarre relationship with Michael Copeland and how he became, in effect, a 'father figure' to the killer. The press initially dubbed William's death the 'Bubble Car Murder' but, given the similarities between what happened to him and with George's murder, they eventually renamed their stories the 'Carbon Copy Murders'.

In these 'Carbon Copy Murders' we can see not only the persistent homophobia I've alluded to, but also within the police's approach the echoes of more recent investigations into the murders of men who identified as gay or bisexual. Discovering the bodies of William and George no more than a few yards apart, for example, is an awful foretaste of finding the bodies (by the same dog walker) of two of the victims of Stephen Port – Britain's most recent male serial killer – in the graveyard of the Church of St Margaret of Antioch in Barking, London in 2015. So too the relationship that developed between Bradshaw and Copeland has a similarity to that between Detective Superintendent Steve Fulcher and Christopher Halliwell. Halliwell, who was arrested after the disappearance and suspected murder of Sian O'Callaghan in Swindon in March 2011, was informally interviewed by Fulcher and gradually, as their relationship developed, Halliwell admitted that he'd also murdered Becky Godden and took Fulcher to where he had buried the poor woman's body.[10]

William's body was found beside a stone wall in Clod Hall Lane, Baslow, which is about nine miles outside of Chesterfield, although his car was found abandoned in Park Road, near the centre of the town. Copeland had clearly driven it back into Chesterfield after the murder. A post-mortem revealed that William had been killed by shock and intercranial haemorrhaging following a fracture to his skull. He'd been repeatedly hit on the head. Some twenty-eight blows could be detected, which, according to the pathologist, had been inflicted with great violence. Copeland may also have stamped on William's skull, and he then seems to have deliberately scattered loose grass over the head and neck in some kind of symbolic ritual. There were no defence wounds on William's body and no signs of a struggle at the crime scene. William's trousers and shirt had semen on them, but there were no signs of anal penetration. Even at the time it was clear that the motive for the murder had been sexual, rather than, for example, theft. Later Copeland admitted that he'd picked up William in the Three Horse Shoes and gone with him to Clod Hall Lane because William wanted to 'suck me and that is why I killed him. I hate things like that.' Did he really? Copeland claimed that he'd used a stone from a dyke to hit William over the head, although he doesn't clarify the stomping allegation or why he had placed grass over the head and neck.[11]

Clod Hall Lane, much like the gents' toilet on Markham Road in Chesterfield, emerges as a secret place where sexual activity could take place, and therefore similar to what today would be called a 'dogging site'.[12] Bradshaw described it as 'a paradise for Peeping Toms',[13] who seem to have informally allocated stretches of the deserted lane and accompanying moorland. They'd then keep a 'regular look out for couples making love or prostitutes who came out from Sheffield with their clients'. These 'Peeping Toms' would come equipped 'with field glasses and periscopes and by pre-arranged signals they'd indicate to each other whether a particular couple were of interest'.[14] Here again we have another form of secrecy, although if it really was a 'paradise' for voyeurs in the way that Bradshaw describes, and if they did actually have their own informally designated areas, we might want to question just how secret Clod Hall Lane's activities actually were. There must have been unofficial 'word of mouth' communication channels that have been lost to history. What can be stated more definitively is this hardly reflects a 'swinging sixties', but rather one which was decidedly hung-up and anxious.

*

George Stobbs arrived in Chesterfield in the middle of May 1960 – less than a month before William was murdered. There's no evidence to suggest that the two men knew one another or ever met, although George would've been aware of the publicity surrounding the murder. During the Second World War he had served in the Intelligence Corps in France, Belgium, Holland and Germany. At the time of his murder George was forty-eight years old, married with two sons – who were both at boarding school – and was employed as an industrial chemist at Robertson & Woodcock (Trebor) Ltd, the sweet manufacturer. Initially he'd been based in London, but then moved to the firm's Chesterfield base, which had been established during the war as a way of escaping the Blitz. When he first arrived, there was no suitable accommodation for his family, and it wasn't until July 1960 that George and his wife Josephine took a house on Mansfeldt Road on the outskirts of the town. He was described by his neighbours and work colleagues as 'polite', 'well-spoken' and as a 'gentleman'.

Josephine would later tell the police that her husband would occasionally 'make excuses' that required him to return to work in the evening, although he was actually visiting a number of the same pubs frequented by William. Helen Crow and Joyce Mitchell, barmaids at the Three Horse Shoes, described to the police how George was a regular in the pub. In any event, Josephine alerted the police on the morning of 29 March 1961 that her husband hadn't returned home after going out the previous evening. She explained that after watching TV together George had left Mansfeldt Road in their Morris Oxford car, ostensibly to go back to work. Shortly after Josephine's call, a lorry driver reported seeing a man's body on

Clod Hall Lane and before the day was out another murder investigation was underway.[15]

George's body was found less than a hundred yards from where William's had been discovered and, like him, had numerous injuries to the head. The Home Office pathologist noted nineteen blows around the head and neck and formed the opinion that the cause of death was shock and cerebral bleeding due to a fractured skull. Copeland later admitted that he'd hit George with a hammer. Semen was found on George's vest, underpants, the front and back of his trousers, the cuffs of his overcoat and also on his penis. There was the same ritualised scattering of grass around the head. The lack of blood at Clod Hall Lane indicated that the murder had taken place elsewhere and the crime scene was eventually discovered nearby in Gladwin Wood. Copeland had then driven George's body to Clod Hall Lane and thereafter took his car back to Chesterfield, where he abandoned it in Park Road – just as he had done with William's bubble car.

This similarity in the geography of the two murders might seem unusual but it's more common than most people imagine. This physical journey made by Copeland also hints at an inner journey of self-discovery. We know comparatively little about Copeland – other than he was tall and well built – but his crimes suggest that he didn't want to stray too far from familiar places that psychologically anchored him, and which made him feel safe while he was experimenting and trying things out. Perhaps becoming a soldier had been an attempt to control the results of that experiment by distancing himself from his home and his family, or, equally plausible, it had triggered a recognition that he liked violence. In any event, being a soldier hadn't worked out for him and so he came home. He also returned home after the murders of William and George because that was his base and where he felt most secure. In fact, a surprising number of violent offenders will seek opportunities to offend within walking distance of where they live. In that sense Copeland was a 'marauder' not a 'commuter'. He wasn't behaving arbitrarily or making a mistake when he duplicated where he left the bodies of his victims or abandoned their cars but was instead revealing the turmoil that he was experiencing about how to make home meaningful, a failure to find authentic love and his identity as a man.[16]

Based on what Copeland eventually admitted to Bradshaw, we know that George had first picked up his killer the night before the murder in the Queen's Head and, on the night of the murder itself, they'd both been drinking in the Three Horse Shoes. This might imply they had by this stage already had a sexual encounter, although we don't know for certain, or merely if one had been promised. When the pub closed, the pair went drinking elsewhere.[17] Copeland explained to Bradshaw that he'd killed George because 'he spoke to me. I knew he was one of them and I hated him.' The murder was premeditated – 'I decided I was going to kill him because he belonged to something I hated most.' This might also suggest that Copeland recognised he too was gay and found it difficult to come to terms with that reality – although it's impossible to know definitively. He made this confession after he'd been remanded at Chesterfield Magistrates' Court on 12 December 1963, although his relationship with Bradshaw stretched further back in time and, as the detective was to acknowledge, he became a 'father figure' to the killer and was 'deeply involved with him'. It's not possible

179

to determine why Bradshaw chose to behave in this way but he gave money to Copeland, drove him about town and offered advice about his relationships and life more generally. In effect, he became a trusted counsellor and mentor.

In late 1961, well over a year before being remanded in custody, Copeland had actually offered Bradshaw a 'pseudo-confession' about his part in the murders. In the company of two other detectives, Bradshaw had picked up Copeland and his girlfriend and they'd then all driven into the countryside around Chesterfield. After they got out of the car, Copeland openly stated to everyone present that he was a 'psychopath', that he associated with gay men and agreed that he had indeed admitted to the murders in a previous conversation. However, despite all of this, it would be more than three years before he was arrested, charged and brought to trial. At best this seems reckless and at worst astonishing. The police had two murders on their hands and a prime suspect who had offered them a confession, so it's difficult to understand their reluctance to bring charges. Might their sluggishness have been a consequence of the sexual preferences of his victims? Copeland was eventually convicted of three murders: of William and George, and also of a young German boy called Guenther Helmbrecht, whom he murdered in November 1960 near to where he was stationed in Verden while he was serving in the army.[18] He was sentenced to death.

There was local feeling at the time about a lack of progress in the case and the *Derbyshire Times* suggested that 'a highly experienced Scotland Yard Murder Squad' should be drafted in. Clearly the unsolved murder of Kelso Cochrane had done little to dent people's confidence about the abilities of the

Metropolitan Police. The paper also wanted its readers to know that 'the victims of these killings are not completely innocent, normal citizens' and that the context for William and George's murders was 'the fringe of undercover activities among men in Chesterfield'.[19]

What emerges from considering these murders is the pervasive homophobia not just of the 1960s but even in the 1970s, when Bradshaw published his article. This is obvious in Copeland's comments about how he 'hated' George and William but also in his observation that they seemed to 'belong to something' which he really 'detested'. Even so, he also freely admitted that he would socialise with gay men. Homophobia is also clearly present in newspaper coverage at the time and expressed quite openly by Bradshaw in his article. More troublingly, how should we interpret the fact that the senior detective leading the investigation into the murders of two gay men became a father figure to their killer and that it was nearly five years before Copeland was found guilty? Is it unfair to Bradshaw to suggest that his relationship with Copeland served to normalise and excuse the violence that had been used against William and George? This might be taking things too far, but it's hard to escape the conclusion that William and George were seen to have brought matters on themselves. We glimpse, therefore, a reality of what it meant to be gay or bisexual, beyond the comparatively liberal confines of London, and the ever-present dangers gay men faced. Paradoxically, given the press coverage of the case, gay men started to travel to Chesterfield in the hope of meeting other men and one local historian has suggested that for a time Chesterfield became 'the gay capital of the north'.[20]

Copeland's death sentence was eventually commuted to life in prison. This is interesting in itself, given the numbers of men he was convicted of killing and his admission that at least one of the murders was premeditated. However, it reflects a judicial and legislative – if not a popular – turn against the death penalty at the time. We also know that Copeland married in 1991 while serving his sentence. In total he seems to have spent more than twenty-five years inside before being released, but he was later reconvicted of other offences. Copeland died at HMP Sudbury in 2013. Ernest Bradshaw died in 2005 at the age of ninety-two. His two sons followed in their father's footsteps and also joined the police.

As for the questions I've posed about the murder investigation and whether it was compromised by the relationship between Bradshaw and Copeland, or if there were other matters that prevented charges being brought, it would've been preferable to have answered them instead of leaving them unresolved. However, the official files remain closed until 2050. Alan Hurndall, the historian who has written most recently about the case, has a subtitle to his book – 'the chilling true story they don't want you to read'.[21] He details the twists and turns of trying to gain access to the official files through Freedom of Information requests and using his own contacts. All of his attempts proved fruitless. When he queried why this should be so, he was advised that it may be to protect surviving family members of the victims. However, William has no direct descendants and George's two sons, who have gone on to have families of their own, were tracked down by Alan and they know what happened to their father. As one of George's sons said to him, 'We can't be shocked.' So, who is being protected? Might it be Ernest Bradshaw? Again, I am posing a question without being able to offer an answer, but our culture of secrecy leaves no other option. Of course, we encountered this in the previous chapter when I discussed the murder of Kelso Cochrane, and it will feature again in our next murder case. However, let's end by suggesting that William and George would have found it much easier to express their sexuality in Britain today than they clearly felt able to in the 'swinging sixties'.

*

For different reasons, secrecy and silence also create a context for the murder of Rita Ellis at RAF Halton in Buckinghamshire in 1967. However, unlike the murders of William and George, Rita's case is unsolved. Again, we have only a few details about her life and, as far as her murder is concerned, a number of questions remain unanswerable. Did she, for example, start a relationship with someone on the base where she was stationed, or perhaps she'd found love with a civilian in one of the towns and villages located close by. Whatever the answer, the sixties didn't swing for Rita either.

Rita was born in 1948 and grew up in Stevenage, Hertfordshire. She was the eldest of four children, with two brothers and a sister called Tina. Rita always struggled at school, partly because she was painfully shy and so, almost inevitably, was described as being a bit of a loner. She was also rather scruffy in her appearance, although Rita was kind, gentle and always willing to offer help to anyone who needed a spare pair of hands. After school she worked in a local toy shop. It was a decent enough life, but Rita wasn't really going anywhere and so, like many other young women, she decided to join the Women's Royal Air Force (WRAF) to 'better her-self'.[22] On the 28 April 1967, when she was nineteen, she was sent to do her basic training at RAF Spitalgate in Lincolnshire.

The idea that Rita was 'bettering herself' fits with a common strand in the memories of WRAFs who've shared their stories with the Royal Air Force Museum. Tass Cotton, for example, joined the WRAF in 1960 and was posted as an air traffic controller at Barton Hall, near Preston in Lancashire. She remembered 'it was the best time of my life and it is where I met my husband who was also in the RAF'. Tass served for three years before marrying and was then posted with her husband to Germany. Iris Johnson (née Taylor) joined the WRAF in the same year as Rita and also did her basic training at RAF Spitalgate. She said, 'it was the best thing that could have happened to me' and trained to be an air traffic controller. She was posted to Cyprus for eighteen months and then returned to work at the operations centre at RAF Waddington, before leaving the service in 1971. Sue Hardy joined the WRAF slightly later, in 1975, and thought that it was 'the best thing I have ever done ... the WRAF helped me to broaden my horizons, gave me a good training, enabled me to go abroad (two years in Cyprus and later a detachment in Nairobi) and last but definitely not least was responsible for me meeting my husband – we married in 1981 and are still going strong'.[23]

After her basic training, Rita was posted to RAF Halton on 21 June 1967 – just when the Beatles' *Sgt. Pepper's Lonely Hearts Club Band* had become the best-selling album in the charts, both in Britain and the USA. Perhaps she got teased about being 'lovely Rita' in her cap and uniform – the title of one of the songs on the album – which asked whether a 'meter maid' might look like a soldier. In any event, she was never to get posted abroad and, from what I've been able to piece together about her life in Buckinghamshire, it would appear she still had few friends and has been described as being rather put upon by other WRAFs. Rita didn't drink or smoke but liked to spend her free time watching television or reading. These are essentially solitary rather than communal activities. Tragically, less than five months after being posted, she was murdered on the night of Saturday 11 November 1967 and her body was discovered the following day – Remembrance Sunday. Unlike many of the WRAFs who have shared their stories online, Rita didn't broaden her horizons or meet a husband, and her post-mortem indicated that she was still a virgin at the time of her death.

These are rather brief, and sketchy, personal details about Rita and nor do they tell us much about her short military career or what happened to her on the day when she was killed. We catch just a glimpse of Rita. We catch even fewer glimpses of her killer, which is explained by a number of interconnected factors. The timeline, for example, of the crucial events leading up to the murder on 11 November remains confused; on that Saturday night, RAF Halton was playing host to a number of local people who had come onto the base for a disco and to play bingo – in other words there were civilian as well as service personnel in the grounds; and there were also a number of sex attacks on women in the local area around the time of Rita's death. Was there a single, predatory sexual offender responsible for all of these attacks, including the murder, or was what happened to Rita unconnected to the local crimes and so should be viewed as unique? These factors serve to confuse rather than help to reveal who might have been responsible for the murder.

In fact, a full DNA profile of her murderer does exist and over time this has been used to eliminate some two hundred suspects from the police's investigation, although there has never been a match on the National DNA Database.[24] Beyond that it's difficult to say anything more about how the cold case team at Thames Valley Police are proceeding. I know from personal experience that they're uncharacteristically protective – we might even say secretive – about their investigation and refuse to consider how others might be able to help by sharing information.[25] It would appear that they're simply waiting for a suspect to emerge who can then be DNA tested, or hope that Rita's killer, who might now be in his eighties, or a member of his family, will be convicted of some other offence and prompt a DNA match on the national database. Of course, we've also the recurring problem of the official files being closed. The authorised records related to Rita's murder will not be made available to the public until 2070 – over a hundred years after she was killed.

In the absence of anything more definitive, we simply don't know if Rita's killer was someone who was employed within the camp, or was at RAF Halton that night to attend the various activities that had been organised. We don't know if her murder was a one-off, or connected to the other incidents that took place nearby. We can't tell if Rita might have known her killer, although there's some evidence that this is possible. She'd had her hair cut and styled just prior to her murder and seemed to be making a new and concerted effort with her appearance. Might Rita have willingly got into the car that took her to her death? In fact, who it was that picked her up is just one of the many confusing features of the case. Ever willing, Rita had agreed to look after the children of Wing Commander Roy Watson and his wife that Saturday night, although she'd never met Watson before. Watson duly turned up in his car at around 19:40 p.m., parking outside where he thought Rita was billeted, but he was late and had actually chosen the wrong house block. He waited for about fifteen minutes, then drove back to his house to fetch his wife, as only women could enter the female quarters. It would seem that Rita, the wing commander and his wife missed each other by minutes on a couple of occasions.[26] She was last seen getting into a car at approximately 8 p.m.

The following morning at about 10:30 a.m., Rita's body was found by a dog walker at the western end of the camp's enclosure – in Rowborough Copse, near a disused railway at an old coal yard. She'd never left RAF Halton. This again suggests that the more likely suspect was someone from the base, or a civilian who worked there and had knowledge of the layout, as opposed to a stranger visiting for the evening. Rita had been beaten, sexually assaulted and strangled with her underwear. There had been some effort to conceal her body, which again also implies that she probably knew her killer. Did perhaps some smooth-talking new boyfriend offer to take her to the wing commander's house, but secretly had other designs? Had things spiralled out of control – as suggested by being strangled with her underwear – and, after 'five minutes of madness', Rita was dead? It's impossible to tell definitively, and with so many people on the camp that night the list of possible suspects is greater than it would normally have been. Further confusion exists because the Thames Valley Police didn't exist in 1967 – it was the old Buckinghamshire Constabulary who policed the county – but in any event Scotland Yard were called in to conduct the murder investigation, while enquiries were also made by the RAF Police. However, no one was, or ever has been, arrested or charged with Rita's murder. When the files officially open for scrutiny in 2070 the mystery might be solved, but it's unlikely that justice will be done. After all, by 2070 Rita's killer will be long dead. A lonely, shy, young woman and a servant of the state was brutally murdered on an RAF base and I'm left wondering if Rita had been the daughter of the wing commander, as opposed to simply being engaged by him as a babysitter, might there have been a different outcome to the case?

There's also a broader context which Rita's case neatly captures. This involves balancing the needs of the state to keep secret information from those who would seek to undermine it, and the rights of its citizens to have access to official documentation so as to judge whether or not the state and its agents have performed poorly, or even outside the law. It's impossible to hold the state accountable when there's widespread suppression of material that has little or nothing to do with national security (notwithstanding the fact that Rita's murder took place on an RAF base). This is further aggravated when the state itself begins to collect information by eavesdropping or spying on its own citizens, especially those who are in a good position to hold it accountable. Done covertly, this seems like the stuff of an Orwellian nightmare and should make us consider how we've come to give the state so much power, or simply looked the other way as it took our liberties from us. This is something that has become more pressing since the 1960s, to the extent that Britain really is obsessed with secrecy, although the origins of that fixation reach far back in our history.

*

Britain has had an Official Secrets Act (OSA) since 1889, although it's the OSA of 1911 that's most relevant to this chapter. This Act, passed in just one day with almost no debate, became a tool to use against whistleblowers as much as deter foreign spies. It made the workings of the state more secret, by criminalising the unauthorised disclosure of any official documentation – no matter how trivial – and was inspired by the work of a popular Anglo-French author called William Le Queux.

One morning in March 1906, people making their way to work in Oxford Street in London were beset by men wearing Prussian military uniform, with spiked helmets on their heads. They shouted warnings that a large army of their countrymen had landed in south-east England and were making their way towards the capital. In fact, this was all part of a publicity stunt organised by the *Daily Mail* to promote the serialisation of Le Queux's latest novel, *The Invasion of 1910*. The book proved to be an immediate success, as it tapped into a widespread fear that had gripped Britain since the Boer Wars that the country was woefully ill-prepared for conflict – especially a war against Germany that was going to come sooner or later. The book was subsequently translated into twenty-seven languages – including German – and earned Le Queux worldwide fame.

His next book was called *Spies of the Kaiser: Plotting the*

Downfall of England and suggested that there was a well-established spy network in the country controlled by Kaiser Wilhelm II, the German emperor. There was little evidence to support this assertion. However, Lieutenant Colonel James Edmonds, an acquaintance of Le Queux, was Head of Counterintelligence at the War Office and he persuaded Richard Haldane, the Secretary of State for War, to investigate the extent of foreign espionage in Britain. Much of what was reported to the committee came from Le Queux himself, or from people who'd read his books and wanted to share their own personal experiences of what they believed were German spies. Much of this was nonsense and the eventual report of their deliberations was in reality an Edwardian 'dodgy dossier'. Life was imitating art, but the committee felt obliged to act and the result was the creation of the Secret Service Bureau. This was later broken up into two new departments – MI5 and MI6 – and in this febrile atmosphere, the 1911 OSA was passed with Section 2 of that Act prohibiting the unauthorised disclosure or receipt of any official information. It's a moot point as to whether this created or merely codified an official obsession with secrecy but in any event it made the actions of the British government more secretive, and in doing so changed the relationship between the state and the citizen.[27]

Section 2 of the 1911 OSA was swept away by the OSA of 1989, although there were earlier iterations in 1920 and 1939. The 1989 Act was in many ways even tougher than its predecessors, as it seemed to have been passed to prevent future government embarrassment in the wake of a number of intelligence scandals. These included: the trial of Clive Ponting, the civil servant who leaked documents that showed that the

Argentinian warship *General Belgrano* had been sailing away from the Falkland Islands and was outside a two hundred nautical mile exclusion zone that had been implemented at the time of its sinking; the revelation that MI5 vetted BBC staff; and the publication of *Spycatcher* by the former MI5 officer Peter Wright.[28] There seemed to be greater hope that our secret state would become more open when Labour came to power under Tony Blair in 1997. In the year preceding his election, Blair had even stated that 'information is power and any government's attitude about sharing information with the people actually says a great deal about how it views itself and how it views power itself, and how it views the relationship between itself and the people who elected it'. He believed that information 'should be, rather than should not be released'.[29]

However, the passing of the Freedom of Information Act in 2000 didn't really open up the work of government to greater public scrutiny at all, and Blair was candid in his memoirs as to why this was the case – he'd changed his mind. 'Freedom of Information,' he wrote, 'three harmless words. I look at those words as I write them, and feel like shaking my head till it drops off my shoulders. You idiot. You naive, foolish, irresponsible nincompoop.' Blair realised that he'd been 'stupid' – an 'imbecile' – to have said what he had in Opposition because freedom of information was not, in his view, going to be used by the public but rather would be deployed by journalists as a political weapon.[30] As if to support his realisation and change of heart, the Freedom of Information Act didn't come into force until 2005 – eight years after Labour had been returned to office. In the meantime, a series of amendments to the Act had made it easier for public bodies to refuse access to information – a situation that continues to this day.

If all of this wasn't bad enough, in May 2013 Edward Snowden, a conscience-stricken computer intelligence consultant working for the US National Security Agency (NSA), absconded to Hong Kong and met with a number of journalists there. He shared classified materials that he'd had access to, which proved the existence of several global surveillance systems. Not only did this secret surveillance network have the cooperation of Britain's own surveillance infrastructure, spearheaded by the Government Communications Headquarters (GCHQ), but it was also evident that the NSA had an extraordinary ability to monitor almost every aspect of our lives through our digital footprints. Stories based on the files Snowden leaked soon started to appear in the *Washington Post* and the *Guardian*, and the US Department of Justice quickly charged him with espionage and theft of government property. For some he became a hero whistleblower, but to others he was a traitor. For this latter group, proof of his unpatriotic behaviour was his decision to seek asylum in Russia. Since 2022 Snowden has had Russian citizenship.

In September 2022 a US Federal Court ruled that the NSA activities revealed by Snowden's leaks were illegal and possibly unconstitutional. Even so, several years before in 2013, two British intelligence officers had called into the offices of the *Guardian* to oversee the destruction of the hard drives of several of the newspaper's computers and the editor was threatened with prosecution under the Official Secrets Act if he failed to comply.[31]

Sadly, it's this odd history and febrile state of affairs which explains why it's still impossible to know who really killed Kelso Cochrane or Rita Ellis, and just why Ernest Bradshaw waited so long to charge Michael Copeland with murder.

CHAPTER EIGHT

Cases Eleven and Twelve

The Murders Committed by John Childs, 1974–78, and the Murders Committed by Trevor Hardy, 1974–76

The Seventies were grim. The Seventies were a hangover from the Sixties. The Seventies were violent. The Seventies were a dead end. Above all: we don't want to go back to the Seventies.

ANDY BECKETT,
When the Lights Went Out (2009)

Margaret Thatcher had more impact on the world than any woman ruler since Catherine the Great of Russia. Not only did she turn around – decisively – the British economy in the 1980s, she saw her methods copied in more than fifty countries.

PAUL JOHNSON, *Wall Street Journal*, 2013

On the evening of Tuesday 15 August 1972, Graham Arthur Hills, a sixty-eight-year-old widower and retired railway worker, was returning home from a night at the theatre. He was smartly dressed and carrying a briefcase, which must have given him an air of respectability, perhaps even prosperity. As Mr Hills crossed the York Road footbridge that once led to Waterloo station in London, he was attacked from behind by three people, at least one of whom was carrying a knife. Despite being outnumbered, he fought back and, as was later reported, 'a stiletto flashed and an old man fell dead – stabbed in the heart'.[1] His briefcase was later found near the crime scene, containing nothing but his prayer book.[2]

This grim murder, for which three youths aged between fifteen and seventeen would later be convicted, might never have come to wider public scrutiny. In the normal course of events, it would have been a local rather than a national story and soon Mr Hills's murder would've been forgotten and transformed into a sad statistic among many other such statistics. Given the ages of the culprits, they were never publicly identified. However, the press picked up on something about this murder which they thought of as new and therefore newsworthy. As Tom Tullett of the *Daily Mirror* put it, 'as crimes of violence escalate, a word common in the United States enters the British headlines: mugging. To our police, it's a frightening *new* strain of crime.'[3] Mr Hills's murder was therefore not just the first British 'mugging' but also a mugging that had 'gone wrong'. Suddenly the newspapers were filled with stories of muggings, and the muggers themselves were seen as posing particular problems for the police, leading to widespread and increasingly desperate calls for there to be more 'bobbies on the beat'.

Of course this was not a new crime at all, but merely a new term for a very old type of street robbery. Paradoxically, it seemed to reinforce another British myth – that things were somehow better in the old days. So, the story of Mr Hills and his muggers got caught up with news values but, as we shall see, not every 'new' or extraordinary crime makes the news agenda. There's a selection process through which stories become news. As for Mr Hills, Tullett also helpfully explained the term for what had happened to him for his readers: 'a mug, easy prey for a quick steal', and the story was dramatically illustrated with a photograph of a man holding a knife.

Mr Hills's murder might not have been a new form of violent crime, but it was the beginning of what's often described as a 'moral panic' – especially about those crimes committed by young people and often focused on crimes where young black men were, or were suspected of being, the perpetrators. A group of sociologists and cultural theorists based at the University of Birmingham thought that these stories were driven by racial prejudice as much as they reflected genuine fears about rising crime rates. They even proposed that the word 'mugging' be abolished, as it had done 'incalculable harm – raising the wrong things into sensational focus, hiding and mystifying the deeper causes'.[4] As far as they were concerned, the reaction to what had happened had been disproportionate.

What the Birmingham academics failed to describe was what would have been a proportionate reaction to muggings – such as the one in which Mr Hills was murdered. Nor did they acknowledge genuine public fears about increases in crime, and street crimes in particular, in the early 1970s. For example, prior to Mr Hills's mugging, the recorded crime rate had been rising by about 5 per cent year on year and there had been a 62 per cent increase in recorded crime between 1967 and 1971. Recorded crime would increase from 1.6 million crimes in England and Wales in 1970 to 2.8 million by the end of 1980.[5] In these circumstances it is disingenuous to suggest that the public were simply panicking, or that their fears were out of kilter with what they saw happening in their communities. For some people, in certain locations, it was perfectly legitimate to be worried about becoming the victim of a mugging.

*

I've started with the murder of Mr Hills and the idea that the public's concerns about muggers and muggings were a moral panic as it illustrates one of the themes that I want to discuss about those seemingly oppositional decades – the 1970s and the 1980s. What is the 'truth' about these two decades and how might we go about separating reality from opinion, or fact from fantasy? At what point does history simply become a form of political propaganda? If the 1960s were our most mythologised decade, the 1970s has become a period that seemingly no one has a good word to say about, and which needed the 1980s as a corrective. The two murder cases that I'm going to use, both from the 1970s, have been chosen because they also allow me to reflect on the 1980s. However, first it's important to describe how these two decades are usually presented.

The 1970s are seen as a time characterised by terrorist bombs exploding on our streets; riots and disorder more generally; strikes disrupting the status quo; and life being lived through one economic crisis after another. All of this leads to a three-day week; power cuts that plunge households into darkness; the pound being devalued; entry into the Common Market; and a more generalised understanding that Britain's best days were over. Britain was 'in decline' and competing explanations for the causes of that decline still retain a hold on the popular imagination. For some, the problems of the 1970s were caused by trade unions with far too much power and more generally the failure of left-leaning, or indeed centrist, governments which had become over-extended. That prevented, so this argument goes, individuals from using their entrepreneurial skills to create wealth through 'free enterprise'. Generous welfare provision inhibited people from taking the new risks that were needed to survive within the world economy. For others, what the 1970s got wrong – and now represents – was the growth of an essentially militaristic state, clinging to notions of empire and using an increasingly politicised police force to trample on those who wanted to protest and transform society along socialist, or at least more egalitarian, lines irrespective of race, class, gender or sexuality.

These two political traditions, both describing a similar, depressing story, often fly in the face of evidence about the 1970s. Living standards were rising, there was full employment, real wages doubled between 1950 and 1974, and society was opening up with, most obviously, more young people attending university because of the provision of student grants. The Open University enrolled its first students in 1971 and offered education through distance learning to those who were employed, or who'd never previously considered going to university. Feminists campaigned for – and won – equal pay, abortion rights and better childcare provision. The first women's refuge opened in 1971 and the following year the Old Bailey got its first female judge. A number of charity and pressure groups were established to keep the issue of gay rights, the problems of racism in society and the damage that was being done to the environment in the public eye. Most people had access to cars, TVs, telephones and central heating, and in 1978 there were more foreign holidays taken than in any previous year.

The idea that the British economy was in decline in the 1970s is only sustainable if it's acknowledged that this was relative and not absolute decline – it was actually growing, albeit at a slower rate than our European neighbours. Indeed, many of our real economic woes, such as inflation, were the result of forces beyond the immediate control of any national government – such as OPEC increasing the cost of oil and the collapse of the fixed rate exchange mechanism.[6] However, these correctives to the story of the 1970s rarely dent what's become an enduring caricature of the period.

This caricature seems even more exaggerated through a regrettable tendency for history to become 'decadist' and for historians to exercise 'decadist imaginations'. The 1950s, for example, are seen as being boring, whereas the 1960s were exciting and experimental. And, as we've been discussing, the 1970s are viewed as a time when there was one crisis after another. On the other hand, the 1980s (so the argument goes) brought stability back by challenging the power of the trade unions, unleashed the entrepreneurial skills of individuals and re-established Britain's place in the world. This type of reductive history fails to acknowledge the overlaps between periods and so, for example, even the hyper-individualism of 1980s Thatcherism was really a product of the 1960s, when the bonds that had once connected people to a collective society were first loosened and for some broke irrevocably. It's also important to remember that Mrs Thatcher herself got her first Cabinet post in 1970 and became leader of the Conservative Party in 1975 – long before she became the Iron Lady.

Given all of this, I'm deliberately choosing to talk about both decades in the same chapter. For me, the murder cases from the 1970s that I describe represent the hyper individualism and the neoliberal free-market economy that have come to be associated with the 1980s and Thatcherism. Of course, there remains a lively debate about what Thatcherism actually was, although the key terms that it became associated with are illustrative: freedom, self-reliance, individual choice and, perhaps above all, enterprise. All were allied to an authoritarian conservatism that emphasised morality and personal responsibility. These words and phrases often became a shorthand for an oppositional view of the world, which characterised the politics of the 1960s and 1970s as socialist and which had in turn created a 'culture of dependency'. Thatcherism wanted to 'roll back the state', which meant, as far as the economy was concerned, that it opposed central planning and state control of the mines, the steel industry, railways, public utilities and even education. Thatcherism wanted the market to be given its head and to rule unhindered. Individuals should be allowed to make their own way in the world, with as little interference from the state as possible. At its most extravagant, some began to question whether there was actually such a thing as 'society'. These ideas could influence offenders as much as they might have inspired entrepreneurs and industrialists.

Having set that context, let's consider the cases of a Manchester serial killer and, in particular, Britain's most prolific contract killer – two men who were active in the 1970s but, ironically, about whom very few people have ever heard.

*

Trevor Hardy was a Manchester-based serial killer who'd eventually be sentenced for three murders in May 1978. Far from the media creating a news frenzy, as had happened in the wake of Mr Hills's death, Hardy was all but invisible and it's therefore clear that 'news values' have a complexity that transcends the simplicity of 'moral panic'.[7] This is all the more remarkable as serial killers, as I first discussed with Jack the Ripper, offer the perfect story to the news media – they kill, then disappear back into their ordinary lives, only to reappear and kill again. Even so, Hardy's crimes barely made the headlines – an absence so marked that it might reflect that there was already no such thing as society even before Mrs Thatcher came to power. Bluntly, no one seemed to care what Hardy had done or who it was that he killed.

Hardy murdered his first victim, fifteen-year-old Janet Lesley Stewart, on New Year's Eve 1974, although he wouldn't admit to it until August 1975. In the presence of his solicitor Hardy told the police that he had seen Janet getting out of a car at around 22:40 p.m. and, mistaking her for a former girlfriend, stabbed her in the throat, cut her neck and then dragged her body into a hollow. He returned in March 1975 to bury her properly, then came back for a second time and removed Janet's hands, feet and head – either to conceal her identity or satisfy some form of sexual sadism. It may very well be that Hardy had gone back to Janet's grave so as to remove her ring, which he then gave to his new girlfriend Sheilagh Farrow, a divorcee ten years his senior.

His second victim was Wanda Skala, an eighteen-year-old barmaid at the Lightbowne Hotel in Moston, whom he murdered in July 1975. Wanda left the hotel at about 2:15 a.m. and a few hours later her body was discovered on a nearby building site. The clothes on the upper part of her body had been torn open, her breast had been badly bitten and her trousers and underwear had been removed. Wanda's right sock was tied around her neck, and it was obvious that she had been strangled.

Hardy's final victim was seventeen-year-old Sharon Mosoph, whom he murdered in March of the following year. Sharon, whose small stature earned her the nickname 'Titch', had only just arrived back in Manchester the night before she was murdered, and she had walked from the bus stop with a friend. Some time later, screams were heard from the direction of the Rochdale Canal. At around 8 a.m. on 9 March 1976 Sharon's naked body was found. Her tights had been used to strangle her. When the frozen canal melted, a bundle of her clothes and her handbag came to the surface. Detectives believed she'd been attacked while walking along the street and then dragged across a car park and thrown into the canal. One of her nipples was missing. Police suggested that Sharon may have confronted Hardy as he was trying to break into Marlborough Mill, where she worked as a cashier.

As with the murder of Janet, Hardy realised that he may have left clues and so he returned to the scene, found Sharon's body and mutilated it, so as to erase his teeth marks from her nipple. He then appears to have left the immediate vicinity and while living rough he sexually and physically assaulted another woman in a public toilet. It was evidence collected from this attack which brought his criminal activities to an end. In June 1976 Hardy appeared at Oldham Magistrates' Court charged with the murders of Wanda and Sharon. At a second hearing a month later Hardy's mother protested her son's innocence.

After the police charged Hardy with the two murders he confessed to killing Janet, who had up until then been treated as a missing person. Despite his confession Hardy pleaded not guilty to murder at Manchester Crown Court on the grounds of diminished responsibility. On the fourth day of the trial, when Sheilagh Farrow was due to give evidence against him, Hardy sacked his counsel and began to conduct his own defence. The jury didn't believe his account and, having retired for just seventy minutes, Hardy was found guilty on three counts of murder. He was sentenced to life imprisonment. During sentencing, the judge, Mr Justice Caulfield, described Hardy as 'hopelessly evil'.

It's difficult to understand why Hardy's crimes have been so ignored, but there are perhaps a few reasons. For example, he'd been a rough sleeper with mental health issues and therefore he didn't seem to garner the media attention that might have come from a police investigation on the trail of a 'criminal mastermind'. The area where he killed was described as being 'down at heel' and so Hardy's victims didn't generate the same sympathy as those who'd been murdered in more affluent areas. Finally, his confession to a third murder came after having been charged with two murders and, given that Janet had already been listed as a missing person, this again seemed to dampen media interest.

However, it's this absence of interest in Hardy and his gruesome serial of killings of three young women that's important. Sharon, Wanda and Janet might not have been 'ideal victims', but it's difficult to escape the conclusion that they'd already been left behind in a culture that, even by 1976, was stratified into winners and losers – a context which Thatcherism would exploit, rather than create.

This brief account of a 'forgotten' serial killer and his equally forgotten victims has similarities with what we know about John Childs, our most prolific hitman. In particular there are extraordinary and troubling details about the crimes that Childs committed, and a confession to the police about another murder which had previously been listed as a missing persons case. Above all, Childs exemplifies a new breed of offender who emerges in the 1970s and 1980s and sees offending as a career choice. Childs, for example, set up a business called Murder Incorporated offering his skills as a contract killer and assassination as a commodity. As he'd later explain rather proudly to a court, he took the decision to go into the 'murder business'. What follows inevitably has to describe some troubling details.

*

Hitmen occupy a secret world, an underworld, where they make business transactions with others wishing to conduct themselves 'beyond the pale'.[8] This clandestine world makes it difficult to be precise about their activities and also explains why there's been comparatively little academic research about them, or the phenomenon of 'contract killing' more generally, which now often gets described as a 'targeted attack'. What modest research that does exist suggests the majority of hits don't generate a great deal of money: one successful hit cost just £200.[9] It would also appear that most are contracted by former business partners of their erstwhile colleagues, and by spurned or one-time lovers. The little that we do know about hits and those who carry them out is a result of failure – the contract killer gets caught, and it's that which allows us to glimpse this secret underworld. We simply don't know with any certainty if, or how, more successful contract killers – those who don't get arrested – might differ from those who are apprehended and are then prepared to talk about how they went about completing their contract, or why, or indeed by whom, they were contracted. Even if they are prepared to talk, would they necessarily tell the truth?

These are important caveats to bear in mind when we consider the murders committed by John Childs. Between August 1974 and December 1978 Childs, who was, like Michael Copeland, a former soldier, carried out six hits – murders for which he was convicted in December 1979. At his trial Childs implicated two other men as being his accomplices – Terry Pinfold and Henry MacKenney,[10] who were also convicted of murder at the time but then later had those convictions quashed in 2003 by the Court of Appeal. Childs remains in jail and is serving a whole life tariff.

At his trial Childs claimed that in a spirit of free enterprise, he set up Murder Incorporated in 1974. He told the court that he was inspired to do so by successfully carrying out his first murder, and with Pinfold and MacKenney held a 'policy meeting and the result of that was that we were going into the murder business'. He suggested that it was Pinfold's job to find the clients, whilst he and MacKenney carried out the hits.[11] As he was later to say about his own motivation, 'I will kill anyone for money.'

Childs was convicted of six murders: Terry Eve, who went missing in 1974; Robert Brown; father and son George and Terry Brett; Freddie Sherwood, a nursing home proprietor; and, finally, a roofing contractor called Ronald Andrews. The bodies of these victims have never been recovered and no murder weapon has ever been found. In reality we've only Childs's confession to Detective Chief Superintendent Frank Cater, after he had been arrested for a series of bank robberies in 1978, that these murders took place at all. However, none of the victims have ever come forward to confirm that they are in fact still alive and so it's safe to assume that they really are all dead.[12] The stories of how these poor people died and how their bodies were disposed of are truly chilling but, once again, we've only Childs's sensational account on these matters, with very little corroborating evidence.

The story seems to go back to 1965, when Terry Pinfold and Henry MacKenney began manufacturing life jackets. Both had chequered pasts, with MacKenney being described as 'a ruthless villain' and 'an East End hard man'.[13] In 1972 they formed a company called H. J. Marine and took the occupancy of a disused church which now operated as a factory in Dagenham. Two years later Terry Eve, who made teddy bears – and hence was sometimes called 'Teddy' Eve – took some space within the factory. In August 1974, after he'd been released from prison, Childs started to work for Pinfold and

MacKenney. The soft toy business was originally Eve's alone but, just before Childs was released, it was registered as a partnership between Eve and Pinfold's wife. A few months later the business was incorporated with Pinfold's wife as the sole director and owner of 99 per cent of the issued shares. Pinfold, through his wife, effectively had control of the soft toy company.

According to what Childs would later claim, by 1974 the life jacket business had fallen on hard times and so there were discussions about how to get rid of Eve. Of course, it would've been simple enough to have thrown Terry out of the factory, but Pinfold seemingly feared that there would be repercussions from Eve's family if he did so. He therefore wanted Childs and MacKenney to kill him, using a smokescreen that he'd simply disappeared because he owed Pinfold money. What we do know for certain is that Terry was last seen making deliveries to the Barn Restaurant on 1 November 1974 and he must have then returned to the factory. Eve, according to Childs, was lured inside, where he and MacKenney beat him with a length of hydraulic hose to which were attached two heavy metal nuts. He was also hit about the face with a hammer and, as Childs told it, MacKenney then strangled Terry with a rope. While all of this was happening Robert Brown, a friend of Eve's, who was hiding in the factory after he'd absconded from prison, came to investigate the commotion and was ushered away by Childs.

After the murder the factory's floor and walls were covered in blood, and so Childs alleged that he and MacKenney spent several hours cleaning it with buckets of water. As for disposing of Terry's body, Childs says that it was wrapped in a tarpaulin and put in the back of MacKenney's car, then they both drove to Childs's council flat in Poplar, east London. They had intended to cut up Terry's body and feed it into an industrial meat grinder that they'd acquired for the purpose. However, the domestic electricity supply was insufficient to power the mincing machine and so, after attempting to flush the chopped-up body parts down the toilet, they decided to burn them in the grate in the living room. This took several hours, with the pair seemingly working in shifts throughout the night. After the body had been burned, they disposed of the ashes and Terry Eve was no more.

Robert Brown, who came to investigate the noise on the night of Eve's murder, was killed in January 1975 because it was feared that he knew too much about what had happened and that he'd go to the police. Childs would later say that he lured Robert to the flat in Poplar, where he was attacked and then put in the bath. That was where 'I cut the clothes off him [and] then used every knife-sword-chisel-screwdriver-bayonet and hunting arrow in my home to stab the slimy bastard with. When I'd finished he looked like a pin cushion [and] bloody bizarre with all the steel and wooden objects sticking out of him.' Thereafter, just like his friend Terry Eve, Robert's remains were burned on the council flat's fire.

The next to die were George Brett and his ten-year-old son Terry, in November 1975. George lived with his wife and children on a farm near Southend in Essex. There seems to have been some disagreement between the Bretts and their landlord, a man called Leonard Thompson. Indeed, there had been an altercation between George and Thompson in October 1973, which had left the latter with a skull fracture.

It was this running dispute that seems to have been the basis for the contract that was taken out on George's life and the more formal beginnings of Murder Incorporated.

George Brett had been running a haulage business since 1972, and on the afternoon of Saturday 4 January 1975 a man calling himself Mr Jennings had come to the farm driving a dark-coloured Jaguar, with a view to discussing a haulage contract. George had then left with Mr Jennings to discuss the business further, taking his son Terry with him in his blue Mercedes. The Mercedes was later found in a car park at King's Cross station in London, and it would appear that Mr Jennings was in fact an elaborately disguised John Childs.

Childs stated that a friend of MacKenney, known only as Big Lennie, had wanted Brett killed and had agreed a fee of £2,000 for his murder, although this was later reduced to £1,800. Obviously, there was speculation at the time that this had to have been the Bretts' landlord, although no evidence was ever uncovered by the police to implicate Leonard Thompson. Once inside the Dagenham factory, Childs claimed that MacKenney shot Brett twice in the head with a Sten gun and he'd then shot Terry in the head as he was being held by Childs. They'd apparently disagreed as to whether or not this had been necessary but, in the same way that Robert Brown was killed because he would have known too much about how Terry Eve had been killed, so too Terry Brett had to die.

The two Bretts were then taken to a compressor shed at the back of the factory where, according to Childs, MacKenney sawed off their legs. They were then put in dustbins and transported in his van back to his flat in Poplar. They were further dismembered once inside the flat and their remains again burned in the grate – a process that took all weekend. As with the other victims, the ashes were disposed of later. There was some forensic evidence to support this version of events, as traces of human blood were found on a dustbin in the pram store at Childs's flat.

The final two victims were Freddie Sherwood and Ronald Andrews. The Sherwoods had moved from London to Herne Bay, where they converted one of their houses into a rest home for the elderly, which was run by Mrs Sherwood. They subsequently bought another property in 1976 and had that converted into a rest home too, although the substantial building works (undertaken by a man called Paul Morton-Thurtle, whom Childs said he knew as Paul Hammond), hadn't gone smoothly. Childs claimed that they'd been contracted to kill Freddie Sherwood for £4,000. This was to be paid in instalments, and a ruse was engineered about buying Mr Sherwood's car and taking it on a test drive to London, so as to get Freddie into the Dagenham factory.

The final victim, Ronald Andrews, was murdered for a fee of £400 because, it was alleged by Childs, MacKenney was having an affair with Ronald's wife Gwen. Like the other victims, Ronald was shot and dismembered inside Childs's flat, although this time there was a more elaborate smokescreen to cover up his death, which involved taking Ronald's car to Wisbech and then driving it into the River Nene, to make it look like he had taken a corner too fast. MacKenney, Childs alleged, had done this while wearing a wetsuit.

The three Court of Appeal judges who sat in 2003 to consider the appeals of Terry Pinfold and Henry MacKenney described the story of how these five men and a boy had come to be murdered as 'remarkable'. So remarkable in fact that they quashed the convictions – concluding that the evidence provided by Childs that Terry and Henry had been his accomplices was 'wholly unreliable' and so untrustworthy as to be 'worthless'. The judges were helped in reaching this conclusion by evidence provided by a psychiatrist and a psychologist, who suggested that Childs was not only a psychopath but also had a personality disorder which resulted in 'the truth and lies become very difficult for [him] to distinguish'. As a result, the judges couldn't 'determine where the truth lies as to these murders'.

Being wrongly convicted and spending many years in jail had a major impact on the lives of Henry and Terry. Henry, who had been convicted of four murders – George and Terry Brett, Freddie Sherwood and Ronald Andrews – and Terry, who had been convicted of the murder of Terry Eve, would later say that they didn't understand why the cases against them had even got to court. While in jail, Terry had suffered six strokes and left prison with serious heart failure, but not only had he lost his health, he was now penniless and divorced. Henry, once described as 'Britain's most wanted man', emerged from prison frail and gaunt, having developed emphysema and had a near fatal dose of pneumonia. These were the all too human consequences of Childs's claims.

What's not in dispute is that Childs remains behind bars. He has repeatedly given interviews in which he openly admits to these murders and has confessed to more. The only logical (or at least legal) conclusion is that he alone was responsible for the six murders. He has never expressed remorse for what he's done or changed what he's described repeatedly as his motivation for undertaking these killings – he would kill anyone for money. As he put it, 'it was just business. It was a dirty job and lucratively paid for the amount of time you had to undergo unpleasantness.' Clearly the noun 'unpleasantness' is doing a great deal of heavy lifting here, given that what's being described is the killing and mutilation of six people, including a child, and then burning their bodies in a small domestic fireplace. However, that does not necessarily mean that what Childs says is in itself untrue, or that the small amounts of money he was paid were unusual – in total he seems to have made just £7,000 from the six murders. All of this fits with the little that we know about contract killings in Britain, where the average cost of such a targeted attack is the price of a small second-hand family car.[14] Details as to why the hits were contracted would also seem to fit with what we know about this underworld business more generally. Finally, any murderer will have the problem of what to do with their victim's body. Some killers have tried to dispose of body parts by flushing them down the toilet, as Childs attempted. Others have simply buried the body in the back garden or incinerated it with garden rubbish, masking the smell of human flesh by burning tyres, and so it's really not so extraordinary that Childs might have used the grate of his fire as he claimed.

*

In all of this, Childs not only emerges as a psychopath and our most prolific hitman – at least as far as we know – but also as a very early example of a criminal that would become more common from the 1980s onwards. This type of offender has been described as a 'criminal undertaker'. These are ruthless 'movers and shakers' who, in order to make a living, get involved in crime and often go on to achieve positions of dominance and status within the communities where they live. They achieve that position because they are perfect examples of a culture, rather than being an aberration or a deviation from it. Research undertaken by Professor Steve Hall and Professor Simon Winlow, for example, explains the rise in both minor and violent crime in the late twentieth century as a by-product of the Thatcherite deindustrialisation, which left many men in particular locales without work. As Winlow has persuasively put it, a 'new criminality' emerged from the 1970s onwards, which was not just a means of gaining status and money but a process that also saw crime and violence becoming 'careers in themselves'.[15]

Tied up within this argument are the ways that men adapted to late modern Britain. Employment within traditional industries such as mines and shipyards no longer existed, as work was outsourced to developing countries within the neoliberal global economy. In such circumstances, Hall and Winlow argue, men learned that violence could deliver the same benefits as work. Men who use violence, and sometimes commit murder, are usually found within the specific social and cultural contexts characterised by deindustrialisation. In these environments violence becomes normalised, and sometimes expected. As Winlow explained, based on the results of his research with violent men in Sunderland, 'it's just the way it was'. In other words, within this specific, impoverished and disadvantaged location, violence quickly became routine and predictable, and led to various 'joys' being experienced – from people laughing at your jokes or becoming more generally deferential, to gaining access to consumer society. All of this indicates the emergence of forms of status, respect and prestige that are different from what might be expected in other less disadvantaged locales, where masculinity could be performed in different ways.

This might take us too far from John Childs. After all, he was murdering in the 1970s and therefore before the effects of the deindustrialisation and in a different part of the country. However, it does seem possible to explain his behaviour not simply through a psychological lens – he was a psychopath – but also as a product of a trend that would become more pronounced and visible in the Britain of the late twentieth century. Not only did Childs find a way of unleashing his own entrepreneurial skills to satisfy a demand within the perverted market for death, but he also gained significant pleasure from having done so. As Jeff Edwards, one of the journalists who interviewed him in prison has put it, 'the only way to make Childs laugh is start talking about killing people'. Rather than having taken things too far, Hall and Winlow's analysis seems to fit perfectly.

Of course, Childs wasn't behaving morally. That's why his actions had to be curbed by the state through the criminal justice system. But what about the market – the commodification of death – that he exploited? As the political philosopher Michael Sandel has reminded us, commodification can spoil the moral norms that should otherwise guide our actions, such as loyalty, altruism and civic duty.[16] Markets have developed to sell blood and human organs. However, if we want to live in a good society we have to allow the state to intervene and place a moral limit on these markets, or others that might emerge but which would be unfair, inequitable or ill advised. Not to do so is to open up the possibility that criminal undertakers like Childs will become even more pervasive. Politics, in other words, has to do much more than manage the economy and free up the entrepreneurial aspirations of individuals; it has to intervene in our lives – in society – to shape and support how those lives are being lived within the community as a whole.

*

And what should we make of the 1970s and 1980s more generally? The caricatures of these decades can only take us so far and the two seem far more interconnected than has previously been acknowledged. However, if history is written by winners, then the victor during this time was Mrs Thatcher. Is it any wonder, then, that we're perpetually encouraged to see the 1970s as a time of strikes and strife, shortages and decline? A decade when we read by candlelight[17] because the electricity was cut off, and of the Winter of Discontent in 1978–79 that left rubbish on the streets and some of the dead unburied. Of course, this narrative ignores the changes that took place for the better. We even entered Europe with comparatively little fuss, or at least with less fuss than when we left several decades later. This same caricature implies that the 1980s and Mrs Thatcher was a corrective to the 1970s, and I now turn to a murder of one of the architects of Thatcherism to pursue these issues further.

CHAPTER NINE

Cases Thirteen and Fourteen

The Murder of Airey Neave, 1979, and the Murder of Elsie Ansell, 1939

I have the honour to inform you that the Government of the Irish Republic, having its first duty towards its people the establishment and maintenance of peace and order here, demand the withdrawal of all British armed forces stationed in Ireland.

PATRICK FLEMING, in an ultimatum sent to the Foreign Secretary Lord Halifax, 12 January 1939

The explosion had so badly disfigured the driver of the blue Vauxhall Cavalier that, at first, no one was quite certain who it was, or even if he was alive or dead. Smoke engulfed New Palace Yard, which added to the confusion, and several passers-by noted that sheets of headed House of

Commons notepaper were blowing gently in the breeze. Police officers rushed to the scene and found the victim slumped over the steering wheel, dressed in a black coat and striped trousers. He'd lost his right leg below the knee; his hair had been scorched and his face was very badly burned. Some thought he might be the Labour MP Alan Lee Williams, who was parliamentary private secretary to Roy Mason, the Secretary of State for Northern Ireland. So, it was clear even at this very early and confusing time, that this had been another terrorist attack, most likely connected to the Troubles – the conflict within and associated with Northern Ireland, which started in the late 1960s and would continue until the Good Friday Agreement of 1998.[1]

These first attenders soon realised that the driver was unconscious but alive, and then a police officer called Peter Dickens retrieved a wallet containing correspondence addressed to the Conservative MP Airey Neave. Now at least they could identify the victim. It was Airey who'd masterminded Mrs Thatcher's rise to power as leader of the Conservative Party and who was himself, after a political life that had been dominated by service on the back benches, now Shadow Secretary of State for Northern Ireland. He was a 'coming man' and the impending general election, which the Tories were expected to win, would cement his power. An ambulance crew arrived and within half an hour the badly injured MP was on his way to Westminster Hospital, where he underwent emergency surgery. Sadly, however, Airey was to die on the operating table on 30 March 1979.

There was yet more confusion. In the immediate aftermath of the bombing, both the Provisional Irish Republican

Army (PIRA) and the smaller, less well-known Irish National Liberation Army (INLA) claimed responsibility for Airey's murder. It would be established over the coming days that it was the INLA which had planted the bomb under the car. The INLA would later claim that Airey's murder 'had a tonic effect in Northern Ireland where there had been celebrations in Belfast [and] a recruiting boom for the INLA', which, prior to this terrorist attack, had approximately sixty members. The INLA stated that Airey had been specifically targeted because he was 'well-known for his rabid militarist calls for more repression against the Irish people'.

We don't need to accept this obviously one-sided editorial about Airey's opinions or conjecture about the role that he might have played as Secretary of State for Northern Ireland after the Conservatives duly won the general election of 7 May 1979, little more than a month after his assassination. It's clear, however, that his death affected Mrs Thatcher deeply. Her first words on hearing about the bomb, when she was preparing for a party political broadcast at the BBC, were reportedly, 'Please God, don't let it be Airey.' When her worst fears were confirmed, she was said to be 'numb with shock' and later told a reporter that 'some devils got him and they must never, never be allowed to triumph; they must never be allowed to prevail'.

Two questions would dominate the next few weeks. Was the bomb planted within the Palace of Westminster, or had it been placed under the car earlier, outside Airey's flat at 32 Westminster Gardens in Marsham Street? And even if it had been established that the INLA were responsible, could an individual culprit be identified and brought to justice?

For propaganda purposes, the INLA wanted to claim that the bomb had indeed been planted within the Palace of Westminster – the very heart of the British state. However, on balance, it would appear that it had been fixed on Marsham Street, where there were significantly fewer risks of being detected. Airey was a 'soft target'. His home address, for example, was listed in *Who's Who* and he'd rejected police protection, despite it being offered as far back as 1975. He claimed that if he couldn't walk the streets of London freely, then life wouldn't be worth living. He was also a creature of habit and so his daily personal and professional routines could easily be established. Sadly, all of this conspired to create the circumstances in which Airey came to be murdered.

Most of the details about the assassination were laid out by the security services in a report given to the then Labour prime minister, James Callaghan, just five days later. This report described how the bomb had consisted of a mercury detonator device attached to a kilo of TNT, secured to the underside of the car with a magnet. This same report also stated that six members of the INLA had been sent to England to carry out the attack, although there's debate as to whether this sextet were all male or included at least one woman. In any event, no one has ever been arrested for the assassination, and despite Airey's prominence this shocking murder soon disappeared from the headlines as other terrorist atrocities related to the Troubles multiplied.

Given the security considerations, perhaps it's no surprise that the official files remain closed until 2079, although there have been a number of credible suggestions about the identities of at least two of the six INLA members. The first is Patsy

O'Hara, who's alleged to have smuggled the bomb materials into England from France, and who died as a result of his hunger strike while serving a sentence on another matter at HMP Maze in Belfast in May 1981. The second suspect is Harry Flynn, who in 2019 was tracked down to Majorca, where he was running a pub called The Celts Well in Santa Ponsa, which was decorated with INLA slogans and Irish flags.[2] Flynn has never been questioned, arrested or charged with Airey's murder, although, having been named as the leader of the INLA in 1982, he's widely regarded as being one of the six who planted the bomb.

*

Airey's death stunned the House of Commons. It remains a deadly reminder that issues related to British involvement in Ireland, and specifically Northern Ireland, have often been ignored or sidelined and so we've tended to forget the awful, bloody consequences. We look away, rather than engage with the repercussions of our historic, tortuous and not always honourable role in Ireland, almost as if that failure of acknowledgement absolves us from bearing any responsibility. And yet this responsibility and the corresponding terrorist reaction goes back a long way – as our second murder case will tragically demonstrate.

There are multiple ways of defining terrorism. In this context I'm suggesting that it's a type of communicative violence by non-state actors fighting against a more powerful adversary.[3] The terrorist's goal is to mobilise their supporters and to intimidate the public, even if the terrorists are rarely in a position to overthrow the state. In that sense the wider threat that they pose is symbolic rather than existential. That symbolic threat can of course still cause severe injury and even death. Is this also 'freedom fighting', or a form of social control 'from below'? Whatever the case, the reaction by the state was – obviously – to treat these incidents as criminal matters to be pursued through the justice system. Airey's assassination, even if he was a politician and about to become Secretary of State for Northern Ireland, was therefore a murder, as opposed to, for example, his being a victim during a period when the state was at war with an enemy combatant. It's also interesting that Shadow Secretary of State for Northern Ireland was a position that Airey had asked for, rather than one he had to be pushed into. He didn't look away or ignore what was happening.

It's quite clear that Airey was an extraordinary man. He had a *Boy's Own* backstory: as a soldier – the first man to escape from the Colditz prisoner-of-war camp during the Second World War; a spy; and latterly a bestselling author, as well as becoming an MP in 1953. However, Airey was an instinctive rather than ideological Conservative and so he played little part in the philosophical development of Thatcherism. What he did do was to convince Margaret Thatcher to stand against Edward Heath for the leadership of the party, at a time when female politicians were rarely seen as electoral assets, and then served as her campaign manager.

Airey's murder serves as an awful example of more general attacks on the state and, in turn, the state's defence of its sovereignty. Here I'm using sovereignty to mean parliamentary sovereignty, by which Parliament is the supreme authority and final arbiter of legality within the United Kingdom. I'm also referring to the idea that the United Kingdom is a sovereign state. In other words, that it's independent and not under the authority of any other country, although this clearly leaves room for particular discussions about the place of other nations who are constituent members of the United Kingdom, such as Northern Ireland, Wales and Scotland.

There's an irony in all of this. It could be argued that sovereignty was what PIRA and the INLA were themselves demanding in the form of the withdrawal of British troops and the creation of a united and sovereign Ireland. They used violence in the pursuit of that political objective, although it cannot be denied that this led to them often killing, whether intentionally or not, members of the public, rather than the political representatives of a more powerful state adversary. This issue of sovereignty wasn't just important for the 1970s and 1980s but remains significant in today's political landscape – and not just within or about Ireland. Sovereignty, for example, is at the heart of the calls for an independent Scotland and Wales. It also played a crucial role in the decision of the United Kingdom to leave the European Union so that we could, we were assured, 'take back our borders', as the Treaty of Rome had meant that Parliament was not the only source of law and some of our sovereignty had been surrendered to Europe. It was a principle that even saw us fight a war with Argentina in 1982.

This discussion is not tangential to, or divergent from, the murder of Airey Neave but at its very heart. And, in keeping with not being 'decadist', let's consider the background to the Troubles, which would see 175 terrorism-related deaths in Britain between 1971 and 2001, and then consider our second murder case – the death of Elsie Ansell in Coventry in 1939.

*

The origins of the Troubles can be traced back hundreds of years and so concentrating on associated terrorist attacks on mainland Britain in the twentieth century can only ever be a fragment of the whole story. Most obviously, it ignores all those who died on the island of Ireland. Even using the twentieth century as a time frame – from the Easter Rising of 1916 to the Good Friday Agreement of 1998 – overlooks significant Irish republicanism within Britain in the nineteenth century. Michael Barrett, for example, was the last man to be publicly hanged in England in May 1868, for his part in what became known as the 'Clerkenwell Explosion' of December 1867. This was an attempt to free the Irish Republican Ricard O'Sullivan Burke, who'd been arrested and remanded in custody at Clerkenwell. Barrett attempted to blow a hole in the prison's wall, but the explosion was misjudged and instead of freeing Burke, the bomb killed twelve local people and injured more than 120.

The Easter Rising of 1916 involved Irish Republicans seizing various government buildings in Dublin, including the General Post Office, and this inevitably led to clashes with the British Army. The Republicans were quickly overwhelmed and fifteen of their leaders, including Patrick Pearse – for many the embodiment of the rebellion – were subsequently executed. What's of interest to this chapter is that the state's response to the uprising merely galvanised further support for the Republican cause and led to the Irish Republican Army (IRA) fighting a guerrilla campaign against the army and loyalist Irish forces. That would last for some two years, until the Government of Ireland Act came into force in May 1921, which was followed by the Anglo-Irish Treaty of December 1921 and the partition of Ireland.

It's also of interest that the Easter Rising took place two years after the outbreak of the First World War, when the British were focused on fighting in mainland Europe. War would again provide the Republicans with an opportunity just as hostilities with Germany were about to begin in 1939. However, Patrick Fleming's ultimatum to Lord Halifax, quoted at the start of the chapter, didn't have the desired effect and so the IRA declared war on Britain, claiming that they were the 'Government of the Irish Republic'. This war took a specific form and was to be conducted through a campaign of sabotage, and so it's sometimes known as the 'S-Plan', or the 'Sabotage Campaign'. Others have described it as the 'English Campaign'. This involved attempting to disrupt civil and public utilities in England, such as water, gas and electricity; blowing up telephone kiosks, public lavatories and post boxes; and attacking commercial premises, armament factories and some industrial plants.

Coventry was specifically mentioned in the S-Plan, because of its importance to the electricity supply in the Midlands, but civilians were not supposed to be targeted. However, just as there were unintended victims in Clerkenwell, Coventry would experience its worst-ever terrorist attack at the hands of Irish Republicans, which resulted in a number of civilian deaths and multiple casualties.

*

Elsie Ansell was twenty-one years old and worked as a shop assistant at Millet's in Cross Cheaping in the city centre.[4] She was engaged to be married to Harry Davies. On 25 August 1939, Elsie was using her lunch break to window shop in nearby Broadgate. She was looking at jewellery in H. Samuel, no doubt thinking about Harry and their impending marriage, which was planned for 9 September. Like most Friday lunchtimes, the area was busy with shoppers, probably just as eager to discuss the threat posed by Hitler's Germany as what they wanted to buy. Alexander Ballinger, the manager of Astley's, which was also situated on Broadgate, was standing watching the crowds from the window of his shop when the bomb went off. The explosion blew him off his feet. He was lucky to survive. Robert Kinsella, another survivor, who had been walking towards Astley's, remembered:

> There was a violent explosion which threw me to the ground. I picked myself up and I could see that there had been terrible damage done. There were a lot of people lying about on the ground, but the first person that I went to was, I believe, old James Clay, whom I picked up: I could see from his injuries that he was almost dead. Of course, I then found I was bleeding very badly myself, and I went to the hospital.

Robert's wounds were relatively minor, but 'old James Clay' – a former president of the Coventry & District Co-Operative Society – died from his injuries. So too did Elsie. Her face had been blown off by the explosion and she was identified only by her engagement ring and some fragments of her clothing. Five days later, she was buried at St Barbara's Church in Earlsdon with perhaps as many as seven hundred people in attendance. On top of her coffin was a spray of cream roses from Harry and a card that read 'With everlasting love and remembrance, from your husband to be Harry'. Elsie was buried in her wedding dress and her mother Laura was so overcome with grief that it's believed she died just a few months later of a broken heart.

Along with James and Elsie, three other people died in the explosion. John Arnott, just fifteen years old, was the youngest victim. After leaving school he worked at W. H. Smith and, with his curly hair and spectacles, was described as a 'familiar face to many Coventrians'. Rex Gentile, a Welsh trainee manager who was lodging with the Arnott family, had been sent to provide holiday cover at W. H. Smith. He'd only been in Coventry for a couple of weeks and his body would later be buried back in Wales. The third victim, Gwilym Rowlands, was also Welsh. Known as Bill, he'd worked down the mines – dangerous enough – before moving to England to be closer to his son. He worked as a road sweeper for the Highways Department of the Coventry Corporation.

Nearly seventy people were injured – some very badly. Most of the survivors were treated at the Coventry and Warwickshire Hospital and such was the extent of their injuries that appeals had to be made for more blood donors. In Broadgate itself Ted Cross, the first ambulance man on the scene, remembered that 'the glass had been sucked out of all of the windows and there were a great many casualties'. One newspaper was later to describe the city centre as a 'miniature battlefield' with more than forty businesses damaged in the blast. Inevitably there was resentment against and hostility towards Irish people living in Coventry – estimated at around two thousand people, who had mostly come to work in the city's factories. Some were thrown out of their accommodation and there were demands that they be fired from their jobs. Captain Stanley Albert Hector, the Chief Constable of

Coventry Police, who was from Somerset, had to deny rumours that he was Irish.

The police investigation into the bombing was led by Chief Inspector Cyril Boneham of Coventry Police, although he was assisted by detectives from Special Branch. There was security intelligence that linked what had happened to the ultimatum sent to Lord Halifax, and very quickly, specific information emerged about who might have been involved. On the day after the attack Special Branch arrested Peter Barnes at his flat in Westbourne Terrace in London. His role as an IRA transport officer was to ferry explosives from ammunition dumps that they'd established in Liverpool and Glasgow. When his flat was searched, potassium chlorate was found in a chest of drawers and there was also an incriminating letter in his coat which clearly alluded to the S-Plan. The Special Branch detectives were able to establish that he'd travelled to Coventry on 24 August – the day before the bombing – and that he had not actually been in the city when the bomb exploded. Other intelligence information led the security services to rented accommodation in 25 Clara Street, Coventry, which was in effect a safe house for the IRA. The house was rented by Joseph Hewitt, who'd come to the city from Belfast in search of work in 1936, and his wife Mary. Also living in the property were Mary's mother Brigid O'Hara, the Hewitts' baby daughter Brigid Mary and a lodger called James McCormick, also known as James Richards. McCormick was the leader of the IRA unit active in Coventry and he and Peter Barnes knew one another from County Offaly in Ireland.

The house at 25 Clara Street was searched by Special Branch, assisted by Chief Inspector Boneham. In it they found bomb-making equipment and a new brass key to an alarm clock, which didn't fit any of the clocks in the house. It was suspected that this key would've been part of the clock used as the timer for the bomb. As a result, the Hewitts, Brigid O'Hara and James McCormick were all arrested and, along with Peter Barnes, were charged with the murder of Elsie Ansell. As this was a capital offence, if the prosecution failed with regards to the Ansell charge, the Crown could bring further murder charges on behalf of the other four victims at a later date.

Special Branch suggested that the bomb had been constructed in 25 Clara Street, weighed about 5lb and had an alarm clock as a timer. It had then been parcelled in a box, wrapped in brown paper and tied up with string. The box was put in the basket of a Karnwell bicycle, bought a few days previously in Halford's by McCormick and another man, who gave his name as Mr Norman of Grayswood Avenue in Coventry. This other man has never been identified, but the person who pushed the bicycle and delivered the bomb is widely believed to have been Joby O'Sullivan, a native of Cork, and not an active member of the Coventry IRA unit. O'Sullivan would later give an interview to an Irish journalist just prior to his death in which he admitted that he was responsible for leaving the bomb outside of Astley's. He claimed that the intended target had been the Coventry police station, although others have suggested that the bomb was more than likely planned for the electricity power station. According to O'Sullivan, the bike kept getting stuck in the city's tramlines and so he'd simply abandoned it out of frustration, and the civilian casualties were therefore a 'terrible accident'. This excuse seems disingenuous at best. O'Sullivan knew that he was carrying a bomb and leaving it in a busy city centre simply because he was frustrated by the tramlines doesn't strike me as sincere.

None of the five who were arrested ever revealed O'Sullivan's name – they claimed that they didn't know it, although it has been suggested that Mary Hewitt and Brigid O'Hara had found him 'a strange man'. O'Sullivan seems to have evaded capture at the time by travelling to London, rather than heading for the ferry at Holyhead, and then keeping a low profile until the coast was clear.

McCormick (who was tried under his alias James Richards), Barnes, O'Hara and Joseph and Mary Hewitt were tried at the Warwick Assizes in Birmingham in December 1939 – by which time Britain was once again at war with Germany. The Hewitts and O'Hara were acquitted but Barnes and McCormick were found guilty and hanged on 7 February 1940 in Winson Green Prison in Birmingham. As his guilty verdict was passed McCormick said: 'I wish to state that the part I took in these explosions since I came to England I have done for a just cause. As a soldier of the Irish Republican Army I am not afraid to die, as I am doing it for a just cause.' In any event, the executions didn't result in the end of the S-Plan, which continued until the end of March 1940 and saw attacks in London, Oxford, Birmingham, Manchester and Liverpool. The attacks seem to have come to an end because by then Hitler was doing far more damage than any Republican soldier could have hoped to have achieved.

*

The attack on Coventry is often described as 'forgotten'. This would seem to fit with the general pattern of how we've reacted to other similar attacks on mainland Britain. They create an immediate storm but, as with the assassination of Airey Neave, quickly fade from the headlines and then from historical memory. This amnesia might be seen as a form of British cultural stoicism – we just keep 'carrying on' irrespective of what's happening. More negatively, it also allows us to stubbornly refuse to engage with some of the more demanding political issues that cause these attacks. These would include, for example, Britain's historic role as an imperial power, that imperial legacy, and current issues of sovereignty. A failure to deal with such issues can have tragic – sometimes deadly – consequences. Frankly, it's quite staggering how many people have been killed or injured in terrorist attacks by Irish nationalists on mainland Britain and how we've chosen to ignore or simply dismiss why they were occurring.

The mainland campaign by the Provisional IRA (PIRA), which started in the early 1970s in response to Bloody Sunday, claimed at least 175 lives, injured more than ten thousand people and is estimated to have caused property damage in excess of £1 billion.[5] The targets of these attacks included politicians, infrastructure needed for the state to function, state officials and commercial enterprises. It also included – whether deliberately or not – ordinary men, women and children.

If we look at these two basic types of terrorist incidents – those targeting the state at large, and those involving civilians – the most notorious of the latter would include the following three incidents. First, a wave of PIRA bomb attacks in British pubs between October and November 1974, which killed twenty-eight people and wounded more than two hundred. The most infamous of these were in Birmingham, where twin blasts destroyed two pubs – The Tavern in the Town and The Mulberry Bush. The Birmingham Pub Bombings killed twenty-one people and injured 182 others. The bombings led to the arrests of six innocent men, and their eventual exoneration. A reinvestigation by the West Midlands Police in 2019 raised hopes that the guilty parties would at last be arrested (if they were still alive). However, in August 2023 it was announced that there would be no criminal charges following that reinvestigation – to the disappointment of the campaign group Justice 4 the 21.

The second incident focused on civilians took place on 17 December 1983 when a car bomb exploded outside the side entrance of the Harrods department store in Knightsbridge, London. Six people were killed – three police officers and three members of the public. Ninety other people were injured, including nine children. Finally, on 20 March 1993 two small bombs detonated in litter bins on the crowded Bridge Street shopping precinct in Warrington in Cheshire. The explosions killed two children – three-year-old Jonathan Ball and twelve-year-old Tim Parry – as well as injuring fifty-four people.

Those attacks which were aimed at politicians, military personnel or other state officials would include, at the very least, the following cases. First, the M62 Coach Bombing of 4 February 1974. The bomb, hidden in the luggage locker, killed twelve people – nine soldiers and three civilians – and injured another thirty-eight passengers. Second, on the morning of 20 July 1982 there was an attack on the Queen's Life Guard as they rode through Hyde Park to take up their sentry duty in Whitehall, and two hours later a second bomb exploded in Regent's Park, where the band of the Royal Green Jackets was performing a concert. A total of eleven soldiers were killed and fifty-nine others, including civilians, were injured. We should also include the assassination of Ian Gow, Conservative MP for Eastbourne, who was killed when a bomb attached to the underside of his car exploded outside his home on 30 July 1990. Less than a year later, in February 1991, there was a mortar attack on 10 Downing Street, which was aimed at killing John Major, the prime minister, who was meeting with his Cabinet to discuss the Gulf War. This attack on Downing Street came seven years after the bombing of the Grand Hotel in Brighton, where the Conservative Party were holding their annual conference. That attack was aimed at killing Margaret Thatcher. Five people, including Sir Anthony Berry, MP, died in the explosion and a further thirty-one were injured. Mrs Thatcher narrowly escaped the blast.[6]

These were persistent as well as traumatic terrorist incidents, which obviously had a far-reaching impact on victims and their families. However, while the state readily condemned what had occurred, and the media were similarly critical, their reaction was fleeting and didn't lead to any fundamental questioning as to why these incidents kept happening. Once the initial horror was over, Britons got on with their lives. It was almost as if these attacks were accepted like natural disasters such as floods or hurricanes, rather than the product of British history and our troubled involvement in and with the island of Ireland. In the same way that we've tended to responsibilise a murderer for killing his victim and rarely consider the broader context in which the death occurred, Irish terrorist atrocities were also viewed within a framework of individual criminality, rather than as an outcome of the policies of the British state.

Let's consider another country's demand for its own sovereignty: Scotland. In this history of Britain in twenty murder cases I could find none related to Scottish demands for independence, and perhaps that absence is just as important to reflect on.

*

In the early hours of Christmas Day 1950, a patrolling police officer found Kay Matheson and Ian Hamilton, two students from Glasgow University, locked in a passionate embrace inside their Ford Anglia. That wasn't so unusual for two students, but their car was parked outside Westminster Abbey and so the officer asked the couple what they were doing there at that hour of the morning. Ian and Kay explained that they'd just arrived from Scotland and hadn't been able to find a hotel. It all sounded innocent enough, and after sharing a cigarette the officer sent them on their way, watching as the car disappeared towards Victoria. He'd no idea that hidden inside was a sizeable chunk of the Stone of Destiny – more formally, the Stone of Scone – which Hamilton had just stolen from the Abbey. Before the sun could properly rise on Christmas morning, he and two other students – Gavin Vernon and Alan Stuart – had stolen the remainder.[7]

The four students were all members of the Scottish Covenant Association, which supported home rule for Scotland. Their theft of the Stone of Scone – which Hamilton termed a 'liberation' – was therefore a daring form of gesture politics rather than a student jape. After all, the stone was an ancient symbol of the nation, which Hamilton would years later call the 'soul of Scotland'. For centuries it had been used during the coronation of Scottish monarchs, until it was taken as a spoil of war in 1296 by King Edward I – the 'Hammer of the Scots' – during the Scottish Wars of Independence. The students were going to bring the stone home and hoped that by doing so they could generate renewed interest in Scottish nationhood and independence. When it was realised that the stone had been stolen, the border between Scotland and England was closed for the first time in four hundred years, and King George VI sent a personal reprimand to the Dean of Westminster for allowing the theft to happen.

Once in Scotland, and after having been repaired, the stone was left by the Scottish Covenant Association in Arbroath Abbey. This deposition site was again meant to send a message. It was here in April 1320 that a formal statement about Scottish sovereignty and independence had been proclaimed. The Declaration of Arbroath (although in reality a private missive to Pope John) states that 'as long as a hundred of us remain alive, never will we on any conditions be subjected to the Lordship of the English'. Although the true purpose of the declaration is now much debated, it has proven to be inspirational for many Scottish nationalists who see within its text a statement about an independent, sovereign Scotland free from interference from their more powerful southern neighbour.[8]

The stone was eventually returned to England in April 1951, and two years later would be used in the coronation of Queen Elizabeth II. In less dramatic circumstances, it again came back to Scotland on St Andrew's Day in 1996, after a campaign led by the then Conservative Secretary of State for Scotland

Michael Forsyth, to be housed in Edinburgh Castle. Kay Matheson was present for its return, although Ian Hamilton refused to attend the ceremony.[9] However, it travelled back to Westminster Abbey for the coronation of King Charles III in 2023 and Ian's son Jamie thought that his father, who'd died the previous year, would've been opposed to the stone's return south of the border as it sent out a message 'of oppression'.[10]

I've spent a little time describing the comings and goings of the Stone of Scone, its history and importance to the Scots, and the symbolic and constitutional importance that it retains today, for it serves as a useful mirror when considering the claims of Irish nationalists and how these might be acknowledged and then achieved. As Ian Hamilton was to reflect, when thinking about what he'd done in 1950, 'we drove down the bleak narrow road to London to hurt no one. Rather to puncture England's pride. To save no one but the ruined hopes of our country.' Stealing the stone was a form of 'communicative' violence by non-state actors in pursuit of a political agenda, but one which broadly took a social democratic form, rather than a type of communication which sought to terrorise and take lives. It was also a politics from 'below', intended to express a clear agenda, a sense of present and historic grievance about English conquest, imperialism, colonisation and the Scots' right to self-determine. As the years passed, these issues would become even more pressing, to the extent that the constitutional future of Scotland has a place in British politics today not unlike the 'Irish question' before 1922, although without, as Professor Sir Tom Devine, Scotland's leading historian, has put it, 'the element of real or potential physical force'.[11]

Why Scotland's claims for independence didn't have the same bloody impact as demands for Irish nationalism is worth considering a little further. For, as we've seen, it's quite clear that Scottish nationalists were just as passionate in their demands for sovereignty over their own affairs as the Irish. However, what seems to have taken them on a social democratic course is the reality that, for a significant period of time, union with England (and Wales) had suited the Scots and had allowed the country to prosper. Many Scots might have taken exception to the idea that 'Britain' was 'England', but Union had created enough opportunities for shared interests to develop between the two nations and even for common goals and sensibilities to evolve.

This state of affairs would continue until June 2016, when in the EU referendum Scotland voted decisively in favour of the UK staying in Europe by 62 per cent to 38 per cent, with all thirty-two council areas voting to remain. However, by 52 per cent to 48 per cent the overall vote of the country was to leave rather than remain in the EU and our withdrawal took effect in January 2020, forty-seven years after the UK had joined in January 1973, when the Europhile Ted Heath was prime minister.

*

What might the famously Eurosceptic Margaret Thatcher, who died in 2013, have made of all of this, and why was she so hated in Scotland? Her former foreign policy advisor Lord Powell of Bayswater, who helped her to draft her 1988 Bruges speech, in which she warned against ever closer EU integration, has commented that it was a mistake and a misjudgement to have allowed a referendum on Europe – a mistake that

Mrs Thatcher would never have made. He pointed out that she 'never had any truck with referendums and frequently spoke out against them'. He also said that, for all of her Euroscepticism, he believes Thatcher would have preferred to battle the EU 'from within, whatever the scale of her frustrations, rather than opening the door to exit'.[12]

We've no way of assessing these observations definitively, but they do at least have a ring of truth. It's more difficult to understand why Thatcher was so disliked in Scotland. Such was Scottish hatred for her that Charles Kennedy, the former leader of the Liberal Democrats who was MP for Ross, Skye and Lochaber, is reported to have described her ironically as 'the greatest of all Scottish Nationalists'. One of her former Scottish Cabinet ministers, Sir Malcolm Rifkind, thought that she fell victim to the strongly masculine, perhaps misogynistic culture of Scotland at the time – 'she was a woman, she was an English woman; she was a bossy English woman' and, moreover, one who did not know her place. Mrs Thatcher was therefore simply 'that bloody woman'. Did she flout gender expectations to such an extent that she grated on the Scots? The Scots-born former editor of the *Daily Express*, Sir John Junor, who was part of Thatcher's inner circle, thought that she was 'too damned good for you [the Scots]'. He further suggested that even though she was 'pulling you out of the shit that you've put yourself into', the Scots were a 'male chauvinist race', 'whingeing' and no longer intelligent enough to understand her abilities.[13]

Let's leave Junor's rantings to one side but at least acknowledge that some of the antipathy towards Thatcher was likely to have been gender based. Accepting this as true brings us full circle to Airey Neave. Following his wartime experiences, when he worked with a number of female British and European agents, he became only too well aware of their skills and competence in the field, which helps to explain his readiness to encourage Thatcher to stand for the leadership of the Conservative Party against Ted Heath. He didn't see her gender as a liability but as an asset. Airey would also have been aware that, when the occasion demanded, the women that he'd worked with during the war had been capable of using violence. That's also seen as breaching gender expectations, and is the subject of the next chapter.

CHAPTER TEN

Cases Fifteen and Sixteen

The Murder of Melanie Stourton, 1999, and the Murders Committed by Joanne Dennehy, 2013

When piety and maternal sentiments are wanting and in their place are strong passions and intensely erotic tendencies, much muscular strength and a superior intelligence for the conception and execution of evil, it is clear that the innocuous semi-criminal present in the normal woman must be transformed into a born criminal more terrible than any man.

CESARE LOMBROSO, *La Donna Deliquente* ('The Female Offender', 1893)

Sugar and spice but not at all nice.

Sunday Times, 27 November 1994

239

I t might seem odd to begin this chapter with the story of an ephemeral but much discussed female subculture of the 1990s – 'ladettes'. However, this fleeting anxiety about ladettes helps to contextualise those women who've historically been seen as 'dangerous'. It also allows us to reflect on the changing position of women over our time frame and consider whether these changes have led to what criminologists rather grandly describe as a 'sociological-emancipation-crime hypothesis'. Put more simply, that social and economic changes have led to more women committing crime. As far as the media were concerned in the 1990s, matters came to a head when a prominent ladette was broadcasting on the BBC during the birthday celebrations for a member of the Royal Family.

Queen Elizabeth, The Queen Mother was born on 4 August 1900. At the time of her birth, Queen Victoria was still on the throne and British troops were continuing their fight with the Boers in South Africa. A century later, on the occasion of her hundredth birthday, the Radio 1 DJ Sara Cox was presenting the station's popular breakfast show live from Ibiza. She led her audience in a chorus of 'Happy Birthday', played music from the year 1900 and then commented, 'It's the Queen Mum's birthday today. Ah, she smells of wee but we all love her.' The station's bosses immediately issued an apology, even though only twelve people actually complained. As was explained, Cox had simply been trying to 'convert the love and affection of the younger generation towards Her Majesty on this day, with the humour and respect her audience would expect'.[1]

Cox was one of the public faces of ladette culture – a term first used in 1994 in the men's magazine *FHM*. Along with other media personalities such as Denise van Outen and Zoe Ball, Cox and the ladettes were a mid-1990s phenomenon that turned gender stereotypes on their head. They were, it has been claimed, 'a product of women's increased equality' that had freed young women from the strictures of conservative forms of femininity. The ladette was 'mouthy, up for a laugh, took her clothes off and could out-do any male companion in the drinking stakes'. This was about women going out, invading what had historically been seen as male space and taking what they wanted. If men were permitted to binge drink and be outrageous, then so could women.[2]

Even if these taboo-breaking claims are exaggerated, the print media was unimpressed. Here were young women who weren't silent or servile, and nor did they see their role as confined to becoming wives and mothers within a domestic sphere. Quite quickly, and at times ludicrously, ladette culture was blamed for rises in female alcoholism, heart disease, child neglect, road accidents and, of course, crime. There was a rise in women committing violence against the person between 1990 and 1999, and a corresponding increase in the numbers of women being sent to prison for offences of violence. However, these figures fluctuated widely during the 1990s and the vast majority of women imprisoned were sent down for non-violent and minor property offences. It also remains unclear if the rise in the female prison estate was a result of women committing more crime through becoming more aggressive, or simply a greater willingness of the courts to use prison rather than a community-based penalty.[3]

Nonetheless, criminal and especially violent women have always been troubling cultural figures and the need to explain their existence has exercised popular audiences, commentators and academics since the time of Cesare Lombroso. Lombroso, who achieved great fame in the Victorian period and is quoted at the start of the chapter, is often described as the 'founding father' of modern criminology. He was a doctor and professor of psychiatry, and crucially he worked in prisons. Based on his prison experiences, Lombroso claimed that criminals were an 'atavistic throwback' to an earlier form of species on the evolutionary scale and suggested that the offenders' distinctive physical and biological features more resembled apes than those of humans. He was the first modern criminologist to write about the woman as a criminal in *La Donna Delinquente*, which was published in 1893.[4] A century later, the ladettes continued to offer up endless opportunities to discuss what in reality has become a favourite cultural preoccupation – interpersonal violence, especially when the perpetrator is a woman.

Violence is primarily seen as the province of masculinity, whereas femininity has traditionally been conceived in terms of nurture and the maintenance of stability and order. Yet in the 1990s these violent and 'dangerous' women seemed to be everywhere – a phenomenon that Hollywood captured in the 1995 movie *Tank Girl*, starring Lori Petty as the tank-driving, nose-picking, spitting, vomiting protagonist, who was prone to random acts of sex and violence. Tank Girl started life as a British comic book character in 1988, created by two men – Alan Martin and Jamie Hewlett. Here we should note other Hollywood characters from the time such as Ripley in the *Alien* franchise (1979–97), Sarah Connor in *Terminator 2* (1991) and the leads in *Thelma and Louise* (1993). All of these women were capable of using violence, albeit in different circumstances, and paved the way for The Bride – a deadly assassin played by Uma Thurman in *Kill Bill* (2003). These female characters were fetishised, often for the male gaze, although criminal and especially violent women were framed in real life as being 'doubly deviant' – not only did they break the law, they also breached the norms of gender.[5] So our response to such women, especially those who have killed, is to make them 'monstrous'. They're not women – or human – at all. Alternatively, some try to rehabilitate and recover them as women, by explaining that the violence they'd used was beyond their individual control.[6]

These issues are of great interest to both historians and criminologists. Crime, violence and especially murder really are male phenomena, to the extent that there's a discernible and historical gender gap between the numbers of men who commit crime and the much smaller number of women who offend. Explaining why that gender gap exists intrigues many academics and, of late, there's been a new debate as to whether it is shrinking. That debate gets us back to the ladettes, and what they might – or might not – represent. After all, it's a very shaky basis to argue that some young women 'living it large' can explain any significant increase in crime. That in itself is nothing new: think back to Edith Thompson and controversies surrounding the flappers of the 1920s. Even so, there remains an argument that, with more women participating in public life, working outside the home and when gender expectations change, there will be a corresponding increase in the numbers of women who commit crime.[7] One journalist has even argued that the numbers of women committing violent crimes has 'increased significantly over the past three decades'.[8] As I will explain, that's true only if we accept that large-percentage increases of small absolute numbers remain small absolute numbers.

*

Let's think about all of this further by journeying again to Aberdeen to discuss a murder, and then back to England for the case of a female spree killer who was active in 2013. We last visited Aberdeen in the 1930s to discuss the murder of Helen Priestly, killed by Jeannie Donald at 61 Urquhart Road. This time we're in the Granite City to consider a more recent murder which, even if it seems to echo some of the issues that we examined in relation to tenement life, also takes us into different territory – why women kill, and if that might be connected to the sweeping cultural changes and legal status of women in the late twentieth and early twenty-first centuries.

Women at the start of the twentieth century (recall the crimes committed by bigamist and serial killer George Joseph Smith) were still subsumed by the legal identity of their husband, and as late as the 1970s women had to fight for equal pay, abortion rights and access to better childcare provision. As British society has become more gender equal, or at least more aware of the need for gender equality, and girls can have realistic expectations about what they might achieve beyond the domestic sphere – aspirations which their grandmothers would never have had – has there also been a corresponding rise in female violence and murder committed by women, as suggested by the 'sociological-emancipation-crime hypothesis'? And, even if there has been *no* increase, how are we to explain why some women kill?

Before we arrive in Aberdeen, it's important to note that these are not new questions at all, for the violent woman has been a troubling figure for centuries. Lombroso would even have us accept that women who kill are 'more terrible' than men who murder and that, as a gender, women are in fact 'more deadly than the male'. That, at least, would put the ladettes in a much more benign context. If Lombroso made you smile – how quaint, you might be thinking – consider an initiative by the European policing agency Europol from 2019. Their *Crime has No Gender* campaign revealed the faces of fugitives 'most wanted' by twenty-one EU countries on charges as diverse as murder, organised crime and human and drug trafficking. On the campaign's website, the suspects were at first hidden behind a mask, before their faces were slowly revealed. Eighteen of the twenty-one were women. As Tine Hollevoet, a spokeswoman for Europol said, 'People think that usually these crimes are not being committed by women, but they are and they are equally as serious as those committed by men.'[9] Hollevoet might not be in the same league as Lombroso, or even making the same argument, but her message amounts to the same.

Thinking about these issues allows us to reflect on the course of our own history. It does this by bringing the narrative closer to the present day, and several of the murder victims that I'm going to describe still have immediate family members alive. In other words, these are murders which took place within living memory and so it's possible to interview those who policed, investigated or reported on these crimes, and I'll use a number of these interviews in the chapters which follow. This also helps us to identify themes which have remained consistent over time, as well as those which have all but disappeared.

*

Melanie Stourton was a twenty-two-year-old care worker who lived alone in a flat on Great Western Road in Aberdeen's West End and was training to become a nurse. She'd moved into the city from the village of Ballater, which is about forty miles to the west of Aberdeen. Melanie had a partial facial paralysis, which made her face seem slightly lopsided, especially when she smiled. Her sensitivity about her face and the fact that she had a club foot sometimes made her shy. However, she didn't let any of this hold her back and her family and friends remembered Melanie as being cheeky, funny and, above all, kind. She would, for example, buy multiple copies of the same *Big Issue* magazine from different sellers in Aberdeen.[10]

On the morning of 9 October 1999, as she was preparing to go to work, Melanie was murdered by twenty-year-old trainee chef Pamela Gourlay, who lived in another flat at the same address. Sometime after 8:30 a.m., Gourlay changed into black clothing, put on some rubber gloves and a carnival sun hat and armed herself with a Sabatier boning knife before knocking on Melanie's door. From what can be gleaned from the evidence presented at court, once she was inside the flat there followed a frenzied and sustained attack. Gourlay chased Melanie around her room, stabbing her as she did so, and eventually slit Melanie's throat as she crawled towards the door. Such was the force of the blows that Melanie was almost decapitated. Once she was dead, Gourlay then stole about £30, a few of Melanie's personal items and some Marks & Spencer gift vouchers.

After the murder Gourlay returned to her own flat and removed her blood-stained clothing, which she put into two black bags. She calmly dealt with two police officers who came to look for Melanie, as she'd been reported missing when she failed to turn up for work. After speaking with the officers, Gourlay went shopping in town with her mother, paying for their lunch with the money she'd stolen. She also used Melanie's bank card to withdraw £10 from a cash machine. With the gift vouchers she bought a flower vase for her grandmother. A couple of days after the murder, Gourlay went with her parents to pick up a relative at Edinburgh airport. It was as if everything was normal and nothing untoward had happened at all.

Given the ferocity of the attack, the police initially believed that Melanie's killer must be a man. So, even though Gourlay was interviewed several times, at this early stage of the investigation she wasn't seen as being a suspect. She was finally arrested when she was captured on CCTV withdrawing the money from Melanie's bank account and, of course, her blood-stained clothes were still in her flat. These provided a wealth of incriminating forensic evidence. Gourlay did eventually admit to two policewomen that she'd murdered Melanie, although she soon changed her story. At her trial she tried to blame her boyfriend Kris Taylor for the murder and explained away the forensic evidence, claiming that she'd simply been present when Melanie had been killed. None of this was accepted by the jury. Both Gourlay and Taylor were drug addicts, although the money stolen from Melanie was insignificant, and it has never been established what might have motivated the killing. Gourlay herself has never spoken about the attack. As one

Glasgow newspaper put it, in an eerie foreshadowing of how the female spree killer Joanne Dennehy would later come to be described, 'the trial failed to reveal what turned a once well-behaved schoolgirl into a brutal executioner'.[11]

Lord Marnoch, the trial judge, in sentencing Gourlay to life imprisonment, with a minimum tariff of fourteen years before she could be considered for parole, noted the premeditation of the murder, 'the degree of depravity' within the attack and Gourlay's 'lack of remorse'. He said, 'I can only conclude, Miss Gourlay, that you are a very evil young woman indeed.' Gourlay was released from prison in October 2013, despite being caught dealing heroin to other inmates earlier in her sentence. However, it was accepted by the Scottish parole board on the completion of her minimum tariff that she was no longer an addict or a danger to members of the public. Since her release, Gourlay has rebuilt her life, found work and formed a new relationship. As Isla Traquair, who originally covered the case as a young journalist working in Aberdeen – and has since released a detailed and compelling podcast about the murder – put it, 'she's leading a normal life'.

Isla spoke to me about her experiences of the case and what it was that drew her to this particular murder as a subject for her podcast. She explained:

> It was my first big murder case as a reporter, and I was just nineteen years old. We were all about the same ages – Melanie, Pamela and me – and we had all grown up in the countryside around Aberdeen and then found work in the city. I covered the case all the way through to the trial, and so that was really the initial attraction. The podcast

just allowed me to go deeper into the murder, and I was always intrigued by the 'Why?' It wasn't really about theft, and so this was a complicated story, and a deep story for me, and for Susan – Melanie's mum. I was also interested in the human stories behind the headlines. Of course, it was also about a woman who killed and that makes this complicated. It's a more fascinating story because it is a woman who was the murderer. If it had been a young man living upstairs from Melanie and who had murdered her it wouldn't have had the same level of fascination. Because of the level of violence even the police had been looking for a man, and so when it emerged that the perpetrator was female everyone's jaw just dropped – 'What?!' And when we realised that it was a young woman who had no relationship to Melanie, that did make it intriguing. It is so unusual to have a woman who kills – it is usually men – and so when a woman carries out something so extreme and the effort it would have taken to do it was all just so unusual. I am fascinated by women who kill because I am a woman. We can all get our heads round crimes of passion, but in relation to this murder, it was planned but also different. What is it that happens to these women?[12]

Isla's background is in journalism. Beyond her immediate, personal connections to what happened – her age being similar to the victim and perpetrator, and a shared geography – her professional interest is reflected in her repeated reference to the case being 'unusual'. The police had been looking for a man as the culprit, given the levels of violence that had been used, which explains why jaws dropped when it transpired that the perpetrator was a young woman. Gender was clearly an attraction to the story for Isla. Her comment that people can get their 'heads round crimes of passion' perhaps also reflects something which continues to puzzle Isla – a puzzle which gives this murder the 'depth' that she describes – and that relates to motive. The mystery of motive propels stories such as this into the headlines and then sustains our interest over the years. It's not so much that we are obsessed with *who dunnit*, but *why dunnit*. This is something that even Melanie's mother Susan is regularly quoted in Scottish newspapers as asking, and also in Isla's podcast. What was it that had actually driven Gourlay to take Melanie's life – or, as Isla puts it, 'What is it that happens to these women?'

Like Jeannie Donald in the 1930s, sixty years later Gourlay offered no explanation to the policewomen that she confessed to, and of course at her trial she attempted to blame her boyfriend. Nor did she ever reveal while in prison, or since her release on parole, what might have motivated her to kill Melanie. Perhaps these silences can be interpreted as an inability to understand what she herself had done, or they are being used more generally to retain control over her story. Silence might also be seen as a return to femininity, for historically it represents an expected role of women – that they are submissive, and so don't express an opinion or have anything to say. Perhaps that was why ladettes were so often described disapprovingly as 'loud and mouthy'.

For Gourlay, robbery seems like the most obvious motive, especially if she needed money to buy drugs, although what she stole amounted to very little. She quickly spent the money on a meal for her mother and used the gift vouchers to buy a vase, and therefore robbery to feed an addiction doesn't really make sense. However, to the criminological eye there are clues both in the levels of violence used and then Gourlay's extraordinarily calm behaviour after the murder. The fact that Gourlay did not go on a spree and attempt to kill as many other people as possible, as if she was a 'killing machine', is also significant. These factors suggest that Gourlay might have committed the murder during what's known as a 'catathymic crisis', which moves us on from simply attributing her motives as stemming from her being 'evil', as the trial judge would have us believe.

The concept of the catathymic crisis was introduced in 1912. It's used to explain different forms of violence which are the consequence of a latent and unconscious motivation that results in an 'emotional explosion'. This is different from the popular idea of anger or violence being the result of a 'red mist'. A red mist would be ephemeral, whereas the emotional explosion of the catathymic crisis could last for hours, or even a day or two, before finally stopping. When that happens, the perpetrator once again appears 'normal'. The victim, whom the perpetrator might or might not know, has simply triggered and brought to the surface some unconscious meanings for the offender. The violence is therefore a means to resolve this deep-seated and often previously unexpressed conflict. The catathymic crisis can be acute – triggered by a sudden and overwhelming set of emotions which have a deep significance for the perpetrator – or chronic, which would be character-ised by a build-up of tension over time, with corresponding feelings of frustration and above all a sense of helplessness.

If we think about Gourlay's attack on Melanie as being

an acute catathymic crisis, it would explain the sudden and ferocious nature of the murder, and also how she was able to behave calmly after the murder had been completed. After the emotional explosion, and when previously unexpressed feelings had made their way to the surface and been acted upon (and therefore resolved), the crisis subsided and so Gourlay could go back to living her life as she had done before. She could eat a meal with her mother, buy a vase for her grandmother, drive to Edinburgh airport to pick up a relative and talk sensibly to the police officers who'd come to check on Melanie's well-being. But how might Melanie have triggered and then brought to the surface some unconscious meanings for Gourlay, to the extent that the end result was murder? When I first explained this concept to Isla, she said, 'I think that this idea of her having a catathymic crisis is right, and I'll explain why.' She went on:

Melanie was very shy, and because of her facial paralysis when she smiled it might have appeared as if she was giving you a funny look, as some of the muscles on one side of her face didn't work. Her facial expressions were often misinterpreted. I've heard from several people that Pamela had a chip on her shoulder about other women looking down at her, or not accepting her. They shared a bathroom at the property where they lived, and it might have been that morning Melanie gave Pamela a quick smile on her way back from the bathroom, but in her shyness she then hurried back to her bedsit from the bathroom, still in her bathrobe – she was killed in her bathrobe. I just wonder if that smile was misinterpreted by Pamela and then that became the trigger for what happened.

Using the concept of a catathymic crisis to explain Gourlay's behaviour is not to excuse it. What she did is still awful and appalling and, of course, Melanie lost her life. However, does it get us closer to the truth? The context for the murder of Helen Priestly in Aberdeen in the 1930s was a loss of face and social standing – a belief that respect wasn't being given where it was due. It's just as likely that Melanie's death over half a century later in the same city was also the result of a mistaken social clue by her perpetrator – the 'funny look' being misinterpreted – rather than Gourlay's inherent 'evil'.

*

Joanne Dennehy killed three men in Peterborough in frenzied knife attacks between 19 and 29 March 2013. She then attempted to murder two other men in Hereford, in the company of an accomplice called Gary Stretch – a man who stood 7 feet 3 inches tall and who had changed his surname by deed poll from Richards to better reflect his height. Dennehy's first three victims were all known to her. Lukasz Slaboszewski was a Polish builder who had come to England in 2005 to work in a DHL warehouse in Peterborough. He had a cocaine habit and seems to have met Dennehy in the city's Queensgate shopping mall just days before he was murdered. He described her in a text that he sent to a friend as his 'English girlfriend'. Lukasz was last seen alive on 19 March. He was stabbed once through the heart with a three-inch lock knife. With the help of Stretch, Dennehy temporarily hid Lukasz's body in a green wheelie bin in the garden to await disposal – at that time she didn't have access to a car.

Her second victim was John Chapman, who'd served in the navy during the Falklands War. He was an alcoholic and lived in the same set of bedsits as Dennehy in Orton Goldhay on the outskirts of Peterborough. He was killed in the early hours of 29 March, while he was asleep at home. A post-mortem revealed that he'd been stabbed five times in the chest, and that two of the stab wounds penetrated his heart – one was inflicted with such force that it passed through his breastbone. Once Chapman was dead, Dennehy used his mobile phone to contact Stretch, all the while singing 'Oops! . . . I did it again' – the lyrics of a Britney Spears song.

Her final murder victim was Kevin Lee, a property developer who, along with his wife, was a director of Quicklet Limited, a firm with a number of bedsits that were rented out to those with limited resources – including Dennehy. Paul Creed, the office manager for Quicklet, hadn't wanted to let a property to Dennehy, but seemingly Kevin had fallen for her story that she'd just been released from prison, having served thirteen years for murdering her father, who had abused her from the age of five. She had indeed just been released from prison, but the rest of her story was untrue. Kevin would go on to employ Dennehy as an 'enforcer' – accompanied by Stretch – to collect rents or evict tenants from the property and in return she got free accommodation. It was Kevin who gave Dennehy money to purchase a car, which was then used to dispose of the bodies of Lukasz and John. He also started a sexual relationship with Dennehy, and he told his friend Dave Church that 'Joanne told me that she wanted to rape me while I am wearing a dress. She is like Uma Thurman from *Kill Bill* and the woman from the *Terminator*.' Kevin was last seen alive at 2 p.m. on the afternoon of 29 March and seems to have gone to visit Dennehy at her bedsit. He was stabbed five times in the chest, with the wounds penetrating both his heart and his lungs. When his body was found, he was wearing a black sequinned dress that belonged to Dennehy. The dress had been pulled up to expose his buttocks, and an object had been pushed into his anus. This form of *post mortem* humiliation hints at the sadomasochism that interested Dennehy.

These three murders are sometimes called the 'Peterborough Ditch Murders' because of where the bodies of the victims were discovered. Kevin's body was found lying face down in a dyke near Newborough, on the outskirts of Peterborough, by a dog walker on 30 March, and a Cambridgeshire farmer found the bodies of John and Lukasz on 3 April, lying together in a drainage ditch at Thorney Dyke. The previous day, Dennehy and Stretch had travelled to Hereford, and been arrested after Dennehy had randomly attacked two men in separate incidents – first Robin Bereza, and then John Rogers, who'd both been out walking their dogs.

Dennehy pleaded guilty to the three murders and the two attempted murders at her trial in November 2013. She was sentenced to a whole life tariff by Mr Justice Spencer due to the premeditation of the crimes and the severity and brutality of her murders. The judge added that he thought that Dennehy was sadomasochistic and lacked the normal range of human emotions. Her sentence means that she joins the serial killers Myra Hindley, Rose West and, more recently, Lucy Letby as the only women in British history to have received such a punishment. Stretch was found guilty of attempting to murder Robin Bereza and John Rogers and was sentenced to life imprisonment with a minimum tariff of nineteen years. It was

Stretch who had driven Dennehy to Hereford, and who had taken her from the first to the second attack in Peterborough.

These are the simple, basic details of the case, but they don't consider what might have motivated Dennehy to kill, or how important Stretch was in the commission of these crimes. It's also intriguing how the media and wider public made sense of Dennehy as a killer. As with Myra Hindley, this was often done through the use of an image. Newspaper stories that accompanied Dennehy's case were often accompanied by a particular photograph where she's holding an elaborate silver dagger, which she's pointing towards her pierced tongue. It looks like she might be about to cut herself and so taste her own blood. However, this wasn't the murder weapon. This same photograph also shows her facial tattoo, and she has her eyes closed almost as if she's in ecstasy. It's an image which serves to 'other' Dennehy and so suggests to the public that such killers are easily spotted and therefore we shouldn't be alarmed. There was also widespread media comment focused on her supposed 'taste for blood', her lesbian affairs and interest in sadomasochism – all of which helped distance Dennehy from 'normal' women.

Other media comment tended to concentrate on her middle-class upbringing, and the 'normal' family background she experienced growing up as a child in Harpenden – almost as if only working-class people could commit such crimes. She was a 'good girl gone wrong' – and for some, very wrong indeed. Christopher Berry-Dee, for example, a prolific true crime author who wrote about the case in *Love of Blood*, went as far as suggesting that Dennehy made 'Jack the Ripper appear a light-weight – that's how evil Joanne Dennehy really is', and further claimed that 'Lucifer had a daughter'.[13] Berry-Dee then compared her to a great white shark (so as to make her less than human), with 'unblinking, dead [eyes] devoid of feeling, emotion, and conscience', and concluded 'there's killing and there is killing. It is not the final body count that matters so much, more the manner in which all of her victims were slaughtered that makes Joanne Dennehy so evil.'

To be fair to Berry-Dee, his comments are in line with other popular coverage of the case, and they offer a taste of how Dennehy has been made sense of as a woman – she is 'monstered' and therefore not a woman at all. Much of what Berry-Dee and others have written echoes the 'deadlier than the male' trope alluded to by Lombroso. In all of this we see how Dennehy conforms to a 'doubly deviant' analysis, but it's possible to explore other issues about her and her crimes, which throw a different light on the case. For example, she was still relatively young when she committed the murders. They also took place within a *folie à deux* – a 'madness shared by two' – with her accomplice Gary Stretch. That in itself is rare, and within other such murders, such as those committed by Fred and Rose West, and Myra Hindley and Ian Brady, it was the male of the couple who was the dominant of the two, but not in this case. It was Dennehy who was the 'alpha male'.

The power balance within this particular *folie à deux* was remarked upon by the police at the time of the arrests of Dennehy and Stretch. It was suggested that Stretch, who suffered from gigantism, was scared of Dennehy and so under her control that he'd had to go along with her plans through fear of being murdered himself. This was also his defence in court, but it was undermined by letters that he exchanged with Dennehy while on remand.[14] In one such letter he wrote 'you will never know how much I really loved you babe, and that's a proper shame. You will never meet another like me babe, that I know for sure. Always yours, I love you Joanne, your personal undertaker, love The Drive.' This is a reference to both the role that Stretch played as a driver and the fact that the car that had been bought with Kevin's money and then used to transport the bodies of their victims was described by the couple as 'the hearse'. The letters that the pair exchanged suggest that it's difficult to be precise about the nature of their relationship.

This difficulty merely echoes others about Dennehy. Who was she in reality, as opposed to the persona that she culti-vated and which, in many ways, was a caricature of a violent killer? It was this caricature that the media latched onto, both as a way of telling the story of these crimes – and making them as sensational as possible – and also as an explanation for what had happened. Dennehy had killed, this narrative suggested, because she had a taste for blood; she was a good girl who had gone bad; her sexual interests were abnormal; and she was dominant – she could scare even scary men. As Kevin put it, she was The Bride in *Kill Bill* and Sarah Connor from *Terminator 2*. These are clearly superficial explanations, and there are other ways to explain what motivated Dennehy to kill.

The Freudian concept of the 'death drive' is a helpful place to start. Dennehy seems to give the impression that she felt that she'd nothing to lose and wanted to go out in 'a blaze of glory'. She never seemed to have a sense of her own self-worth, which gets disguised by the middle-class 'good upbringing' that's often reported on, as if that might eliminate personal trauma. The death drive is expressed through an individual being aggressive and self-destructive, and having a repetition compulsion. In other words, the psychological phenomenon when someone repeats an event time after time so that they develop a pattern of behaviour as a way of managing difficult or distressing events from earlier in their life.

We know from an interview that Dennehy's younger sister Maria gave to the BBC in 2014 that she'd been bright, happy and bookish as a child.[15] Things started to go wrong when she was thirteen, when she met an eighteen-year-old man at a football match and they 'ran away together'. We might now describe this as grooming and rape, given her age in relation to the man with whom she 'ran away'. Indeed, why does this not get described as abduction? They were later found living in a hostel in Milton Keynes. Dennehy returned to Harpenden to her parents' home, but this set in motion a pattern of behaviour which involved regularly running away, using alcohol and drugs, petty theft, and so spells in prison and a psychiatric unit followed. Several years before the murders in Peterborough, Dennehy had met and formed a relationship with an older man called John Treanor – whom I've interviewed at some length – and they had two daughters together. However, John eventually asked Dennehy to leave the house as she showed little interest in their children. The relationship ended when she pulled a knife from her boot and plunged it into the carpet screaming 'I wish I could fucking kill someone.'

In all of this we can see attraction and rejection, but also exaggerated responses to both that attraction and then the rejection, or expectation of rejection. Dennehy's responses are self-destructive and angry, and characterised by impulsivity and unpredictability. The eighteen-year-old man and her relationship with John Treanor are most obviously about attraction and rejection, but so too is what happened with Lukasz and Kevin. Did she perhaps want to reject Kevin before he ended their relationship? Why start dating Lukasz only to kill him days later? There's also a streak of narcissism here. This is often mistakenly believed to be about confident, self-absorbed individuals who are in love with themselves, but the opposite is true. Narcissists are usually insecure, and sensitive to any criticism which undermines their sense of superiority, or which fails to give them the attention and validation that they feel they deserve. They also find it difficult to accept fault, lack empathy and are often controlling and manipulative in order to maintain a sense of themselves. These traits would be present during childhood but might only become more pronounced – and therefore noticed – in later life.

These twin insights about narcissism and Dennehy's death drive provide a way of thinking about her and her crimes beyond the stereotypical ones, and especially a means of countering the popular idea that she was simply evil and 'monstrous'. They offer a form of understanding (although not excusing) what she did. We can also assess if she really was 'more deadly than the male' by thinking about how she compares with similar killers. Given the short time span of her three murders – just ten days – Dennehy is a spree killer, rather than a serial killer who would kill over a longer period.

A spree killer was originally defined as a 'rapid-sequence homicide offender', a label which fits Dennehy perfectly. We know that spree killers are usually impulsive and so tend to commit their crimes in an unplanned way. Such murderers were once thought of as 'killing machines' because they were totally preoccupied with carrying out their attacks, rather than thinking through the implications of their actions. That explains why the time spans of their sprees are short, as they are usually arrested quickly. Finally, research about spree killers also suggests that they're motivated by feelings of anger, resentment and disappointment. They perceive their crimes as a way to regain control of their lives, to re-establish their sense of self and what they believe they are entitled to.

All of this seems to much better explain Dennehy and her appalling crimes than continuing to use Lombrosian ideas related to monstrous, deadly women, or simply labelling her as evil. She was repeating a pattern of behaviour that had been established when she was thirteen, and which then involved her behaving in ways that were characterised by impulsivity, unpredictability and anger – exacerbated by her use of alcohol and drugs. Her narcissism prevented her from accepting responsibility for what she'd done. In killing Lukasz and Kevin she could reject them before they rejected her and thereby regain a sense of who she wanted to be and what she expected for herself, before they could threaten that self-concept. Poor John was probably an impulsive mistake, but as she'd already killed Lukasz, death had become 'moreish', as she explained after her arrest. And, just as had happened when she was thirteen years old, she then ran off – this time to Hereford rather than Milton Keynes, and not only with an older man, but one that she could push around. Again, she was repeating a pattern of behaviour that had started when she was a child, only this time she was in charge. She was neither unique nor more of a monster than human. Her behaviour wasn't inexplicable but rather conforms to a well-established pattern about how spree killers act and why they set out to kill.

*

Lombroso thought women were 'congenitally' less inclined to offend than men, and if they did, there was a biological cause for their offending. He asked his contemporaries to accept that women who committed crime, when compared to 'normal women', were shorter, more wrinkled, and tended to have darker hair and smaller skulls. Even worse, they were more ruthless, lustful and immodest. However, he also claimed that, just as for male criminals, the roots of female offending were genetic, and what kept most women on the straight and narrow were 'piety' and 'maternal sentiments'. On the plus side, Lombroso noted that female offenders tended to have more hair than their male counterparts. Well, at least that's something.

So here we have an early but influential and seemingly 'scientific' account of what causes some women to offend. Such was Lombroso's fame, these ideas began to emerge into public consciousness and then quickly took hold – especially in Victorian Britain. They served to act as a warning about how gender should be performed – how women should be women – so that those who lacked godliness and maternal instincts but had instead 'intensely erotic tendencies' were seen to be uncivilised. As ludicrous as all this might seem, some of these ideas still permeate popular discussions about female offenders today.

We might want to question if it's necessary to try to explain why women kill. Perhaps we simply need to accept that some women commit murder. And, as our examples have shown, they can do so in a variety of different circumstances and might be motivated for all kinds of strange, or banal reasons – just like men who kill. Over our time frame it's clear that we've always wanted to 'other' female killers and see them as 'doubly deviant' but are they really more ferocious, monstrous and evil than men who kill, as the old Lombrosian trope would have us believe? As the examples included within the narrative make clear, they're not.

One question remains. Are more women committing murder and manslaughter and therefore closing the gender gap on men who commit such crimes? The short answer is that they're not. However, the smaller numbers of women who offend means that our criminal statistics are always likely to highlight fluctuations in the data for any given year. So, for example, homicide statistics – which include murder, manslaughter and infanticide – from the years 2002–03 to 2005–06 show an overall decrease in the numbers of offences for both men and women, but with the fall greater for women. Over the period only one in ten of those convicted were female. However, the percentage changes year on year were striking, as these reflect smaller absolute numbers. There were, for example, thirty-one convictions of women for homicide in 2005–06, which was 43 per cent fewer convictions than for the same offence in 2002–03, when fifty-four women had been convicted. Over the same time frame the fall for men was much smaller.[16] For the three-year period from March 2019 to March 2021, 94 per cent of those convicted of homicide were male and that figure stayed constant for the three years between March 2021 and March 2023.[17] In other words, there's no evidence that women are committing murder or manslaughter in greater numbers.

However, the media inevitably pick up on these data fluctuations, rather than the overall trend within the crime statistics. BBC News, for example, led with the headline 'Sharp Rise in Women Caught Carrying Knives' and described a 'steep' increase of 73 per cent in knife possession offences for women between 2014 and 2018. This increase represented recorded figures of 1,509 knife possession offences in 2018, as opposed to 872 offences five years earlier. This was in reality a small proportion of the 40,000 offences recorded in 2018 and, as the article itself made clear, often these women were carrying knives in their handbags on behalf of a male companion in the belief that they were less likely to be searched.[18]

In relation to murder and manslaughter specifically, if we look back over British history for a much longer period of time – from the thirteenth century to 2016 – the 'big picture' is that there's been a reduction in the overall homicide rate, and that the rates of violence for female offenders have barely changed at all.[19] In the thirteenth century women were responsible for 8.6 per cent of all homicides (excluding infanticides) – a figure not so dissimilar to the 9.1 per cent that was recorded by the Office for National Statistics in 2013. In other words, the ratios for the rates of murder have remained stable for eight hundred years, despite the fact that women's legal status, educational attainment, work opportunities and gender-role expectations have clearly transformed over the course of those eight centuries. Why this should be so remains unclear and the honest answer is that we still don't understand which social, cultural or economic mechanisms might be responsible for long-term rises or falls in the levels of interpersonal violence committed by either men or women. Given that's so, it's simply nonsense to blame any of this on the ladettes of the 1990s. One possible hypothesis is rarely considered. Might the overall reduction in homicide over time suggest that men might be behaving more like women, as opposed to women behaving more like men?

CHAPTER ELEVEN

Cases Seventeen and Eighteen

The Murder of Jimmy Mizen, 2008, and the Murder of James Bulger, 1993

Why should we expect children to have any sense
of maturity when they grow up in a society where
human life is accorded no value?

Letter to the *Guardian*, 27 November 1993

Edith Thompson, Jeannie Donald, Pamela Gourlay and
Joanne Dennehy are not typical murderers. Most obviously their gender sets them apart, as nine out of ten of the
perpetrators of murder in Britain are male. That statistic
probably doesn't surprise anyone – especially not fans of true
crime documentaries and crime drama. What's perhaps more
surprising is that seven out of ten of the victims of murder are
also men and that the age group most likely to be killed are
those aged between sixteen and twenty-four. The history of

murder in Britain is disproportionately about men, and especially young men, killing other men and boys.[1] I'm going to
discuss one such murder where the victim and the perpetrator
come from within this typical age group and another where
the victim and perpetrators were much younger. As we've
seen, women can and do commit murder and also become
murder victims, but murder really is a male phenomenon –
a phenomenon that therefore needs to be 'owned' by men.
It's men, particularly young men, who need to change their
behaviour. Those changes will involve, at the very least, men
talking to each other and especially to younger men and boys
about how to perform masculinity – a task which, of late,
seems to have been left to social media influencers.[2] It will
also involve schools, as much as the criminal justice system.

As my reference to social media hints at, there have clearly
been dramatic changes to the lives of men and women, and
especially boys and girls, between 1885 and the present day.
Successive Factory Acts from 1833 to 1878 limited the age at
which children were legally allowed to work. Today children
can only work full time from the age of sixteen, and even
then, training has to be a component of their employment.
Education for children between the ages of five and twelve
became compulsory from 1880 onwards and in 1918 the school
leaving age was raised to fourteen. It was raised again after
the end of the Second World War, once more in 1973, and by
2013 children were required to remain in education or be in
work with training until the age of eighteen. These milestones
in education and work arrangements have gone hand in glove
with broader cultural changes related to child welfare, parenting styles and the rights that children now have under the law.[3]

All of this might amount to a 'march of progress' for children, although others have seen these changes as creating 'toxic childhoods' and 'paranoid parenting'. It's even been suggested that childhood has actually 'disappeared'. Within this analysis, childhood is seen as a creation of mass literacy and therefore a consequence of the medium of print. This first established and then imposed a categorical distinction between being a child and what it meant to be an adult. Most obviously the latter could read, while a child had to be taught to do so. This gave a role to teachers, the institution of school and marked out a period of time that became childhood. However, the rise of the internet and social media has created a culture where there's now little difference between being a child or an adult. School can easily be bypassed and increasingly children teach their parents how to navigate online communication and social media interactions, rather than having to read print media.[4] It could be argued that children don't actually need to learn to read or write at all, and in an age of artificial intelligence mass literacy is a thing of the past.

My intention is to use these rather bold suggestions to help us think about what is meant when we describe someone as a child, and what it is that we hope to do with that space in time called childhood. That's no easy matter. Trying to make sense of children and childhood has been problematic throughout British history, largely because the child is always defined by the adult world, which tends to blame the child for any problems, whether that's true or not.

There's also a historic, cultural tendency to think of children in a binary way. Children are innocent or evil; filled with potential and hope, or corrupt and dangerous; in need of the adult world's protection so that they can prosper and thrive or, on the other hand, a group that has to be managed, policed and controlled. Childhood becomes a device for adults to discuss their own anxieties, hopes and fears, so is used to reflect on society more broadly. This often creates difficulties for children, especially those who are sexual, or who use drugs and alcohol. It's even more problematic for children who are violent and commit murder. Some of these violent children get made into adults prematurely – they are banished from childhood, so as to protect our notions of what that space looks like and who it should encompass. Inevitably this process diminishes an individual child's complexity and reduces their existential humanity.

It also results in ambiguity. For example, you have to be eighteen to buy tobacco in the UK but you can consent to have sex from the age of sixteen; in England and Wales you need to be eighteen before you are allowed to marry, although that's possible in Scotland from the age of sixteen; you also need to be sixteen to buy and own a pet, but most young people will have a mobile phone by the age of eleven; it's possible to be granted a firearms certificate from the age of fourteen; and, finally, young people are held criminally responsible for their actions from the age of ten in England and Wales, and from the age of twelve in Scotland.

*

Jimmy Mizen turned sixteen on 9 May 2008. He'd just reached the age when he was legally allowed to leave school and find work, although he wasn't yet an adult. Just one day later Jimmy was murdered by a nineteen-year-old man called Jake Fahri, who was later convicted and sentenced at the Old Bailey to a minimum of fourteen years in prison before becoming eligible for parole. An account in the *Guardian* describes the events on the morning of Jimmy's murder and can be used to set the scene of the attack. I've quoted it here almost in full because the language used is revealing about children, childhood and murder.

A teenager who killed the school-leaver Jimmy Mizen during a frenzied scuffle in a south London bakery was given a life sentence and ordered to serve a minimum of 14 years yesterday after an Old Bailey jury found him guilty of murder.

Jake Fahri, 19, was said to have gone berserk after challenging Mizen and his brother in the shop and throwing a heavy glass dish of sausages at him. The dish shattered after hitting Mizen on the chin and a shard of glass cut vital blood vessels in his neck.

[...]

Mizen, who had celebrated his 16th birthday the day before, died within minutes in the arms of his brother in the bakery's storeroom, in a welter of blood, while Fahri sauntered smiling from the shop. The case is believed to be the first in which a glass dish has been classed as a murder weapon. Fahri, who pleaded not guilty, had claimed that he had been acting in self-defence.

Mr Justice Calvert-Smith told him: 'A trivial incident over absolutely nothing in a High Street bakery ended three minutes later with the death of a blameless young man.'

The court was told that Fahri, who had a history of difficulties controlling his temper, had not wanted to lose face after picking a row with the two brothers as they stood in front of him in the queue at the shop, where they had gone to buy sausage rolls. Fahri demanded that they should get out of his way and became angry when Mizen's older brother Harry suggested he should say please.

He promised to wait for them outside the shop and stormed back in after seeing the Mizens telephoning their older brother for help. The brothers bundled him out of the shop and he then returned a third time, wielding a metal framed advertising sign and kicking through the shop's glass door. As the 6ft 2 inch tall, 14 stone Jimmy Mizen, wrested the sign away, Fahri, 5ft 7ins, picked up the dish from the counter and hurled it at him.

Crispin Aylett QC, prosecuting, said: 'A trivial incident, brought about by the defendant's rudeness, escalated into something horrific. The defendant reached for any and every available weapon with which to attack the Mizen brothers. The whole incident lasted no more than three minutes – three minutes of absolute madness on the part of this defendant.'

[...]

Fahri, who lived close to the Mizen family and had attacked Harry Mizen twice previously, showed no emotion as he was sentenced, but as he was taken to the cells he called out: 'I will be all right, mum, I'll be all right' to his weeping mother in the public gallery.

Detective Chief Inspector Cliff Lyons said: 'Jake Fahri is an aggressive young man who throughout his life continually demonstrated an inability to control his emotions and restrain his temper. As we have all come to know Jimmy was the exact opposite of Fahri; a peaceful, courteous person with only the best intentions.'[5]

There are a number of issues raised here. It's clear, for example, that Jimmy and Harry Mizen knew Fahri and that they had a history which predated the confrontation in the bakery. Fahri had attacked Harry on two earlier occasions and, it would later become clear, these attacks had resulted in Fahri being reported to the police. This also helps to explain why the murder was cleared up so quickly, and Harry could of course identify his brother's assailant. As it happens, Fahri handed himself in to the authorities. We also know that while the weapon used was unusual – a glass dish – what happened to Jimmy fits with the general pattern of how most male victims are murdered in that he was stabbed by a 'sharp instrument', in what was termed 'three minutes of absolute madness'.

A criminological explanation for the murder wouldn't see this as a 'trivial incident over absolutely nothing', but rather one that was filled with meaning. This was about three young men with very different expectations of their future, performing their own versions of masculinity in circumstances that were already tense because of their hostile interpersonal history. It was about anger, 'saving face', status, a demand for respect, and ultimately about survival and death in the most banal of circumstances. We can also question whether Fahri's violence was instrumental, or expressive. In other words, whether his attack on Jimmy and his brother was rational – done to achieve a specific objective – or simply because Fahri had that type of personality.

We can think about what happened in the bakery from a

Freudian perspective. Freud proposed that criminal behaviour was the product of some mental conflict, which could often be traced back to problems in childhood. He posited that there were three core aspects of the human psyche: the id, the ego and the superego. The id contains the unconscious, primitive biological drives for survival, such as aggression and sex, and is said to work on a 'pleasure principle'. It seeks to avoid pain but both satisfy and enjoy these primitive drives, without regard to how others might suffer, or the negative consequences that might flow from following these primitive urges. The id is also the site of the 'death instinct' – a willingness to self-destruct. The ego is the real 'self', that controls the drives of the id by responding to the needs of others and conforming to what is expected of an individual as a result of social convention. The superego, which like the ego develops throughout childhood, is that part of the personality which has internalised the moral and ethical rules of society, largely by the child being socialised by his parents or carers. Freud suggested that criminal behaviour was the result of mental disturbance, or the product of the offender's weak conscience.[6]

A modern application of Freud's psychoanalytical approach to murder can be found in the work of the American psychiatrist James Gilligan based on his interviews with violent men when he was working in a number of prisons.[7] For Gilligan, an internal mental conflict about shame and loss of self-esteem is the key to understanding why some men use lethal violence. He suggests that violent men have often themselves been the objects of violence in the past, especially in their childhood, and that as a consequence they experience feelings of embarrassment, powerlessness and worthlessness. Gilligan maintains that violent men lack the emotional infrastructure which serves to inhibit violent impulses through, for example, having developed a sense of guilt or empathy. So, in a situation where they feel that their self-worth is being challenged, and in which they also reason that there's no other way to diminish that sense of shame, they use violence to rebuild their wounded self-esteem.

This takes us back to instrumental and expressive violence – and, sadly, to the murder of Jimmy Mizen. The 'trivial incident over absolutely nothing', as it was described by the judge, was for Fahri something much more symbolic. From the newspaper report it would seem that the Mizen brothers had been standing in front of Fahri in the queue in the baker's shop and that, when he'd complained that the brothers should get out of his way, he was told that he should say 'please'. This seems to have triggered feelings of shame, to the extent that the outnumbered and physically smaller Fahri believed that the only way that he could re-establish his own sense of self-worth was to strike out and use violence.

He certainly seems to have wanted to continue with the incident – returning to the shop on two occasions – and so wasn't able to rebuild a sense of his self-worth in any other way. This perhaps also indicates that he lacked empathy, guilt or indeed fear for his own safety. While this murder may not have been premeditated, there were nonetheless a number of opportunities for Fahri to walk away, which would have allowed the conflict to have come to a different conclusion. He chose not to do so, as that would not restore what he felt he had lost within the encounter.

We should also note the importance of 'micro' as well as 'macro' explanations for murder. What seems to have mattered in the baker's shop weren't macro sociological or cultural questions about age, gender, race or poverty but rather the micro-dynamics of the incident as it was being played out. This isn't meant to excuse Fahri's behaviour, and nor should we ignore the fact that this type of psychoanalytic analysis is difficult to test in any empirical way.

We can't directly observe the id, the ego or superego and nor can we actually prove (or disprove) that they exist – despite attempts to do so through, for example, psychoanalysis, ink-blot tests or dream analysis. It's therefore impossible to be certain that they play any role at all in shaping an individual's behaviour. We might also criticise psychoanalytic psychology for being overly deterministic. Everything gets explained by internal conflicts and tensions within the individual's psyche, and thus, for example, environmental factors are overlooked. However, especially in Gilligan's work, we glimpse how social situations can influence human behaviour.

My own sense of what happened in the baker's shop comes from a more socio-criminological approach, which analyses the situational and 'foreground' factors of violence. I tend to pay particular attention to the emotional or psychological state of the murderer at the time of the murder. In other words, what it feels and means to kill and what's achieved by the murderer as a consequence. Professor Jack Katz describes the different emotional levels that are involved in the 'typical murder', where the killer commits an 'impassioned attack' or, in his memorable phrase, the 'righteously enraged slaughter' of a victim who has, whether intentionally or not, humiliated the attacker. In many ways, there are echoes here with Pamela Gourlay and even Jeannie Donald, who also believed that their sense of self had been attacked. Through this righteous slaughter the killer defends their sense of 'good' against 'evil', by transforming humiliation into a rage that will prove fatal. In this way, Katz argues, instead of violence being senseless it has meaning and value for the attacker.[8]

Once again, we might want to re-interpret the murder of Jimmy as — at least in the killer's mind — a form of righteous slaughter. Fahri saw *himself* as the victim in this social encounter with Jimmy and Harry and so, as Katz suggests, wanted to transform his humiliation into rage. This might explain why he was described as 'going berserk' in the baker's and then, after having killed Jimmy, 'sauntered smiling from the shop'. The act of murder had been for him righteous as it allowed him to regain his sense of identity — which was why he was smiling.

Much of this analysis has to be conjecture. However, I believe that in trying to save his lost face and wounded pride, Fahri killed Jimmy as a result of a complex set of incident-specific factors which were being played out against a background of more universal circumstances, some of which are more likely to produce violence than others.

One of those circumstances is masculinity and how it's performed by young men. This comes across in the binary ways that Fahri and Jimmy are described in the newspaper report by various people who were involved with the case, or with its prosecution. Fahri had difficulties with his temper, couldn't 'control his emotions' and was an 'aggressive young man'. On the other hand, Jimmy was a 'blameless young man', 'peaceful', 'courteous' and someone who had only 'the best intentions'. I am not denying these conclusions, but they seem to rob both Fahri and Jimmy of the complexity of their lives and their respective identities. And, as we've discussed, there are multiple ways of performing masculinity which might sometimes legitimately accommodate aggression and being prepared to lose control of your emotions, rather than keeping them in check.

Fahri hit the headlines again in early 2025. Having been released on parole in 2023, after serving fourteen years in prison, he reinvented himself as a balaclava wearing drill artist called TEN, and recorded music, some of which was then featured on BBC Radio 1Xtra's *Introducing* show. All of the music which he performed contained violent themes and in one song Fahri seemed to reference Jimmy's murder in lyrics which described 'stuck it on a man and watched him melt like Ben and Jerry's'. The idea of 'sticking it on a man' and watching him 'melt' can be interpreted as a victim dying as a result of a knife attack. In another track he suggested that having 'see[n] a man's soul fly from his eyes and his breath gone ... I wanted more, it made it less wrong', and this can be taken to imply that, instead of being apologetic, he wanted to continue being violent. Margaret Mizen, Jimmy's mother, was understandably 'numb' after hearing about Fahri's music and her husband Barry queried whether his son's murderer was suitable for parole and safe to release back into the community. After all, he seemed to be glorifying what he'd done to Jimmy through these songs, rather than showing remorse. He was now literally performing his own version of masculinity – a masculinity which was violent, uncompromising and unrepentant. Given the lyrics within the music that he was performing, Fahri was deemed to have broken the conditions of his parole licence and was returned to prison.[9]

Jimmy's murder, even with all its odd singularities and

tragedy is, from a criminological point of view, a 'typical' British murder. It was about a young man attacking another young man as a means of saving face and attempting to maintain his self-identity. The victim and the perpetrator knew each other, as opposed to being strangers, and the murder itself, far from being premeditated, was committed in just a few minutes of madness. There were atypical elements to the murder too: it took place within a public space, not a domestic setting, and a glass dish is an unusual 'sharp instrument' to be used as a murder weapon. However, Fahri's inability to regain his sense of self – his idea of what constituted being a man – and his feelings of childish entitlement could only, he believed, be achieved through using violence. That's the context for most murders in this country, rather than those which often generate headlines and editorials. Surely, therefore, this has to be the basis on which to build an understanding of murder and what we must do more generally to reduce the incidence of violent crime in Britain in the future. That reduction can only come when we begin to understand what it now means to be a young man – a child – and how that space in time should be designed to enable rather than diminish, and when it is filled with hope and possibility rather than expectation of failure.[10]

Fifteen years before Jake Fahri killed Jimmy Mizen an equally dreadful, if atypical, murder challenged British expectations about the behaviour of young people and what it meant to be a child. One child was killed and two others became the youngest convicted murderers in modern British history. Even now, the details remain distressing and I have done my best to describe only what's necessary for the purposes of discussion.

*

On the afternoon of 12 February 1993, in Bootle, Liverpool, two ten-year-old boys called Robert Thompson and Jon Venables abducted two-year-old James Bulger from the New Strand Shopping Centre while his mother was being served in a butcher's shop.[11] Venables and Thompson, who were truant-ing from school, had been shoplifting and getting into trouble all morning. They'd also tried but failed to abduct another young child from the shopping centre earlier in the day. Their abduction of James was captured on the CCTV system, and images of him being led away soon became grimly iconic.

Outside the shopping centre James was taken on a journey of two and a half miles through the town, with Venables and Thompson battering him along the way. They were passed by at least thirty-eight witnesses, none of whom intervened effectively to save James, with some being fobbed off with calculated and skilful lies by the two abductors. As darkness fell, Venables and Thompson finally brought the little boy to a railway line, where they covered him in paint, pushed bat-teries into his mouth, kicked and hammered him with bricks and an iron bar before leaving his partially stripped body on the tracks, where it was later severed by a train. The Home Office pathologist who examined James found forty-two in-juries on his body, fifteen of them to the front of his face. He determined that the cause of death was the result of multiple head injuries and that, mercifully, he was already dead before being hit by the train.[12]

Venables and Thompson were arrested on 18 February. They first appeared at South Sefton Magistrates' Court on 22 February, outside which an angry mob had gathered. Popular outrage against Venables and Thompson was instinctive and visceral, and so great was public feeling that it was fortunate for them that their identities couldn't be revealed under Section 49 of the Children and Young Persons Act 1933, and they were simply referred to during the trial as 'Child A' and 'Child B'. Every day a crowd waited outside the court, shouting 'String 'em up', and no one involved in the case underestimated what would have happened if that mob had managed to get hold of the two young murderers.

Venables and Thompson were finally sentenced to be detained at Her Majesty's Pleasure in November 1993 and their tariff was set at eight years. This was later increased to ten years and then Michael Howard, the Home Secretary, partly responding to a public campaign in the *Sun*, increased this further, to fifteen years, in 1994. Eventually, after various appeals based on their ages to the European Court of Human Rights, this was reduced by Lord Justice Woolf to eight years, which was the original tariff and in due course Venables and Thompson were released in 2001. They were given new identities and are legally entitled to anonymity. Venables was re-imprisoned in 2010 for breaching a number of the conditions of his parole licence, released once more in 2013 and was returned to prison in 2017, having been found in possession of 1,170 indecent images of children. Thompson, who's still living under his assumed identity, would seem to have been successfully integrated back into the community.

Denise Fergus, the mother of James Bulger, set up a campaign called Justice for James, which advocated for a whole life tariff to be imposed on Venables and Thompson. She's also campaigned unsuccessfully for the withdrawal of their anonymity.

At their original trial at Preston Crown Court, the floor of the dock had to be raised by a foot so that Venables and Thompson could observe the proceedings. This practical measure served to emphasise their youth. They were children – ten when they abducted James and eleven by the time of their trial. From the outset Richard Henriques, the lead prosecutor in the case, had to rebut the common law presumption of *doli incapax*, which presumed that a child under the age of fourteen didn't know the difference between right and wrong and therefore couldn't be held legally responsible. He did so successfully and would later conclude that the murder had been planned, premeditated and in its commission had showed 'opportunism and daring'. Even so, in December 1999 the European Court of Human Rights ruled that the 1993 trial had been unfair in that it violated Venables and Thompson's right to a fair trial and awarded them respectively £29,000 and £15,000 in compensation.[13]

These simple, horrifying details of the case hardly capture how central the murder of James is to the recent history of criminal justice in Britain and how it fed into a binary analysis of children and childhood. It was a turning point in penal sensibilities, which saw sentences lengthen and prompted the numbers being sentenced to prison increase – not just of children, but also of adults. Michael Howard's famous 'prison works' speech to the Tory Party conference in October 1993, which I quote below, came after James's murder, not before, and what seems to have prompted the growth in prison numbers in the 1990s – a growth which has continued to this day – was James's murder, rather than the political ideology of the incumbent Home Secretary.

The murder of a two-year-old boy by two other children sparked a debate about a range of social and moral issues, including single mothers, 'home alone' children, bad parenting, 'video nasties' and violent video games.[14] It shaped the Criminal Justice and Public Order Act of 1994, lowering the age at which a child could receive an indeterminate sentence, and created the Secure Training Order which allowed twelve- to fourteen-year-old juvenile offenders to be locked up in newly created and privately run Secure Training Centres.

As all of this suggests, politicians were both reacting to the popular and media pressure about the murder and using it for political ends. At a stroke it created a consensus between 'New' Labour and the Conservatives around the idea that each was the party of law and order. This consensus remains at the heart of more recent debates about law and order. Crucial at the time of James's murder was the fact that Tony Blair was the Shadow Home Secretary and had been influenced by a visit to the USA, where he'd come under the spell of Bill Clinton – a Democrat who had nonetheless supported the use of the death penalty. So, in January 1993, the month prior to James's murder, Blair had stated on an ITV political magazine programme called *The World this Weekend* that Labour would be 'tough on crime, and tough on the causes of crime'. Following the murder, he maintained that 'children should be taught the value of what is right and what is wrong'. More broadly, he told a Labour Party audience in Wellingborough that:

The news bulletins of the last week have been like hammer blows struck against the sleeping conscience of the country ... a solution to this disintegration doesn't simply lie in legislation. It must come from the rediscovery of a sense of direction as a country ... not just as individuals but as a community ... we cannot exist in a moral vacuum. If we do not learn and then teach the value of what is right and what is wrong, then the result is simply moral chaos that engulfs us all.[15]

Not to be outdone, John Major, the prime minister, told the *Daily Mail* on 21 February that 'I would like the public to have a crusade against crime and change from being forgiving of crime to being considerate of the victim. Society needs to condemn a little more and understand a little less.' At the Conservative Party Conference that autumn, Michael Howard delighted his audience by reminding them:

Let's make one thing absolutely clear: prison works. It ensures that we are protected from murderers, muggers and rapists – and it makes many who are tempted to commit crime think twice ... This may mean more people will go to prison. I do not flinch from that.[16]

As these soundbites suggest, James's murder became the battleground for a political culture which was oppositional, confrontational and where each side sought to outdo the other, rather than one which attempted to understand, explain or inform. Neither political party, for example, reminded the country that in the mid-1990s, according to figures produced by the National Society for the Prevention of Cruelty to Children, at least one child per week under the age of five was dying at the hands of their parents or carers. No one drew attention to the fact that in the ten years prior to James's murder just ten children under the age of five had been killed by strangers, as opposed to 571 who'd been murdered by someone who was known to them.[17]

The media played a central role in shaping how James's murder was reported and how his killers were viewed. Their treatment of the case was often sensationalist and sometimes irresponsible. Of course, the murder really was appalling and genuinely shocking but there was also a tendency to suggest that Venables and Thompson were without parallel in our history. That's simply not true, as a case from twenty-five years earlier illustrates and which allows us to reflect more broadly on the reaction to the murder of James.

*

On the day before her eleventh birthday in May 1968, Mary Bell strangled four-year-old Martin Brown in Scotswood, Newcastle, and then, a few months later, she also strangled three-year-old Brian Howe. Bell would be convicted of the manslaughter of both boys on the grounds of diminished responsibility at Newcastle Assizes in December 1968, which at the time made her Britain's youngest female killer – a distinction that she retains. She was eventually released in May 1980 at the age of twenty-three, having served almost eleven and a half years in custody. On her release, like Venables and Thompson, Bell was given a new identity and granted anonymity for the rest of her life. She's since given birth to a daughter, who has also been granted anonymity.[18]

Bell's case was shocking and disturbing, and the killing of Martin and Brian was just as awful as the murder of James. However, Bell's murders didn't provoke the same levels of public anger and anxiety or any fundamental questioning about broader social questions regarding the state of the country. Also, not long after James's death there was another murder of a child by other children in Norway, which can again throw some light on the public and political reaction to what happened in Bootle.

Five-year-old Silje Redergard lived in the city of Trondheim and was murdered by three six-year-old boys in October 1994. The boys had Silje strip and then took it in turns to hit and beat her with stones and sticks, before finally stamping on her. They left Silje unconscious in the snow and she'd later die of hypothermia. However, none of the three boys were punished by being imprisoned and were instead given psychological help. There were no cries for vigilante justice, and no manoeuvring by any Norwegian politician to politicise the incident. Silje's death was treated as a terrible aberration – not a symptom of broader political or moral concerns requiring fresh policy developments. A few days after the murder the three boys returned to their schools.

These differing reactions to the murders committed by Mary Bell and then with how the Norwegians viewed Silje's death suggest that James's murder tapped into a broader cultural anxiety that people had about the state in Britain at that time and the role that government could play in shaping society. In the cries of 'String 'em up' we don't just hear the voices of those who wanted the reintroduction of capital punishment, but also the voices of those who'd been left behind. These people lived different lives to those of their parents and grandparents who'd mattered to the state during the 1920s and 1930s, and in the post-war Britain which had rejected

Churchill and voted for Clement Attlee. In contrast, Bell's murders and the reaction to them were contained within the body politic and the culture of the day because the state still seemed to understand the lives of people who might want to stand outside Preston Crown Court.

It's hard to resist the temptation to see the murder of James Bulger not just as a turning point in penal sensibilities, but also as one that made visible a swathe of Britons who no longer felt part of what Britain had become. They lived in a different country – almost as different as Britain was to Norway. The people of Trondheim didn't riot, protest or demand that the boys who killed Silje should be executed. They reacted to her murder with a belief that the state had everyone's best interests at heart and could deliver justice that was fair and proportionate. In the Britain of the 1990s that was no longer the case. These different historical and geographic reactions were not accidental, but the product of conscious choices that had been made through public and economic policies, which had had a profound impact on the lives of people, and especially the lives of children – as one campaigning journalist was to discover.

*

Nick Davies's research took him to several major cities in England, including Nottingham and Leeds, but the book that he eventually produced was about a 'hidden' Britain. As he described it, he would watch from a train window 'the green and pleasant fields go by for few hours', arrive at his destination and then, with the help of a local contact, it was as if 'I crossed an invisible frontier and cut a path into a different country ... to put it more broadly, it is the place where the poor gather'.[19]

Davies was especially interested in 'two small boys' in Nottingham called Jamie and Luke, whom he first observed at a fairground, standing close to the doorway of a public toilet. It was obvious that they were selling sexual services, and more shocking still was their age – Jamie was eleven and Luke, his friend, was two years older. As a result of family break-ups, they'd been put in care, which was where they'd first been sexually abused. They now sold sex to men as a means to survive, which was merely another form of the abuse they'd previously experienced. Davies described how both boys told him about their lives – 'one long sequence of misery and pain' – and how 'they are like little symbols of ruined childhood, guards on the door of darkness'.[20]

This wasn't just Jamie and Luke's story that Davies was describing. Based on his research, he concluded that 'something new is happening – the sheer scale of it, as if there's an invisible conveyor belt tipping an endless supply of children out onto the streets'. What Davies observed and the children that he talked to described was chaos, damage and violence, and he wanted to know when all of that had started. He argued that the world that these children inhabited wasn't an 'accident' but had been 'created quite deliberately, rather like the great penal colony of Australia was planned and created by politicians'. He saw Jamie, Luke and the other children as an inevitable end product of Thatcherism, which no longer wanted to 'sustain the welfare state but [look] where first to cut it'.[21] The state had 'hollowed out' support for the family, making it more difficult for poorer families to support their children. That's where the 'conveyor belt' had come from and was the reason why the supply of children on it was 'endless'.

Davies's startling conclusion is supported by extensive data produced by the Children's Society. For several decades, the charity has been conducting research with children under the age of sixteen who've left home for one reason or another. They make a useful distinction between those young people who choose to leave home and those who are asked to leave. They call the former group 'runaways' and the latter 'throwaways'. Given how Jamie and Luke described their lives to Davies, they'd be characterised as 'throwaways'. The charity's research from the 1990s and then from 2005 makes for depressing reading. By their reckoning, at least sixty-six thousand young people stayed away from home for at least one night in England and Wales during this time and the majority were between thirteen and fifteen years old. Almost 10 per cent of those who ran away were under ten years old.

The charity also identified a link between a child's family structure and the likelihood of them running away or being thrown out. In particular, young people living in single-parent families were roughly twice as likely to run away as children living with both parents, while those living with a step-parent were almost three times as likely. Unsurprisingly, those who ran away from home usually expressed a negative opinion of their relationship with their parent or carer, which suggests a general unhappiness at home. A third of the runaways admitted to having problems with school attendance, while those who'd been excluded from school were three times more likely than most children to run away. That phenomenon has only got worse, with school suspensions and exclusions increasing dramatically. In the autumn term of 2023–24 in England there were 346,279 suspensions and 4,168 permanent exclusions – an increase of more than 1,000 exclusions from the previous year.[22]

Poverty was a significant factor. The Children's Society discovered that many of the young people who'd run away had been entitled to free school meals and that more than 15 per cent of those children came from families where there were no adults in paid employment living in the household. These children, just like Jamie and Luke, also described physical, sexual and emotional abuse and neglect to the extent that home wasn't seen as a safe space for them, and so their childhood had become something to endure and survive, rather than a time that was positive and which allowed for their growth and development.[23]

*

Davies's damning conclusion can be given a more academic description: childhood is a social construction. What we've come to call childhood is not inevitable, fixed and finite but a contingent, changing space. Childhood is defined by and then dependent on an adult world that might support that space by providing the resources to make the lives of children safe, secure and fulfilling. Take those resources away and childhood will change – especially for poorer children. Of course, there's no single universal childhood but multiple childhoods, as Charles Dickens was keen to point out even in the Victorian era. However, for Davies this was the 'something new' and why he discovered Jamie and Luke selling sex outside a men's toilet in Nottingham. That was no accident, nor simply Jamie and Luke exercising free will, but a by-product of policy changes related to families initiated during the 1980s. Those changes were also the basis for all the runaways and throwaways that the Children's Society encountered in their research.

The 'hollowing out' of the provisions of the welfare state is what was different in the 1990s when Venables and Thompson killed James, compared to the 1960s when Mary Bell murdered Martin and Brian. In Bell's day, people mattered to the state and the state, in turn, mattered to people in ways that were no longer reflected in the culture of the 1990s. I think that's why Bell's murders didn't cause the same level of anxiety or anguish as the murder of James. Like the murder of Silje Redergard in Norway, what happened to Martin and Brian was seen as a tragedy, whereas James's death became symbolic of much more than the appalling murder of a child. In that sense not only were Jamie and Luke guards on the door of darkness but so too were Venables and Thompson.

CHAPTER TWELVE

Case Nineteen

The Murders Committed by Derrick Bird, 2010

> Last night I called 999 and declared war on
> Northumbria Police before shooting an officer on
> the West End roundabout in his T5. Rang again
> and told them they're gonna pay for what they've
> done to me and Sam.
>
> RAOUL MOAT, 2010

R aoul Moat's understanding of masculinity meant that
he never expressed remorse for shooting his former girlfriend Samantha Stobbart on his release from HMP Durham
on 3 July 2010; killing Chris Brown, her new boyfriend; and,
the following day, shooting and blinding PC David Rathband.
Two years later, David would take his own life. In a forty-nine-
page letter that Moat wrote and had handed in to the police
by a friend, with a copy for the *Sun* newspaper, not only did he
justify his actions but also blamed everyone else for the deadly

conclusion that he'd come to since his release from prison. This involved not only his two-day shooting spree, but also a near week-long manhunt by the police in an attempt to capture him. It was during this time on the run that Moat 'declared war on the police', before he eventually committed suicide on the outskirts of the town of Rothbury on 10 July 2010.

Moat's letter is a mix of self-pity and self-delusion, but it also offers great insight into a failed masculinity which, even *in extremis*, sought to justify and excuse rather than to accept responsibility.[1] So, he claims he shot his former girlfriend in the stomach so that she could get 'massive compensation', and the scarring would remind her 'not to do this to anyone again'. The 'this' that he's referring to is his former girlfriend choosing to leave him while he was imprisoned and daring to start a new relationship. He claims that he shot PC Rathband because he was waiting to harass someone – 'probably a single mother who couldn't afford her car tax' – and suggests that it was the police's fault that he now found himself in his current predicament. 'The police are going to pay for what they did to me' is, of course, a denial of personal responsibility and one which attempts to relocate the blame, moving it away from Moat and putting it onto others. 'They've hunted me for years,' he claimed, 'now it's my turn.' He's getting his retaliation in first, although even this decision was apparently beyond his control. The former body builder and ex-bouncer claimed the rage that he felt only came after he was 'taken over' by the Incredible Hulk – a superhero who's not necessarily always a force for moral good but can sometimes simply 'lash out'.

Moat liked to think of himself as noble and virtuous, which is why he wrote the letter. It was a blatant attempt to dominate the media narrative, almost as if he was channelling a dark shadow of W. T. Stead. He was trying to control the PR about what was happening in Northumberland, and a surprising number of people seemed to believe what he claimed. After he'd taken his own life, a Raoul Moat memorial page was established on Facebook which attracted 36,500 members and was entitled 'RIP Raoul Moat You Legend'. The page was created by Siobhan O'Dowd, who said, 'We don't condone what he did, as what he did was wrong. I feel sorry for the families but he was still a human being at the end of the day.'[2] She did eventually delete the page in the face of a public backlash.

As he'd intended, Moat captured our attention, but what's less commented on is that his shooting spree was a 'copycat' of events from the previous month in Cumbria. That spree, plus the mass shootings in Dunblane, Scotland in 1996, open up a discussion about what happens when 'righteous slaughter' and a failed masculinity isn't just aimed at an individual, or the police, but when 'war is declared' on the community as a whole.

*

On Wednesday 2 June 2010 Derrick Bird, a fifty-two-year-old taxi driver, shot and killed twelve people and wounded fifteen others before taking his own life in woodland beside Penny Hill Farm, near the hamlet of Boot, in what the *Whitehaven News* described as a 'killing spree' and a 'rampage throughout Copeland'.[3] Copeland consists of six localities in West Cumbria, centred on the towns and larger villages of the area including Gosforth, Seascale, Egremont, St Bees and Whitehaven. Bird used two legally owned weapons during this spree – a shotgun and a .22 rifle, which was fitted with a telescopic sight.

In the early hours of that Wednesday morning, Bird first shot and killed David, his twin brother, and then Kevin Commons, the family's solicitor. He then travelled into Whitehaven and shot and killed Darren Rewcastle, a fellow taxi driver, and attempted to kill two other men who were also employed as taxi drivers. From Whitehaven Bird journeyed back and forth, shooting more randomly and killed, or injured, those people that he encountered as he drove through the villages of Egremont, Thornhill, Carleton, Wilton, Gosforth and Seascale, before driving into the Eskdale Valley, where he committed suicide, some seven hours after having killed his brother.[4]

As the enormity of these events unfolded, an editorial in the local newspaper struggled to capture a sense of the disbelief and unprecedented nature of what had happened in their community. 'People woke up yesterday to go about their normal day only to have their worlds shattered in the space of a few hours. Who could believe in our peaceful close-knit community such horror and devastation could occur?' The editorial was entitled 'Carnage in West Cumbria' and termed it 'the worst mass shooting since Dunblane in 1996'.[5]

What happened in West Cumbria was technically a spree of murders, rather than a mass shooting and Bird was correspondingly a spree murderer. I'm again employing here criminological research, which views spree murder as involving two or more victims, within two or more episodes.[6] This phenomenon is therefore different from serial murder, as that type of murder would require a cooling-off period between attacks. In contrast, a spree of murders involves a swathe of destruction in different locations with no cooling-off period. This is again different from the mass murders committed by Thomas Hamilton in Dunblane, which involved one killing episode within one location. However, both events offer us an opportunity to reflect on righteous slaughter when it transcends an interpersonal feud and becomes focused not on an individual, but on an entire community. To what extent was Bird similar to Hamilton, as the local newspaper suggested, or was he perhaps more like Jake Fahri, or even Raoul Moat?

It's also worth considering why history has been so silent about modern British mass and spree murders. There's only one popular book, but no monographs or peer review articles about the Cumbrian shootings.[7] As for Dunblane, prior to my own work,[8] there was only one academic article[9] and, even though 'Dunblane' appeared within its title, just one monograph which discussed Hamilton's mass murders, and even then only in its final chapter.[10] These 'criminological silences' have helped to create and then maintain a popular narrative about what happened in Dunblane centred on Hamilton's 'oddness' and his not belonging within the local community. This narrative is difficult to sustain and simply making Hamilton himself accountable fails to see his mass murder in the context of a number of more common and universal factors, including his performance of masculinity.

Should Bird also be responsibilised in the same way? Was he too regarded as 'odd' and pathological, or was he instead an accepted and valued member of the wider Whitehaven community? If he was in the latter category, it would be more accurate to explain what happened in West Cumbria in 2010 as being rooted both within the generic culture of that part of Britain at that time, and how some men there come to perform masculinity. He might not have sauntered off with a smile on his face, as Jake Fahri had done after killing Jimmy Mizen, and nor did he leave a forty-nine-page letter justifying his behaviour, but it's still possible to gain some insight into Bird's decision to embark on his shooting spree and then compare what he did with the behaviour of Fahri, Hamilton and Moat.

*

Given the absence of academic writing about Whitehaven, it seems important to explain how I went about developing the material which appears in this chapter. In trying to make sense of Bird's shooting spree I made several research visits to Whitehaven; went in a taxi from the town to the place where Bird would eventually commit suicide, so as to imagine what he might have been thinking about on this forty-five minute journey into the Eskdale Valley; walked Whitehaven's streets, eating in its restaurants and drinking in its pubs; spoke with any local residents who were prepared to talk to me; and visited the memorial to Darren Rewcastle which his family and friends have created in the town. I didn't seek to speak to any surviving members of Bird's family, but I did talk to one of his friends at some length, who was at that time still employed as a taxi driver. Of note, many members of the public were very willing to speak to me about what had happened in 2010 – something which is in itself at odds with my experience of researching in Dunblane. There, it became clear that asking questions about the 'massacre' was simply not acceptable.

All of this has links to what is often labelled as 'ethnography',[11] although I make no claims to have spent long periods of time within Whitehaven, despite undertaking field research there. These research trips allowed me to build up an understanding of what motivated Bird to embark upon his spree of murders. Even so, motivation is often the 'least understood and most neglected'[12] aspect of the work of a criminologist. That does seem to be a strange state of affairs for the discipline of criminology, because it's obvious that we need to consider what drives some people to violence, which inevitably requires us to think about their motivation.

It was possible to gain some understanding about what provoked Bird, and what his emotional state at the time of the spree was like, through speaking with many members of the public in Whitehaven who knew him – some of them very well. Whitehaven and the surrounding villages are small, face-to-face cultures and, as many people explained, it was almost impossible for anyone who lived there to have secrets. Bird himself might have been silent, but that shouldn't imply that other people didn't understand what had driven him to kill, or that he hadn't spoken to them about what was happening in his life. There's also a wealth of newspaper accounts about his shooting spree – almost three thousand articles – and the *Guardian* alone published over a hundred of these, most of them news reports, but also a number of editorials and longer, more reflective commentaries. I'll use these journalistic pieces from the *Guardian* in the account presented below. However, in order to understand better Bird's behaviour, it would be helpful to piece together the sequence of events as they transpired on the day of the spree.

*

In the early hours of Wednesday 2 June 2010 Bird left his home, described as a 'shabby terrace house' (*Guardian*, 2 March 2011) in the village of Rowrah and travelled to Lamplugh, where he shot and killed his twin brother David at his home, High Tree Farm. He chose to kill his brother as a result of what the

Guardian described as 'an act of revenge for imagined family injustices', and further characterising Bird as having 'a persecution complex' (*Guardian*, 3 June 2011). After killing his brother, Bird travelled past his own house in Rowrah and drove to the home of his solicitor Kevin Commons at Mowbray Farm, Frizington Road and shot and killed him in his driveway. He then returned to Rowrah and went to another address in the village, where he knocked on the door but there was no reply. These events seem to have been the first phase of the spree.

Bird next drove to Whitehaven town centre, where he shot Darren Rewcastle at the taxi rank on Duke Street. He had a long-standing grievance against Rewcastle, who had apparently damaged Bird's car tyres. Bird then drove around the town's one-way system and returned to the taxi rank where he shot Donald Reid, and then went on to Duke Street and Scotch Street where he shot Paul Wilson, who was injured. He turned onto Coach Road and shot and injured Terry Kennedy and Emma Perceval, who were both in a taxi.

Clearly taxi drivers were the focus of this second stage of Bird's spree shootings and the *Guardian* noted that there had been 'substantial tensions on the cab rank. Fellow drivers said Bird, who, like many cabbies in Whitehaven, worked for himself, had fallen out with several other drivers whom he blamed for stealing his trade.' Bird had also argued with other cabbies that week, 'over drivers taking fares at the back of the queue, instead of sending customers to the first cab on the rank' (*Guardian*, 4 June 2010). Paul Wilson would later describe how he'd initially thought that Bird had fired a blank at him and that he was being a 'daft bugger', simply 'playing a prank'. He went on: 'As I turned the corner, I noticed Derrick's taxi in the nearside lane coming towards me. I thought nothing of it and I carried on to the police station. He stopped next to me and called my name. I looked directly at him and I took a few steps towards him and ducked down to look in the passenger window. As I ducked to look at him, he fired. He called me over and shot me' (*Guardian*, 8 March 2011). Calling people to his taxi and then shooting them in the face was a recurring feature of Bird's spree and is a violent reversal of his typical working habits in the community where he had once performed a service.

The next phase of the spree involved Bird leaving Whitehaven and taking a minor road through the village of Sandwith and Rottington to St Bees. Driving along Out Rigg towards the market town of Egremont he shot and killed Susan Hughes at Hagget End. He then turned right at the junction of South Street and drove to Bridge End, where he killed Kenneth Fishburn. He headed towards Cringlethwaite Terrace, where he shot Leslie Hunter, who survived the attack. He then travelled out of Egremont on the A595, turning south and heading towards Thornhill. Here he left the main road and drove onto Thornhill estate, where he shot at Ashleigh Glaister, but the bullet missed her. He then drove on single-track roads past the village of Carleton, and on the Egremont to Haile road he shot Isaac Dixon, before turning towards Egremont again. However, he then made a U-turn and drove back to Wilton, where he killed Jennifer Jackson, then a further U-turn and drove back into the village where he shot Jennifer's husband James and Christine Hunter-Hall, who survived.

After shooting Christine, he drove through Haile and shot Gary Purdham on the A595 at Calder Bridge and then turned to Seascale, where he killed James Clark on the Gosforth Road.

Under a narrow railway bridge, he shot and injured Harry Berger and then drove along the seafront onto Drigg Road, where he killed Michael Pike and Jane Robinson. He shot and injured Jacqueline Lewis on Old Shore Road. He continued past Drigg towards Holmrock and the Eskdale Valley. At Eskdale he took a circuitous route via Irton to Santon Bridge and then doubled back through Irton to the Bower House pub. He continued to Eskdale Green, where he shot and injured Fiona Maretta. He then drove to Boot, where he shot and injured Nathan Jones and Samantha Chrystie, and he also shot at Christine Alty, Craig Ross and Phillip Lowe. Finally, he travelled along the valley road, colliding with oncoming vehicles and a stone wall, before turning off the road signposted 'no through road' to Doctor Bridge, Boot. One of his tyres fell off, which brought the car to a halt. He then left his taxi and made his way on foot into local woodland, where he shot himself.

Bird's shooting spree took several hours to unfold, during which time he fired in eighteen different locations, and might best be seen as having three distinct phases (see Table 1, below). The first phase related to the shooting of his brother and the family solicitor; the second to the murder of Darren Rewcastle and the shots that he fired at his fellow taxi drivers in Whitehaven. Of the twelve people who were killed by Bird, nine were unknown to him. He travelled for some forty-five miles, and it's clear that his experience as a taxi driver allowed him to evade detection. One police officer later commented, 'The fact that Derrick Bird had extensive local knowledge, was a taxi driver, was intent on causing as much damage as possible and the route and the amount of terrain he covered . . . made it incredibly difficult to find him' (*Guardian*, 24 March

2011). In the final phase, the more random shootings that took place outside of Whitehaven on his circuitous journey would eventually end in Boot, where Bird took his own life.

Table 1

The Three Phases of Bird's Spree

Phase 1	Phase 2	Phase 3
Targets: David Bird – his brother; family solicitor	*Targets:* Darren Rewcastle – a colleague	*Targets:* Random
Family dispute	Work dispute	Commits suicide

*

As has been described, there were a number of attempts to make sense of what had happened in Whitehaven in the immediate aftermath of the shootings, then at the subsequent coroner's inquest into the deaths and, finally, on the occasion of the first anniversary of the spree. This 'making sense' was essentially a binary process. What happened in West Cumbria was either to be explained through Bird's personal pathology, or through wider, more generic cultural issues which sought to transcend an understanding based solely on responsibilising Bird. This binary process became especially evident when analysing the articles which appeared in the *Guardian*, although it should be noted that journalists working for the *Guardian* would often quote from other newspapers, especially the *Sun* and the *Daily Mail*. Indeed, this binary mode of analysis within newspaper reporting was even extended to the location of the spree itself, with the journalist Marina

Hyde commenting that a recurring trope of a 'rural idyll' being 'shattered' was all too quickly apparent, 'for ease of narrative purposes' (*Guardian*, 5 June 2010).

There was an immediate difficulty in simply making Bird responsible for what had happened, even if he was literally the perpetrator. Virtually everyone in Whitehaven who worked with him or knew him went out of their way to stress that he was 'a quiet fellow', and an 'ordinary bloke'. Mark Cooper, a friend and fellow taxi driver, described Bird as someone who 'owned his house and car. He paid his round in the pub. It's a terrible tragedy. He was just like us. I had never seen him lose his temper with anyone or get angry' (*Guardian*, 5 June 2010). Bird's two sons also put out a press release in which they described their father as 'the nicest man you could ever meet. He was a loving dad and recently became a grandfather ... a loving and cheerful character and was well known throughout the local community and the areas where he worked' (*Guardian*, 7 June 2010).

As Jeremy Seabrook noted in a longer commentary, this picture of Bird as an 'amiable, unassuming man with a quick smile' could be contrasted with a 'more complex picture' which began to emerge as various journalists started to dig a little deeper. This 'complexity' was related to two issues: speculation about Bird's mental health, and secondly his willingness to engage in what was described as 'sex tourism' in Thailand. In relation to the former, Bird was described as 'paranoid' and 'delusional', especially about his financial affairs, and the *Guardian* quoted psychologist Dr Adrian West's evidence at the coroner's inquiry which suggested that Bird was filled with 'bitterness, resentment and depression', which had led him to 'enact vengeful, retaliatory fantasies' (*Guardian*, 26

March 2011). The idea of 'retaliatory fantasies' may have been given some credence when it emerged that Bird had watched Steven Seagal's *On Deadly Ground* only hours before embarking on the spree, given that the film's plot is largely focused on a lone gunman taking revenge. The *Guardian* even quoted my own work for the *Daily Mail*, where I suggested that the spree murders were 'a sadistic act of self-loathing' (*Guardian*, 3 June 2010). Of course, this 'complexity' is still nonetheless related to Bird as an individual with mental health issues. However, it was later revealed that he wasn't known to local mental health services and had rarely needed an appointment with his own GP (*Guardian*, 2 November 2010).

It was Joan Smith for the *Guardian*, in an article entitled 'Derrick Bird Normal? He Was a Sexual Predator', who raised broader issues related to spree murder, gender and masculinity. Writing before the spree murders committed by Joanne Dennehy in 2013, Smith wondered why 'does a very small group of men respond ... by killing people?' Smith was particularly keen to draw attention to Bird's cruelty towards his victims and 'most important of all, [that he] was a habitual sexual predator'. Her source for making this statement was an interview conducted by the *Sun* with Chris Bulmer, a bar owner in Pattaya, Thailand, who said that Bird had visited his bar and had become 'obsessed' with a twenty-two-year-old Thai woman. Smith argued that Bird's behaviour was a manifestation of his need for 'control, a fantasy-driven compensation for the slights and insults they perceive in everyday life'. She concluded there was a 'widespread cultural imperative to normalise sex tourism by Western men' and that 'there is something very seriously wrong with men like Bird'

(*Guardian*, 8 June 2010). This does seem to be an important insight into Bird's performance of masculinity, although it also begs the question as to why other male 'sex tourists' don't engage in spree or mass murder.

What's rarely given much prominence within this binary analysis is the financial pressure that Bird seems to have been under, not just because he believed (incorrectly) that he was being investigated by HM Revenue and Customs but also because of increasing stresses at his place of work. I've already noted that the second phase of Bird's spree was specifically centred on taxi drivers in Whitehaven. The *Guardian* noted that 'there had been a rise in tension at cab ranks in the town because of an increasing number of drivers and a decreasing number of jobs'. One taxi driver said, 'There are so many new drivers out there and not a lot of jobs. There have been fights over fares and accusations that some drivers are coming in from Preston and Blackpool to take jobs' (*Guardian*, 3 June 2010). Bird's best friend Neil Jacques also commented that the day before the spree Bird had wanted to 'talk about his money problems. He thought he was in proper trouble. He was bothered because of the tax demands, he could not cope. He had been doing the taxis for fifteen or sixteen years and he had never paid any tax' (*Guardian*, 9 June 2010). Bird told a different friend that 'Whitehaven would be as famous as Dunblane' (*Guardian*, 2 March 2011) and another resident of the town even claimed that he'd shaken the hands of his fellow taxi drivers one by one and told them 'there's going to be a rampage in this town tomorrow', although they had all 'laughed and didn't take him seriously' (*Guardian*, 3 June 2010).

*

I visited the town to engage in conversation about the spree shootings with residents of Whitehaven in bars, cafés and restaurants, at the hotel where I stayed and with a number of taxi drivers. I spoke with some twenty people and our conversations were mostly spontaneous, although I did use the plaque erected to Darren Rewcastle as a prompt to initiate discussion with taxi drivers waiting for fares at the local cab rank. Having done so, I also hired one taxi driver – whom I will call Bob – to take me from Whitehaven to Boot. Bob was a friend of Bird and therefore knew him well. I also visited the offices of the local newspaper. There was no hesitancy to engage in conversation with me and the most obvious example of a willingness to participate with what I was asking about came from two female employees of the *Whitehaven News*, who gave me a copy of the newspaper from 2 June 2010. I always identified myself as a criminologist interested in Bird's killing spree. Only one man attempted to steer my conversation away from Bird, and on to Mildred Gale, the paternal grandmother of George Washington, who is buried in St Nicholas's Church in the town. It later transpired that this man was a local councillor. I used a reflexive diary to record my conversations and quote freely from them within this section of the chapter, especially in relation to my journey with Bob.

It soon became clear that most people in Whitehaven knew each other and so I was regularly directed from one person to another who might be in a better position to answer my questions. Those people I spoke to did so openly and without any hesitancy. Throughout our conversations Bird was described as an 'ordinary bloke' and as 'normal' and, as a consequence, when pushed to explain why he'd behaved as he had done, the most common response I was given was that he had simply 'flipped'. A number of people described Bird as a 'friend' or stated that they knew someone who regarded him as such. Only the councillor described Bird as an 'aberration'. Aberration, of course, means deviation, abnormality or an oddity, which relates back to the idea that Bird's pathology best explains what had happened, but this wasn't what came across in the majority of my discussions.

One surprising discovery from the field research was the difficulties of navigating the town itself. It took me three attempts to find my hotel, as the one-way system is complicated and, at first glance, seemed to deliberately obstruct people who might want to come and stay. The hotel had no car park, and I soon discovered that Whitehaven doesn't have a car park that allows a visitor to stay for more than four hours. On enquiring where I could park overnight, I was advised to leave the car on one of the local housing estates. During the week, the sole multi-storey car park in the town is reserved for the staff at the Sellafield nuclear site. All of this conspired to make the town centre appear like an island that most people would pass by, rather than a place where they could stop and visit. It was also suggestive of why Bird's knowledge of the local road systems was so advantageous to him in avoiding detection.

The other two common reactions to my questions were that I was the first person ever to ask about what had happened since 2010–11, and then to be given local geography lessons. For example, the hotel receptionist said he'd never been asked anything about Derrick Bird and the shootings. He then reminded me that more people had died in the village of Egremont, a small market town five miles to the south, than in Whitehaven itself; that the first murder took place in Rowrah; and that Bird would eventually commit suicide in the hamlet of Boot. This geographic fragmentation of the spree is in marked contrast to the mass murders committed by Thomas Hamilton, which were concentrated within Dunblane Primary School.

All of these issues would reappear within conversations on my taxi journey with Bob. I've deliberately not used his real name and have also anonymised some of his personal details so as to avoid possible identification. Bob was especially helpful in explaining – and showing – the geography of the spree shootings and allowing me to understand the particular benefits of being a taxi driver. In essence, as he explained: 'I like the freedom; the independence. I just do as I please. I make the money to pay the bills and go out for a drink.' He also admitted that there had been tension in the cab ranks in the weeks and months prior to the shootings. For example, he explained that 'there was bickering among the drivers as some were taking runs from the back; that wound people up. It is better now since the shootings as we now use a first-car system.' He also suggested that he felt that Bird had 'targeted' Darren Rewcastle and confirmed that there had been an incident when Darren had put a dart in Bird's tyre a few weeks before the shootings.

Bob was Bird's friend, and they socialised together. He thought of him as 'placid. He didn't get into trouble or bother anyone,' although, as we have seen, this wasn't altogether correct. When asked to characterise what Bird had done, Bob said, 'I think of it as evil, what he's done, but he was a normal person before that. He had a drink and he went out. Mind you, he could be a loner. He could go and sit in a pub on his own. I couldn't do that.' I suggested that Bird might have been making a point by targeting people whom he felt had insulted him or had not supported him in some way. Bob simply replied, 'I just think he lost his mind. He had a mental list [of people] – a paper list has never been found. I don't think that he was trying to achieve anything.' In his longest musings on what had happened, Bob described Bird as 'as a loner, although he did mix with people'; talked about his visits to Thailand; and then described an incident which had resulted in Bird being physically attacked by some of his passengers. Even so, Bob described the people of Whitehaven as 'friendly. I can say hello and they would say hello back. We are just calmer people here.' Bob thought that this contrasted with a large city like London, as 'You could blend in and disappear in London, but not here. If someone runs away from my taxi without paying their fare, they will eventually get back into the taxi. Everyone knows everyone. We're close even though we don't know each other.'

As we drove further into the countryside, we lost radio coverage in the car and my mobile phone signal disappeared. Despite Marina Hyde's insistence that the countryside outside of Whitehaven had been set up as a 'rural idyll' for 'narrative purposes', I really was struck by how beautiful, isolated and picturesque the area was that Bird had chosen to take his own life. Despite the isolated nature of the country, we also passed a number of walkers and four campsites. As we did so Bob joked, 'They're giving way to me as they see the taxi stripes and they're thinking the last time I saw a taxi driver up here he had a gun. I'm surprised they haven't run for cover!' I asked Bob why he thought that Bird hadn't shot at more people – perhaps by going onto one of the campsites – to which he replied he thought that he'd 'run out of ammunition'. Bob also suggested 'the police didn't want to catch him; they were scared. We are a small town with no armed response. This kind of thing doesn't happen here. Our police are just village blokes that we all know.'

There are clearly a number of contradictions in what Bob said. For example, he described Bird as a loner, but also as someone who mixed with other people; that Bird had no motive, but also that he was taking revenge; that Whitehaven's face-to-face culture of everyone knowing each other made it 'calmer' than London, although it was this very same culture which had produced a spree murderer. I was also aware that Bob had refused to speak to the media as he thought that it was 'wrong' to accept money in the wake of the shootings, although, as agreed, albeit in a different context, I paid a £70 taxi fare to discuss exactly the same event. Finally, Bob's idea that Bird had simply 'lost his mind' is at odds with the fact that he'd been threatening to exact revenge on his fellow taxi drivers for some time prior to the shootings. In short, Bird hadn't simply 'flipped'. This public threatening to act is also reminiscent of Hamilton at Dunblane but, while Hamilton was a prolific letter writer and had repeatedly made these threats in print, Bob reminded me that Bird had only a mental note of those that he wanted to shoot, so that there was no 'paper list' to be found.

*

I've already described how Dunblane was referenced by the local newspaper almost immediately in the wake of the spree shootings, as a means to try to make sense of what had happened in Cumbria, and how this comparison cropped up in what was said to me in my field research. Bird himself threatened to make 'Whitehaven as famous as Dunblane', although his spree shootings were fragmented over a much wider area. I list in Table 2 (below) other similarities and differences between these two events.

Table 2

Dunblane and Whitehaven

DUNBLANE	WHITEHAVEN
Mass murder – majority of victims children	Spree murder – victims all adults
Concentrated	Fragmented
Face-to-face culture	Face-to-face culture
'Dunblane massacre'	'Cumbria shootings'
Formal civic memorial to victims	Private memorial to Darren Rewcastle
Genteel	Low income
Defined by murders	Not defined by murders
Hamilton viewed as 'odd'	Bird viewed as 'ordinary'
Closed to discussion with researchers	Open to discussion with researchers

It's clear that there are a number of criminological and interpretive differences between these two events and that these have had a long-lasting impact on how both incidents are perceived. The most important relate to the fact that almost all of Hamilton's victims were children, while all of Bird's were adults aged between twenty-three and seventy-one years old. Hamilton was viewed by many people as 'odd'; Bird was almost universally seen as an 'ordinary' bloke, who had family and friends and was integrated into the community. More generally we should note their similarities as mass and spree murderers in that they both legally owned the firearms they used; took their own lives at the conclusion of the murders that they committed; that they were both self-employed and had financial worries.

Of the interpretive differences, I've drawn attention to how Dunblane is historically defined by mass murder, despite the sporting success of local tennis stars Jamie and Andy Murray, who come from Dunblane and who both knew Hamilton, whereas Whitehaven has largely avoided being characterised in this way. This undoubtedly relates to the difference between the concentration of the mass murders within one location and the ages of the victims, whereas Bird's spree murders took place over a wider geographic area. So too Dunblane was closed, guarded and secret, while Whitehaven positively welcomed me as a researcher. In this respect, making sense of Whitehaven was closer to the 'noise' that Norwegian journalist Åsne Seierstad encountered while researching the spree shootings of Anders Behring Breivik on Utøya island in July 2011. Her book about these murders, she explained, had been written as a result of

all those who told me their stories ... Parents and siblings have shared their family histories. Friends have spoken of comradeship ... Some of the conversations went on for days and nights, others were short phone calls ... it is the multitude of conversations that have made this book possible.[13]

Finally, I also suggest that Dunblane is a rather 'genteel' place, whereas Whitehaven and its environs are much more impoverished, and this economic reality had an impact on the financial status of Hamilton and Bird. This is an issue which needs to be discussed more fully.

*

A starting point for making sense of all of this has to be to remember that violence often occurs when some men feel that their self-worth has been challenged. The immediate context for what happened in Whitehaven is that Bird had been attacked by passengers in his taxi and picked on by so-called friends, and as a consequence he seems to have felt embarrassed, powerless and worthless. In these circumstances, some men will use violence to regain power and control, and to rebuild their wounded self-esteem. As one academic has put it:

> The purpose of violence is to diminish the intensity of shame and replace it as far as possible with its opposite, pride, thus preventing the individual feeling overwhelmed by the feeling of shame.[14]

This observation would fit with what had happened in the Three Cooks Bakery between Jimmy Mizen and Fahri and, seen in this way, Bird's spree murders are not 'instrumental' but rather a form of 'expressive violence'. They have less to do with rational thinking and are much more about expressing an underlying identity which feels under threat and attack. So, we might see Bird's ongoing paranoia about his fellow taxi drivers, his brother and HMRC as a grand form of cognitive distortion, whereby he came to view himself as the victim who would have to fight to regain his sense of identity. Above all, the final phase of his spree reveals Bird's gradual moral disengagement from the community and, as such, the mechanism which allowed him to exaggerate differences between himself and others in that community. This moral disengagement facilitated an 'us and them' form of thinking or, more accurately, a 'me and them' mentality. Like Moat he was declaring war, but on the community rather than the police – although he was still 'getting his retaliation in first'.

This is where we can again usefully employ the concept of 'righteous slaughter'. Bird's spree shootings were not 'cold blooded' but committed in a highly emotional state to restore a wounded sense of self. The spree was his way to gain revenge on those whom he saw as damaging his business and his reputation – a revenge that was going to be obtained in a butch and brutal way. I've chosen that phrase with care, as it once again raises the issue of the link between violence and masculinity. The resort to violence by some men can often be explained by a desire to avoid 'shame' – the sense of dread that comes for some with the knowledge that the social bonds that had previously connected them to a community had been broken and therefore produced their isolation. For others, that shame will be experienced as a form of humiliation which results in their loss of identity.

Bird could only regain his standing in the local community by destroying it and, echoing his friend Bob – the taxi driver who took me to Boot – he could therefore 'just do as I please'. It was a form of power. In that respect his shootings were a form of 'hyper-masculinity'. As Elliot Rodger, the British-born perpetrator of a spree of murders in California in 2014, would put it, 'Who's the alpha male now, bitches?'[15] His question of course implies that he'd previously thought of himself as a 'beta male'. Rodger used this phrase in the online 'manifesto' that he left to be read after having taken his own life. He's therefore like Moat, who produced a forty-nine-page letter, although Bird left no such document explaining his behaviour. However, to what extent was his 'sex tourism' in Thailand similar to Rodger's 'fantasies of becoming powerful and stopping everyone from having sex'? One can almost imagine Bird echoing these sentiments and he emerges as someone desperate to order the world in a way which gives him power – perhaps even omnipotence. His comment that 'there's going to be a rampage in this town' perfectly captures his need to control others and how in doing so Whitehaven will at last be dazzled by him. Bird saw all this as rightly his but believed that he'd been frustrated by others who had unfairly accused, shunned or dismissed him. Often, he saw this as a conspiracy to prevent him from having what he believed was rightly his. A conspiracy, therefore, which stopped him from living his life less ordinary and thwarted his being a 'somebody' in a world where he was, or believed he was, viewed as a 'nobody'. Bird was a beta male, desperate to be an alpha, with all the benefits that he believed would result from that designation.

There seems to be something of this in every incidence of mass or spree murder, albeit acknowledging that each murderer will have some extra ingredient added or missing. So too there are echoes here of Fahri's murder of Jimmy Mizen. Of course, we're rightly always shocked and surprised by mass or spree murder. There's therefore an understandable tendency to view the murderer as different; as odd in some way – as extraordinary. However, this understandable overestimation ignores what we know all too well – that ordinary people can commit acts that are dreadful. Perhaps we can therefore only conclude that what Bird did was extraordinary, but the man himself was not. This 'banality of evil' serves to increase the horror of what happens, but it should also make us question the true causes of why some men use lethal violence in the form of mass or spree murder. That questioning inevitably involves us considering how some men have come to accept a way of being a man that all too often results in death. Hamilton, Bird and Moat were really just beta males within the model of masculinity that they'd been brought up with and still clung to, but which increasingly did not define what it meant to be a man for men in Britain more widely. That development is to be welcomed. However, what might happen if some of these beta males were to gain positions of trust and authority – such as becoming a police officer – and were still desperate to become alphas?

CHAPTER THIRTEEN

Case Twenty

The Murder of Sarah Everard, 2021

Ps. ACAB

Tweet by PATSY STEVENSON,
14 September 2023

M ike Todd, the Chief Constable of Greater Manchester
Police (GMP), died on Mount Snowdon in Wales in
March 2008. An inquest held seven months later concluded
that 'Todd died of exposure when the state of his mind was
affected by alcohol and drugs and confusion, due to his personal life'.[1] This was suicide in all but name. The reference to
Todd's personal life was at the heart of the circumstances that
led him to leave his wife and three children and head for the
mountains, as it was widely suspected that Todd feared his
three-year affair with the head of Manchester Chamber of
Commerce was going to be exposed by a Sunday newspaper.
More than this, the Chief Constable was known within GMP

as 'shagger Todd' or 'hot Toddy', and it was later alleged that he'd had affairs with five female police officers or personnel staff within his force, and sexual liaisons with at least thirty-eight other women.

Predictably the media covered Todd's death extensively, as well as the inquest. It also reported on the official inquiry that had been set up to 'conduct an examination of the circumstances to ensure that nothing in the conduct of Mike Todd's personal life had adversely impacted on the professional discharges of his duties as Chief Constable'. This inquiry was headed by Sir Paul Scott-Lee, at the time Chief Constable of the West Midlands Police. Potential witnesses couldn't be compelled to give evidence, and several chose not to do so. The inquiry eventually cleared Todd of any professional wrongdoing and found that his private life, while 'complicated', hadn't affected his duties. The inquiry concluded that:

> It is clear that throughout his career Michael Todd was an exceptional Police Officer and the professional qualities that he brought to Greater Manchester Police must not be underestimated. Michael Todd used his rare talents to the benefit of the people of Greater Manchester and in doing so led the Police Force to a new level of public service.

Todd, in other words, not only represented the best that the police had to offer – and hence his promotion to one of the most senior ranks – but had come to symbolise a 'new level of public service'. His was a career to celebrate, not to denigrate, and so he was in effect being rehabilitated by the police through the inquiry as 'one of us'. Even if his lifestyle might have been less than one might have expected from a police officer, he was an exemplar of the values, skills and sound judgement that the police expected of their personnel. He embodied the culture of the police, which has been characterised as having a sense of mission, a need for action, cynicism and suspicion, isolation from others who are not in the police, solidarity with fellow officers, conservatism, prejudice, pragmatism and machismo.[2]

We can see this machismo reflected in Todd's 'complicated' personal life and his many affairs. One former senior police officer described Todd's love affairs as 'torturous', thought that it 'beggars belief' that he'd been promoted to chief constable and asked 'what went wrong with the promotion process?'[3] However, no woman ever claimed that their relationship with Todd had been other than consensual, although there was obviously a power differential. Should this not have suggested to Sir Paul Scott-Lee that the 'new level of public service' that he described was, at the very least, compromised as far as Todd was concerned? Had this really not 'adversely impacted on the professional discharges of his duties as Chief Constable'? Perhaps this simply suggests how widespread sexual misconduct was within our police at that time and therefore how easy it was to turn a blind eye and excuse Todd's behaviour. Over a decade later a more junior police officer, in a different force but with an equally well-known reputation for sexual impropriety – he was known to his colleagues as 'The Rapist' – would commit murder.

*

The years since Mike Todd's death have not been good ones for the police. Policing has been mired in scandal and controversy after an unending series of shameful and dishonourable acts by individual police officers and by the police as an institution. In other words, when the police are acting as an arm of government and therefore as part of the state. As has often been the case, these issues first came to a head across the Atlantic. Things have now got so bad in the USA that there are repeated calls to 'defund' the police – in 2020 the policing budget was $115 billion – and Alex Vitale, Professor of Sociology at Brooklyn College, scored a surprise bestseller with *The End of Policing*. There's no question mark in the title of his book. Vitale was literally predicting that the police as an institution as it's currently organised was ending. Emblazoned on the front cover was an extract from his text: 'The problem is not police training, police diversity, or police methods. The problem is the dramatic and unprecedented expansion and intensity of policing in the last forty years, a fundamental shift in the role of the police in society. The problem is policing itself.'[4]

The tipping point for much of this anger was of course the murder of a black man called George Floyd on 25 May 2020 in Minneapolis, by a white police officer called Derek Chauvin. George had been arrested on suspicion of using a counterfeit $20 bill. As part of the arrest Chauvin knelt on George's neck for almost nine minutes, after he'd been handcuffed and was lying face down in the street. Chauvin's colleagues prevented passers-by from intervening after they heard George pleading 'I can't breathe'. Several members of the public took mobile phone footage of the incident, and this quickly went viral. Almost overnight George's murder led to national and then global protests about historic racism and police brutality. It also brought to greater prominence the Black Lives Matter movement, which had been established in 2013.

The Black Lives Matter movement was a response to the killings of Trayvon Martin, Michael Brown, Eric Garner, Rekia Boyd, Pamela Turner and many others – all African Americans who'd been fatally shot or killed by the police, or other law enforcement agents. And it cannot be denied that the various US police forces do kill far more civilians than any other Western nation. In 2020, for example, the year that George was murdered, 1,020 people were fatally shot by the police – a figure that rose to 1,055 the following year. In 2022 US law enforcement killed 1,176 people, which is an average of three people per day, or a hundred people every month.[5] Nor can it be denied that African Americans are disproportionately more likely to be killed by police officers than white Americans. For example, the rate of fatal shootings for the black population is forty per million, and for the white population sixteen per million.[6]

As a way of comparing these numbers of police shootings leading to fatalities, figures produced by the British charity Inquest show that in 2019–20 there were three such deaths in England and Wales. The following year there was only one fatal shooting by the police, in 2022–23 there were three and the year after there were two.[7] The numbers are greater for deaths in police custody. The IOPC – the Independent Office for Police Conduct – reported that there had been twenty-four deaths in or following police custody in 2023–24, which was an increase of one from 2022–23 and the highest figure since 2006–07.[8]

While the figures are different between the two countries,

it was nonetheless also the murder of a member of the public by a serving police officer that acted as a tipping point for a fundamental questioning about our own police. This questioning has often focused on the activities of the Metropolitan Police Service (MPS), usually known as simply the Met. This isn't to imply that there have been no scandals connected to the activities of police officers working elsewhere in England and Wales, or for Police Scotland, which is controlled by the devolved Scottish Parliament. However, there's one very good reason for concentrating on the Met – it is the largest police force in the UK in terms of officer numbers, and as well as having responsibility for law enforcement and the prevention of crime in the Greater London area the Met has a number of specialised roles throughout Britain, such as counter-terrorism.

The specific murder that frames this chapter followed in the wake of a number of scandals for the Met. These included: the wrongful shooting of Jean Charles de Menezes at Stockwell station in 2005; the failure of the Met to catch the serial killer Stephen Port, who murdered four young men between 2014 and 2015; police officers who were supposedly protecting the crime scene sharing images of murdered sisters Bibaa Henry and Nicole Smallman; and officers at Charing Cross police station between 2016 and 2018 exchanging racist, sexist and homophobic messages and openly using derogatory language about people with disabilities.

We can see this fundamental questioning about the police in, for example, an August 2022 report by the Policy Exchange think tank, written by David Spencer, a former detective chief inspector in the Met, which stated quite simply 'British policing has lost its way', and that our police were not 'a force fit for the future'.[9] The police's own think tank – the Police Foundation – wrote that policing in the UK was in a 'long crisis', and the *Observer* summed up what many people were thinking with a headline 'Crisis after Crisis: What is Going Wrong at the Met Police?'[10] Zoe Williams, one of the newspaper's columnists, commented, 'Isn't it frightening that a lone woman seeing a policeman now feels afraid, not reassured?'[11] The case that prompted this anguish and soul-searching related to the murder of a young white woman called Sarah Everard.

*

Sarah was a thirty-three-year-old marketing executive, walking home from a friend's house in Clapham, south London at about 9:30 p.m. on 3 March 2021, when she was stopped by Wayne Couzens, a serving Metropolitan Police officer. Sarah was described by her friends as 'intelligent, articulate and caring', and as someone who 'always put others first – she was strong and principled and a shining example to us all'.[12] A former Durham University student, Sarah was looking forward to visiting Ibiza with her boyfriend Josh Lowth and their friends in a few months' time, but in the meantime there was her work to be getting on with, and COVID-19 restrictions to navigate. In March 2021 there were, for example, still restrictions on mixing indoors with anyone except for members of 'your household', and it was against government guidelines to stay overnight away from your home. Sarah was less than a mile from her flat in Brixton when she was stopped by Couzens.

Sarah didn't know Couzens, although we still can't be

certain whether this was a random attack or if she'd been more specifically targeted by him. What we do know is that he'd been driving around in a white Vauxhall Astra that he'd hired in Dover for more than four hours that night, looking for a suitable victim. Couzens had joined the Met in 2018, having transferred from the Civil Nuclear Constabulary, where he'd been employed since 2011. Two years later he began working for the Parliamentary and Diplomatic Protection Command, as an authorised firearms officer at diplomatic premises around central London. On the morning of 3 March, he'd finished working a twelve-hour shift at the US embassy. It's now known that Couzens had been planning to carry out a violent sexual assault on a yet-to-be-selected victim for months. It's likely that he used his knowledge of working on COVID-19 patrols in January 2021 to trick Sarah, under the guise of making a fake arrest for breaching the guidelines.

It has also been established that he used his Metropolitan Police warrant card, his uniform belt and police handcuffs during his abduction of Sarah, and that she was eventually strangled with his police belt. The abduction was witnessed by a couple travelling in a car, but they presumed they'd seen an undercover officer carrying out a legitimate arrest and so they didn't intervene. The kidnapping was carried out in less than five minutes, which offers some insight into the premeditation of the attack and, more worryingly, how practised Couzens seems to have been in undertaking this sort of abduction.

After he had Sarah in the hired car, Couzens drove to Dover, where he transferred her into his own vehicle and then drove to a remote, rural area where he raped and strangled her. By 2:30 a.m. on 4 March Couzens had left the crime scene and was caught on CCTV at a service station buying drinks. He appeared perfectly normal. Couzens also bought petrol, which he used to burn Sarah's body, and then put her remains in two green rubbish bags which he later dumped in a pond near an area of woodland that he owned in Hoad's Wood in Ashford, Kent. He also seems to have taken his wife and two children on a picnic in the woods where he'd burned Sarah's body. A week after she disappeared, Sarah's remains were found in a woodland stream and Couzens was arrested on 9 March at his home in Deal. He suggested to the police at the time of his arrest that he'd been threatened by an East European gang, who were demanding that he hand over to them 'another girl' after he'd failed to pay a sex worker. He claimed that when he'd given Sarah to the gang in a lay-by in Kent, she was alive and uninjured. This was all nonsense and easily disproven by DNA, CCTV and other pieces of evidence that linked Couzens to Sarah's murder.

Couzens was sacked by the Met on 15 July 2021, a week after he admitted in court to murdering Sarah. At a disciplinary hearing chaired by Assistant Commissioner Helen Ball, it was established that he'd 'breached the standards of professional behaviour in respect of discreditable conduct' and the Assistant Commissioner also commented that Couzens 'has betrayed everything we, the police, stand for and following his guilty pleas and convictions I have dismissed him today'. All that may be so, although it's also important to remember the culture of the police that I described in relation to 'shagger Todd'. Indeed, the Met are now also facing questions over chances that were missed concerning Couzens' predatory sexual behaviour, which date back to 2015, when he was involved in an alleged flashing incident while he as working for the Civil Nuclear Constabulary. A member of the public spotted him driving around Dover naked from the waist down, and this incident had earned him the nickname 'The Rapist' among his colleagues. In January and again in February 2021, he was also involved in two alleged incidents of indecent exposure. Other allegations of indecent exposure have subsequently come to light, although Couzens has continued to deny them all.

There was a further scandal relating to the police's response to the case. An organisation called Reclaim These Streets (RTS) was started by four women who wanted to arrange a vigil for Sarah on 13 March 2021, to draw attention to issues surrounding women's safety in public spaces. Despite the best efforts of the organisers to engage with the Met, they weren't given official approval to hold the event on Clapham Common, as the capital was still subject to strict COVID-19 restrictions. Even so, thousands of women attended the unofficial vigil, which descended into chaos and disorder. Officers were filmed dragging women away from the bandstand where a crowd had gathered to hear speeches, and this was captured by TV cameras and on mobile phones. The policing of the event seemed heavy-handed and disproportionate, and a number of arrests were made. One of those arrests was of a young women called Patsy Stevenson and a photograph of her, held face down in her COVID-19 mask by two police officers, but looking upwards at the camera, captured the front pages of several newspapers the following day. She would subsequently receive an apology and financial compensation for what had happened to her, and on the day that this settlement was announced she tweeted 'Ps. ACAB' – All Cops Are Bastards.[13]

Four of the female organisers – Jamie Klingler, Anna Birley, Henna Shah and Jessica Leigh – also took legal action against the Met claiming that their rights to assemble had been breached, and that they'd been threatened with £10,000 fines and criminal prosecution if the vigil went ahead. Ruling in the women's favour, Mr Justice Holgate stated that the police had focused on 'issuing their press release' rather than engaging with the organisers. Jamie Klingler said that what the police had done was 'not a normal reaction', but an attempt 'to try to silence women who are mourning a woman who one of their officers had killed'. She went further and stated that 'they should have handed out tissues. They should have facilitated a safe space for us to grieve.' Instead, as Zoe Williams was later to argue in her *Guardian* article, 'they had used COVID-19 restrictions self-servingly to try to block the protest, in what would later turn out to be a chilling echo of the murderer's own violence'.

Sarah's murder and the subsequent handling of the vigil brought to the fore fundamental debates about how our police are organised and managed, what it is that they do and, perhaps most important of all, who it is they do that work for. Those fundamental debates had often been silenced beneath a cliché – our police are 'the best in the world' – which simply isn't true. This is just one of the many myths that have been attached to the police – a myth perpetuated by crime dramas, and sometimes by the police themselves. It has come to operate in the same way that we're assured that we were 'all in it together' during the Blitz. It creates a comforting story about a British institution that keeps criticism at a distance and so helps to preserve working cultures and practices that should've been changed a long time ago.

Many police officers and ex-police officers across a variety of ranks and forces would secretly agree with this analysis. Others have gone further and publicly stated that police culture is damaging, corrosive and needs to change.[14] And even if most might shy away from criticism that's levelled at the police as an institution, they're all acutely aware that there's a wide gulf between the media portrayal of police and policing and the usually mundane responsibilities that fill their working day. They also know that many of their colleagues are less than professional. Yet, paradoxically, they also understand how the media portrayal of policing has come to shape the public's perception of who they are and what they do, and how that in turn influences the way that they behave – how they 'perform policing' – on the streets. Frankly, a few actively perpetuate many of the myths that we've come to accept about our police and policing, despite the fact that they know this creates an understanding which isn't accurate.

*

There are so many myths about our police that there's only space to discuss a few. However, it's also important to remember that since 2010 police numbers have been significantly reduced. There were fewer police officers in England and Wales at the time of Sarah's murder than there'd been in the preceding decade. In the three years since 2020 there has been an attempt to recruit twenty thousand new police officers, but as of June 2022 there were still only 142,750 police officers, compared with the 143,734 employed in March 2011. During this period the population of England and Wales grew by about 3.5 million, and so while there were 264 police officers per 100,000 in 2011, there are now 235 police officers per 100,000 of the population. This is all related to funding, and the amount of money that government spends on policing. In 2021–22 total police funding in England and Wales was £15.88 billion, which is almost exactly the same as it was in 2010–11 – £15.86 billion. Taking inflation into account, this means that there has been a reduction of what is spent on policing, and should we want to bring police spending back in line with 2010–11 levels, there would need to be an increase in their current budget of £1 billion a year. Things don't appear to have changed since Labour came to power in 2024. The Home Office is to have its budget cut by over 3 per cent in 2025–26, although the impact of this on police spending is still unclear.[15]

Three police myths are of interest here: having more 'bobbies on the beat' would help to reduce crime; that the police spend most of their time fighting crime – they are, in effect, a 'thin blue line' that keeps the barbarians from destroying our civilisation; and 'stop and search' helps in the fight against crime. In passing it's also worth noting that officers (of various ranks) make up only about 60 per cent of the police workforce in England and Wales. So, if a member of the public was asked to think of 'the police', most would conjure up a picture of a police officer in a uniform, or a police car with flashing blue lights speeding to an incident. However, about 40 per cent of 'the police' are performing a diverse range of roles that don't fit this symbolic – mythical – representation.

Patrolling on a beat remains one of the most common

activities undertaken by our police and up to half of a force's strength is classed as 'operational patrol'. This patrol was established way back in 1829 with the formation of the Metropolitan Police, when Richard Mayne, one of the two original commissioners, stated that the purpose of the police was 'the prevention of crime, the protection of life and property and the preservation of public tranquillity'.[16] A uniform constable patrolling the streets is a way that the police can reassure the public through a visible presence. It also helps to forge links with local communities, allows for the gathering of intelligence and reduces problems related to crime and disorder. All of this is laudable enough, although it's the idea that patrolling helps in the fight against crime that has been cemented in the public's consciousness. Police drama series, and in particular the iconic *Dixon of Dock Green*, which ran between 1955 and 1976, helped to create this myth. In *Dixon of Dock Green*, George Dixon – the archetypal 'bobby on the beat' – understood the complexities of the community that he policed, knew the people who lived there, and it was this knowledge that helped him to solve crime. However, in reality the use of a patrolling constable has no impact on crime.

One of the first investigations about the effectiveness of the police patrol was undertaken in Kansas City, Missouri in the 1970s. The study found that increasing or decreasing the levels of vehicle patrol had no significant effect on crime levels, fear of crime or even satisfaction with the police. Nor did research suggest that foot patrol by the police was any more effective. Research in Newark, New Jersey in 1980 demonstrated that manipulating the numbers of police officers on foot patrol had no impact on levels of crime, although it did seem to provide the public with greater reassurance. This type of research was also carried out by the Home Office in England and Wales in the 1980s, and the most startling conclusion that emerged was that a patrolling constable in London was likely to pass within a hundred yards of a burglary in progress once in every eight years. The same study went on to acknowledge that the patrolling officer wouldn't necessarily realise a crime was actually taking place or stand much of a chance of catching the burglar. However, many people do feel reassured when they see a patrolling police officer, but what they're doing on their beat is not preventing crime. Rather, they are responding to requests from members of the public and acting as 'peace' officers rather than 'police' officers. They are providing a police 'service', not acting as law enforcers or even crime fighters.[17]

The police don't actually spend that much of their time fighting crime. In 2012–13, for example, according to the College of Policing, 19.6 million non-crime offences were recorded by the police, which equated with an individual officer attending to approximately 150 non-crime issues per year. The police deal with suspected suicide incidents, missing people and, until recently, people with mental health problems. They're hardly a crime-fighting force at all, which tends to undermine the myth of the 'thin blue line'. That reality doesn't go down well with many police officers, who see 'crime control' as 'real police work', and often as 'a man's work'. Many police officers like to think that what they do involves danger, strength, action and using their policing skills to bring offenders to justice.

The BBC police procedural *Dixon of Dock Green*, which started in 1955, created a picture of what policing was all about in the 1950s and 1960s. Later, it was the ITV series *The Sweeney*, which ran from 1975 to 1978, that seemed to strike a chord with the public – and the police themselves – about policing in the 1970s. This iconic series focused on the Met's Flying Squad, which targeted organised crime, and used the narrative arc of Jack Regan (played by John Thaw, who would go on to play the title role in the ITV series *Inspector Morse*) – a tough, individualistic detective who used violence and broke the rules. In other words, a million miles away from the cosy paternalism of George Dixon.

The Sweeney was not a faithful representation of policing in London in the 1970s, even if it was perceived to be authentic by viewers. The audience wanted to identify with Regan and his no-nonsense approach to bringing offenders to justice, especially at a time when there were ongoing debates about law and order. In fact, the idea that a character such as Regan was a force for good and could be viewed as a crime-fighting role model was specifically taken up by the series *Life on Mars*, which ran between 2006 and 2007. The premise in this series was that Detective Inspector Sam Tyler, a forensically minded officer from the present day, gets hit by a car, falls into a coma and when he wakes up finds himself transported back to Manchester and the GMP of 1973. There he meets Chief Inspector Gene Hunt – a hard drinking, rule-breaking detective just like Jack Regan. From his vantage point, DI Tyler finds DCI Hunt 'an overweight, over-the-hill, nicotine-stained, borderline alcoholic homophobe with a superiority complex and an unhealthy obsession with male bonding'. Hunt merely replies, 'You make that sound like a bad thing.' The series was not only playing on the idea that policing had become too politically correct, but also implicitly criticising the managerialism that had begun to creep into how the police were being organised.[18] A more recent series – *Line of Duty*, which ran between 2012 and 2021 – tackled police corruption, but still continued to portray the police more generally as crime fighters.

If the police aren't really a crime-fighting force, is it fair to criticise them when they don't actually have much of an impact on crime? Just 5.6 per cent of all offences recorded by the police led to a suspect being charged or summonsed in 2021–22, down from 7.3 per cent the previous year, and from 16 per cent in 2014–15. The police therefore aren't clearing up much crime, but if they aren't actually a crime-fighting force why should that be a problem? Well, for one thing it changes the way that the public think about the work that the police do, and the confidence that they have in them more generally.

We might also want to ask, if the police aren't actually crime fighters why do they have specific powers such as 'stop and search', which is specifically described as a tactic which helps to combat crime? The police have a range of statutory powers to stop and search someone if they have 'reasonable grounds' to suspect that they're carrying drugs, weapons, stolen property or something that could be used to commit a crime. Being stopped and searched doesn't mean that you're arrested, but it could lead to an arrest. The use of stop and search peaked in 2008–09 when more than 1.5 million stop and searches were carried out, although the numbers have now fallen dramatically. However, stop and search is still used disproportionately against black and minority ethnic groups and young people – black people are ten times more likely to be stopped and searched than white people. Three in every thousand white people were stopped and searched in 2017–18, compared to twenty-nine in every thousand black people. But does stop and search act as a deterrent and reduce crime?[19]

There's scant research on whether stop and search prevents and deters crime. The little that does exist suggests that it has only a very weak and inconsistent association with crime, and there's no evidence of any impact on violent crime. Almost 17 per cent of stop and searches did lead to an arrest, and most of these related to drugs offences and theft. That means that 83 per cent had no positive outcome, and that the 'reasonable grounds' that had caused the stop and search were wrong.[20]

Our policing is supposedly based on consent. We pride ourselves that our policing is local in character and that there's an unspoken – but firmly based – understanding that the police know what's expected of them when performing their duties to us as citizens, and that they'll ensure that those expectations are fulfilled. Yet the notion that we are policed by consent is dubious at best, and the disproportionality of stop and search falling on one ethnic group emphasises that communication and trust between the police and some groups can easily break down. In turn this creates problems about police relations with various local communities and the public more generally. We might even want to view what happened on Clapham Common through the lens of whether or not this was local 'community policing', or even policing by consent. This also brings us back to the murder of Sarah Everard, the vigil that was held in her memory and the broader goal of drawing attention to the dangers women face.

*

Commander Bas Javid was the executive lead for frontline policing within the Met during the COVID-19 pandemic. He therefore has a particular view about what happened on Clapham Common. He has since left the Met, becoming Director General for Immigration Enforcement at the Home Office in 2023. Bas's own biography is also of interest, echoing themes and questions that have emerged throughout this history of modern Britain.

In an interview Bas described to me how he was born in Rochdale. His mother and father were Pakistani Muslim immigrants who'd first moved to England in the 1960s. Bas and his older brother Sajid – who would go on to become a Conservative MP, and later the Health Secretary and Chancellor of the Exchequer – were brought up in Bristol, after their parents had left the north and moved to the West Country, where his father had at first driven a bus and then run a shop. The Javid family lived in a flat above the shop.

Bas left school at sixteen in 1988 and joined the Royal Navy. He spent much of his service on HMS *Brilliant*, including patrolling the Persian Gulf during the 1991 war, for which he received a commendation. After his discharge from the navy, he joined Avon and Somerset Police in 1993, at a time when policing was being rocked by the murder in London of the black teenager Stephen Lawrence by a gang of racist thugs. Then after thirteen years within Avon and Somerset, he joined the West Midlands Police in 2007. Thereafter he became a commander in the Metropolitan Police in 2019 and was then promoted to the rank of deputy assistant commissioner.

Bas shared a very interesting anecdote about his life with his brother when they were growing up in Bristol.[21]

I think that my policing career began when I was a child with the Javid Brothers' crime-busting gang! Our gang had just two members – Sajid and me – and back then we were still in primary school and we'd circle the neighbourhood on our bikes, communicating by walkie-talkie, looking for crimes to report. Whenever we saw something we would go to the phone box and dial 999. It was just kids being kids. Saj was the chief constable, but I was the leader of the gang and by far the more street smart. It was about the values that came from our dad – he gave us a sense of right and wrong, and a belief that family came first but then be part of a community.

Here's a very powerful, personal story about two young Muslim boys trying to 'police' their community, which at the time, according to Bas, was plagued by a great deal of anti-social behaviour. They wanted their community to be better than it was, and even if it was just 'kids being kids', it was the children of two first-generation immigrants who were riding around on their bikes and dialling 999 if they saw something that they felt needed to be reported. This surely suggests that from an early age the Javid brothers wanted to take the initiative and lead; they wanted to stand out as much as they wanted to fit in – personal qualities and values that they'd both use in their subsequent careers. It's also possible to glimpse Bas's sense of humour in this anecdote, which was not something he could often show in his public-facing role with the Met.

In relation to the policing of the vigil for Sarah Everard and, more generally, the loss of public trust, Bas said:

I want to start by offering my condolences to Sarah's family, and to her friends. Her murder clearly sent shockwaves throughout the country. It made people angry – including people who work in the Metropolitan Police. We also need to remember that we still have a global pandemic, and I lost my thirty-nine-year-old cousin, who was an asthmatic, to COVID-19 and so I know personally the impact that COVID-19 can have. We wanted to work with the people who were organising the event to talk about the gathering and suggest that perhaps they could have an electronic event – an electronic gathering. We were caught between a rock and a hard place. We understood that people wanted to express their anger, but a small group did go against the rules. Should we have enforced the rules, or turned a blind eye? The difficulty is finding the right balance. I think that the majority of the public want us to uphold the law, based on the threat and risk that exists. My colleagues are professionals. They didn't want it all to end in arrests, but the whole pandemic has had a major impact on our thinking.

On one level Bas's response is formulaic and intended to close down criticism. After all, the courts did eventually rule against what the Met had done and awarded damages to various people involved with the vigil. Nor should we ignore the fact that a serving police officer had used the lockdown restrictions to abduct, rape and murder a young woman. It's also true that there were outdoor demonstrations and gatherings in London during lockdown which had been policed in different ways – including a number of anti-lockdown marches.[22] A few months after Sarah's murder, Rangers fans had gathered in George Square in Glasgow to celebrate their team winning the Scottish Premier League, despite the fact that large gatherings outside weren't permitted in Scotland at this time. Presumably the decision to allow these events to go ahead – or at least to step back and not get directly involved – had also been ones where a balance had to be found and where the police were also caught 'between a rock and a hard place'.

This raises the issue of trust between the public and the police so as to ensure that people were safe – including being safe from Bas's colleagues. He felt that the solution 'comes back to local policing – community policing. We need to ensure that the police are seen as part of the solution not the problem. You can never arrest yourself out of a situation. I think that the vast majority of people still respect the police. Not all, and there is a small minority who don't, but I really believe that the vast majority do respect the police.' While this might well be true, it seems hard to identify who this 'community' in 'community policing' is, or who might repre- sent it. Nor does there appear to be a way that would allow a 'community' to carry on with an event – such as the vigil on Clapham Common – if this is proscribed by law.

In an article that Bas had written for the *Spectator* before Sarah's murder and the subsequent vigil, he'd said that 'any- one who's looking for certainty about how the virus will behave, or how we will respond, will be disappointed. But isn't it better to be careful?'[23] In the same article he also sug- gested that 'we don't want to alienate the public but we need to uphold the law, and we must find our way without being too distracted by the media'. Looking now at what he'd writ- ten, this seems to have guided the approach of the Met on the night of Sarah's vigil. They were being 'careful', even if they didn't want to 'alienate the public' by 'upholding the law'. That seems like a tricky balance to achieve at the best of times, and all the more so given that other outdoor gatherings had gone ahead, and that Sarah's vigil was about the murder of a young woman by a member of their own force. This rather makes a mockery of the idea of 'policing by consent', especially if the public feel very strongly about an issue which might be against the law or proscribed by national guidelines. And while Bas felt that community policing could re-create a sense of trust, this does appear to be wishful thinking on his part. According to London's mayor Sadiq Khan, the public's trust in the police, even several years after Sarah's murder, remains fragile and he concluded it would 'take years' to repair.[24]

However, some measure of Bas's comments that the police on the night of the vigil didn't 'want it all to end in arrests' and, more generally, his view that 'you can never arrest yourself out of a situation' can be gleaned from comments made by a number of officers who were on duty that night. PC Darryl Mayne, for example, stated that he and his colleagues had sensed that the gathering was turning into an 'anti-police protest', rather than a vigil in the memory of Sarah. He also shared that 'I recall the crowd screaming what I believed to be the following: "Go away", "Murderers", "Arrest your own"', and that some members of the crowd had shouted at him 'It should be you', which had caused him distress.[25] This seems to offer some counterbalance to the criticism that the policing was heavy-handed and echoed the actions of Couzens himself.

I also asked Bas about budget cuts, and the impact that these had had on police performance. He admitted that it was a 'strategic problem' and then, using less managerial language, he also admitted that 'our capacity [as an organisation] doesn't match the demands we have on a day-to-day basis – 999 calls, or even the required footfall on a particular street. It just doesn't match. We don't have the budgets to plan ahead . . . and without the funding you are on the back foot.' So it's not really about having more bobbies on the beat, as they're sometimes simply not on the beat at all. Bas's answer also gives some credence to his belief that most of the public are still on the side of the police. After all, if they weren't, why would they continue to make these demands?

*

The murder of Sarah Everard by a serving Metropolitan Police officer will continue to foster a level of distrust between the public – especially women – and the police. Sarah's murder was followed by a number of other scandals for the Met, including the conviction of a firearms officer called David Carrick, who pleaded guilty to eighty-five serious offences, including forty-eight rapes, in February 2023. He was sentenced to life imprisonment and was described by Mrs Justice Cheema-Grubb, the trial judge, as an example of the 'malign abuse of power by a man against a woman'. His offences spanned nearly two decades. Carrick believed that his position as a police officer made him 'untouchable' and gave him 'exceptional powers to coerce and control'. Mrs Cheema-Grubb, the first Asian woman to serve as a High Court judge in the United Kingdom, said that he'd 'betrayed his oath' to protect the public and had caused 'irretrievable devastation'.[26]

There's clearly a great deal of work that has to be done by our police to repair the damage that Couzens, Carrick and others have caused. Nor are there 'bobbies on the beat' as they were in the past, police numbers and budgets have fallen and, unsurprisingly, arrest and charging rates are at their lowest ever levels for most offences. Frankly, the police have already been defunded, although not in the way that their critics in the USA are demanding. Where all of this will end will depend on political decisions that need to be taken about appropriate levels of funding. However, funding that will allow for the recruitment and training of new officers will only begin the process of repairing the police's reputation. That can only happen when there's leadership which is robust enough not only to challenge existing – and toxic – police cultures but also replace those cultures with values that reflect what Britain is like today, rather than what it might have been like in the past.

Of course, there's something to admire about Bas Javid's decision to join the police and in his success as a Muslim of Pakistani origin to reach the very highest ranks of policing. And what about Mrs Justice Cheema-Grubb? Born to Indian Sikh Punjabi parents who came to Britain in 1960, she was called to the bar in 1989, became a QC in 2013 and a High Court judge two years later. If ever there's a way of assessing how much we have changed over time, having Bas and Mrs Justice Cheema-Grubb in senior roles within the criminal justice system is surely something to be celebrated. It feels a very long way from where we were in 1885, and perhaps just as far from the days of 'shagger Todd'.

Let's end by thinking about Sarah and give the last word to Rose Woollard, one of her closest friends since they'd been at university together. Rose had even contacted the BBC to raise awareness of Sarah's disappearance before it had become an official police investigation. She remembered that Sarah was an 'exceptional friend, dropping everything to be there to support her friends whenever they needed her'. Rose continued, 'she was sunshine and light and made you feel warm and good and safe'.[27]

At The End of a History

B as Javid, Mrs Justice Cheema-Grubb and the murder of Sarah Everard offer one way of considering the changes and continuities that it's possible to discern within Britain over the last 140 years. These changes would relate to the gender and race of two criminal justice professionals working at the highest levels of public service, but there are continuities too in that what was being described, or managed, by them were a series of rapes and yet another murder of a young woman on the streets of London.

The temptation becomes simply to list the changes and count the similarities, as if that in itself would form a meaningful conclusion. That temptation has to be resisted, for it really doesn't tell the story of Britain or the British I've described.

This isn't to deny that there have been changes in relation to, most obviously, gender, race and sexuality, although there will surely be some who'll want to question whether those changes have gone far enough, and others who'll argue that there's been no substantive change at all. However, I've no doubt that if we could go back to 1885 the Britain that we'd encounter would look, feel, sound, smell and act differently from the island that we inhabit today. That's an easy point to make.[1] More difficult conclusions don't lend themselves to a simple totting-up, or by imagining that we can travel back in time and have a look around the Victorian era. A conclusion can only emerge from thinking carefully about what this history tells us about the place that we call Britain and who the British have become.

What has, I hope, been made clear is that history isn't so much written by winners, but by certain types of winners whose story then gets harnessed by the state to tell a tale about modern Britain and the people who live there. We become that tale. So, not all winners make it into the historical record, because their story does nothing to contribute to or enhance the way that we're supposed to think about ourselves, explain our past and therefore judge the present. That was most obvious in the story of Billy Hill, who thought that his 'halcyon days' came during the Blitz, because of all the money that he and his gang were able to make from stealing and looting in the burning ruins of bombed-out London. He wasn't 'all in it together', but out for himself; he was a winner – he even left us a compelling autobiography – but not the right type of winner. Hill's story exposes that history becomes not only what's remembered, but also what gets forgotten and discarded. His story is seen to be meaningless and therefore lost to history – despite the fact that the overlooked and disregarded often tell very different but equally important tales.

This preferred version of the past is consciously and deliberately created by the state. Time after time, as I've shown, it was literally impossible to answer questions about a murder, or a series of murders, because the official files were still secret and hidden away under lock and key. That wasn't being done to protect Britain from the prying eyes of a foreign enemy, which is surely the point of having an Official Secrets Act, but often, I would argue, to prevent an alternative narrative being constructed, which was less flattering of the state and how it functioned. As I've discussed, the state was even prepared to manipulate the murder rate. People wanted and still want to hold the state accountable but are often powerless to do so, given the obstacles put in their way. Why should it *not* be possible to read the case files on the murders of Kelso Cochrane, Rita Ellis, William Elliott, George Stobbs or indeed Airey Neave? It would appear the answer is that the state and its employees would emerge in a less favourable light. That would surely undermine their claims for efficiency and administrative competence and shatter the myths that we've come to believe about ourselves. It might also erode our continuing support at the ballot box. The conclusion has to be that there really is no freedom of information in Britain and until there is we can't democratically hold the state to account. My demand therefore has to be for more openness, candour and honesty about what's done in our name by those with power.

The opposite of being a winner is to be a loser, although I don't think of the people who form the backbone of the text in that way. These were ordinary people, living ordinary lives but that doesn't mean they were losers. Their stories are no less valuable – or heroic – than the stories of the winners who normally make it into the historical record. Their ordinary lives also give us an insight into different forms of historical change and, perhaps more revealingly, stubborn continuity across the decades: Maud Clifford breaking up with and then getting back together with her husband who then kills her; Percy Thompson sharing his house with his wife's younger lover and eventually being killed by him; Rachel Dubinski having to fight for the meagre allowance that her former husband rarely paid and then ending up dead; George Stobbs lying to his wife about going back to work so that he could slip out of the house and meet up with gay lovers in Chesterfield; and Jimmy Mizen, killed the day after his sixteenth birthday by another young man who simply didn't know how to be a man.

These ordinary lives were also patterned by a complexity that's usually hidden beneath history's surface. I imagine that few people would have realised that a tenement was so much more than a 'slum' and hid its very own status-driven subculture. Or that tensions on a taxi rank in Whitehaven could sow the seeds of spree murder. These were ordinary, banal, everyday places where people demanded respect and wanted to be thought of as respectable to the extent that small slights could lead to murder. Who knew that there was a thriving gay subculture in Chesterfield in the 1960s, and that the surrounding countryside was filled with voyeurs armed with binoculars? Did we really not appreciate that, in the absence of suitable ways of earning a living in a deindustrialised landscape, a propensity that some men have for violence could become a precious commodity? Of course, these subcultures were also the context for murder, and that's when ordinary people became extraordinary, and when the state began to take an interest in who they were and what had happened to them. And what *had* happened to them? Far too often the official conclusion personalised and othered the problem – they were murdered – rather exposing how decisions of the state had a much broader impact on how people lived and so created the circumstances in which they died.

The Britain that emerges from weaving together these stories of ordinary lives is rather different from the one that's commonly described in our history books. We uncover a Britain that was much less peaceable and benign and a British Empire that was more grasping, warlike and self-serving. Britons took what they wanted when they could and were prepared to kill if that was necessary, even if the story they told about themselves at the time – and ever since – would have us believe otherwise. Billy Hill once again captured all of this when he suggested that Sir Walter Raleigh and Sir Francis Drake had been 'gangsters – weren't they nicking something that didn't belong to them? Only because it was on behalf of their government that made it legal.' He has a point.

At the same time, these ordinary lives demonstrate the continuing importance to Britons of family, communality, loyalty, the right to vote, a determination to get justice, forgiveness, and the hazards that still exist for those who are female, black, Asian, gay, or who seem to threaten the status quo. However, the Britons who emerge from the text are not one-dimensional and it's their vagueness and imprecision which is surely of greater interest, even if it leads to more questions. Why did Percy Clifford volunteer to fight in South Africa, and was Edith Thompson simply fantasising when she wrote to her younger lover about killing her husband? Is John Childs really our most prolific hitman? To acknowledge this complexity is to give agency to those who've been described and recognises that their existence was much more dynamic, vital, vibrant, astonishing and surprising than history has previously allowed. That should make us question our acceptance of what the state claims are 'British' values and also how we're supposed to think of Britain as a nation. There are, in other words, no neat and precise characteristics that can describe Britain, or what it means to be British, and there never have been.[2]

This makes it even more important to consider more critically our origin myths – the things that we like to say to describe ourselves and so give meaning to Britain. Obviously, myths can change, although for hundreds of years they've tended to have an English, as opposed to British, patina. For a considerable time that shiny gloss also served the needs of the Scots and the Welsh. That no longer seems to be the case and so these origin myths have started to come under pressure and increasingly seem to be out of step with nationalist demands. That pressure was already evident in Scotland from the 1980s onwards because of the 'democratic deficit' and became more intense as a result of Brexit. Every region of Scotland voted to remain in the EU, and although Wales voted to leave, they did so by a narrow margin – there's even some evidence to suggest that it was made to look like a Brexit-supporting nation only because of so-called English settlers.[3] These nationalist pressures have somewhat dissipated but they could easily become more passionate again, and while there's currently no willingness to allow the SNP to have another referendum on independence, their arguments to do so are valid and have merit.

However, even if there was another referendum that doesn't mean the Scots would necessarily vote to leave the United

Kingdom, although, frankly, there have been precious few attempts to explain why they should stay. Would it be a surprise if the Scots were to leave the United Kingdom? Would it even be a shock if we were to see a United Ireland in the decades to come? These seem like unlikely scenarios but the cultural glue that once held Britain together has become weaker, and so less persuasive.

The title of these concluding remarks is an allusion to Francis Fukuyama's article, published in the *National Interest* in the summer of 1989 and called 'The End of History?' In essence he suggested that with the imminent collapse of the Soviet Union the last ideological alternative to liberal democracy, Western thought and market capitalism had been eliminated. History had reached its end goal because the world had at last stumbled towards a stable equilibrium. Unfortunately for Fukuyama, history had a few more tricks up its sleeve. There may well be other tricks up history's sleeve for Britain and the British too. The Scots and the Welsh might happily re-embrace the Union, and Ireland will continue to have a north and south.

Murder disrupts and destabilises; it unsettles the rhythms of a community; and, above all else, it tragically steals time from people, who can't live their lives as they once had hoped and planned – just like Elsie Ansell, buried in the wedding dress that she never got to wear down the aisle. With their lives being taken too early, we just don't know how the jazz-loving Kelso Cochrane would have experienced the swinging sixties, or how Rita Ellis might have progressed in her WRAF career and Melanie Stourton as a nurse. What might James Bulger's school days have been like, and would Jimmy Mizen have settled down, found a partner and perhaps by now have children of his own? These murders are scars on the face of the future.

Murder also requires the state to question and investigate. This in turn involves officials speaking to people and recording what they said – perhaps after looking in places where they might not have chosen to go and describing what they found there. Murder gets recorded and those records tell a story. So, murder creates an official, as well as a personal, story of Britain and the British that continues to echo through space and time – long after the perpetrator might have been caught and punished. Those personal and official stories – these grains of sand – have helped me to uncover a different Britain, by allowing me to describe those Britons who rarely make it into the pages of history. What a tragedy that they had to die to do so.

Secondary Literature

Freda Adler (1975) *Sisters in Crime: The Rise of the New Female Criminal*, New York: McGraw-Hall

John Alderson (1979) *Policing Freedom*, London: Macdonald and Evans

Laurence Alison and Marie Eyre (2009) *Killer in the Shadows: The Monstrous Crimes of Robert Napper*, London: Pennant

Alan Allport (2020) *Britain at Bay: The Epic Story of the Second World War, 1938–1941*, London: Profile

Christopher Andrew (2009) *The Defence of the Realm: The Authorised History of MI5*, London: Penguin

Nick Appleyard (2009) *Life Means Life: Jailed Forever*, London: John Blake

Marc Auge (2009) *Non-Places: Introduction to an Anthropology of Supermodernity*, London: Verso

Peter Aylward (2012) *Understanding Dunblane and other Massacres: Forensic Studies of Homicide, Paedophilia, and Anorexia*, London: Karnac

Victor Bailey (2019) *The Rise and Fall of the Rehabilitative Ideal, 1895–1970*, London: Routledge

Paul Baker (2020) *Fabulosa: The Story of Polari, Britain's Secret Gay Language*, London: Reaktion

Peter Baker (1962) *Time Out of Life*, London: Quality Book Club

Anette Ballinger (2000) *Dead Women Walking: Executed Women in England and Wales, 1900–1955*, Aldershot: Ashgate

Roland Barthes (2009) *Mythologies*, London: Vintage

Curt R. Bartol and Anne M. Bartol (2014) *Introduction to Forensic Psychology: Research and Application*, London: Sage

Nancy K. Baym (2010) *Personal Connections in the Digital Age*, Cambridge: Polity

Simone de Beauvoir (1965) *Force of Circumstance*, London: Weidenfeld & Nicolson

C. E. Bechhofer Roberts (1944) *The Trial of Harry Dobkin: Edited, with a Foreword and Note on Capital Punishment*, London: Jarrolds

Andy Beckett (2009) *When the Lights Went Out: What Really Happened to Britain in the Seventies*, London: Faber

Paul Begg (2006) *Jack the Ripper: The Facts*, London: Robson

Walter Benjamin (1999) *The Arcades Project*, Cambridge, MA: Harvard University Press

George L. Bernstein (2004) *The Myth of Decline: The Rise of Britain since 1945*, London: Pimlico

Christopher Berry-Dee (2015) *Love of Blood: The True Story of Notorious Serial Killer Joanne Dennehy*, London: John Blake

Patrick Bishop (2019) *The Man Who Was Saturday: The*

Extraordinary Life of Airey Neave – Soldier, Escaper, Spymaster, Politician, London: William Collins

George Blake (1934) *The Heart of Scotland*, London: B. T. Batsford

Ian Brady (2001) *The Gates of Janus: Serial Killing and Its Analysis by the 'Moors Murderer'*, Los Angeles: Feral House

John Brewer (2000) *Ethnography*, Milton Keynes: Open University Press

Fiona Brookman (2005) *Understanding Homicide*, London: Sage

Libby Brooks (2006) *The Story of Childhood: Growing Up in Modern Britain*, London: Bloomsbury

Becky Brown (2020) *Blitz Spirit: Voices of Britain Living Through Crisis, 1939–1945*, London: Hodder & Stoughton

Philip Brown and Richard Sparks (eds) (1989) *Beyond Thatcherism: Social Policy, Politics and Society*, Milton Keynes: The Open University

Martin Brunt (2023) *No One Got Cracked Over the Head for No Reason: Dispatches from a Crime Reporter*, London: Biteback

Rex Butler (ed.) (2017) *The Žižek Dictionary*, Durham: Acumen

Angus Calder (1991) *The Myth of the Blitz*, London: Jonathan Cape

Peter Calvocoressi (1978) *The British Experience, 1945–1975*, London: Penguin

David Canter (2005) *Mapping Murder: Walking in Killers' Footsteps*, London: Virgin

David Canter (2007) *Mapping Murder: The Secrets of Geographical Profiling*, London: Virgin

Rory Carroll (2023) *Killing Thatcher: The IRA, the Manhunt and the Long War on the Crown*, London: Mudlark

D. Chambers (2013) *Personal Relationships and Social Media*, Basingstoke: Palgrave Macmillan

Fred Cherrill (1954), *Fingerprints Never Lie: The Autobiography of Fred Cherrill*, London: Macmillan

Wensley Clarkson (2008) *Billy Hill: Godfather of London*, London: Pennant

Ian Cobain (2016) *The History Thieves: Secrets, Lies and the Making of a Modern State*, London: Portobello

Marianne Colbran (2014) *Media Representations of Police and Crime: Shaping the Police Television Drama*, London: Palgrave Macmillan

Mark Connelly (2005) *We Can Take It: Britain and the Memory of the Second World War*, London: Pearson

Patricia Cornwell (2002) *Portrait of a Killer: Jack the Ripper – Case Closed*, London: Little, Brown

Merlin Coverley (2006) *Psychogeography*, Harpenden: Oldcastle

Edward J. Cowan (2014) *For Freedom Alone: The Declaration of Arbroath*, Edinburgh: Birlinn

David Crouch, *Medieval Britain, c. 1000–1500*, Cambridge: Cambridge University Press

Shani D'Cruze, Sandra Walklate and Samantha Pegg (2006) *Murder: Social and Historical Approaches to Understanding Murder*, Cullompton: Willan

Roger Dalrymple (2020) *Crippen: A Crime Sensation in Memory and Modernity*, Woodbridge: Boydell

Martin Daly and Margo Wilson (1989) *Homicide: Foundations of Human Behaviour*, Piscataway: Aldine Transaction

Nick Davies (1997) *Dark Heart: The Shocking Truth About Hidden Britain*, London: Chatto & Windus

Nick Davies (2014) *Hack Attack: How the Truth Caught Up with Rupert Murdoch*, London: Chatto & Windus

T. M. Devine (2000/2012), *The Scottish Nation: A Modern History*, London: Penguin

T. M. Devine (2016) *Independence or Union: Scotland's Past and Scotland's Present*, London: Allen Lane

David Edgerton (2018) *The Rise and Fall of the British Nation: A Twentieth-Century History*, London: Allen Lane

Clive Emsley (1991) *The English Police*, Harlow: Addison Wesley Longman

Richard English (2004) *Armed Struggle: The History of the IRA*, London: Pan

Colin Evans (2007) *The Father of Forensics: The Groundbreaking Cases of Sir Bernard Spilsbury, and the Beginnings of Modern CSI*, Cambridge: Icon

Stewart Evans and Keith Skinner (2000) *The Ultimate Jack the Ripper Sourcebook*, London: Robinson

Steven Fielding, Bill Schwarz and Richard Toye (2020) *The Churchill Myths*, Oxford: Oxford University Press

Byrne Fone (2000) *Homophobia: A History*, New York: Metropolitan

James Alan Fox and Jack Levin (2005) *Extreme Killing: Understanding Serial and Mass Murder*, Thousand Oaks: Sage

Stephen Fulcher (2017) *Catching a Serial Killer: My Hunt for Murderer Christopher Halliwell*, London: Ebury

Frank Furedi (2001) *Paranoid Parenting: Abandon Your Anxieties and Become a Good Parent*, Harmondsworth: Penguin

Juliet Gardiner (2004) *Wartime Britain, 1939–1945*, London: Headline

Malcolm Gaskill (2022) *The Ruin of All Witches: Life and Death in the New World*, London: Allen Lane

Nicci Gerrard (2004) *Soham: A Story of Our Times*, London: Short Books

James Gilligan (2000) *Violence: Reflections on our Deadliest Epidemic*, London: Vintage

Ralph Glasser (1986) *Growing Up in the Gorbals*, London: Chatto & Windus

Ralph Glasser (1988) *Gorbals Boy at Oxford*, London: Chatto & Windus

Ralph Glasser (1991) *Gorbals Voices, Siren Songs*, London: Pan

A. C. Grayling (2021) *The Frontiers of Knowledge: What We Know About Science, History and the Mind*, London: Viking

David Green (2008) *When Children Kill: Penal Populism and Political Culture*, Oxford: Oxford University Press

B. D. Grew (1958) *Prison Governor*, London: Herbert Jenkins

Alison Halford (1993) *No Way up the Greasy Pole*, London: Constable

Steve Hall, Simon Winlow and Craig Ancrum (2008) *Criminal Identities and Consumer Culture: Crime,*

Exclusion and the New Culture of Narcissism,
Cullompton: Willan

Steve Hall (2012) *Theorizing Crime & Deviance: A New
Perspective,* London: Routledge

Steve Hall and Simon Winlow (2013) *Revitalizing
Criminological Theory: Towards a New Ultra-Realism,*
London: Routledge

Stuart Hall, Chas Critcher, Tony Jefferson, John Clarke and
Brian Roberts (1978) *Policing the Crisis: Mugging, The
State, and Law and Order,* London: Macmillan

Andrew Hankinson (2016) *You Could Do Something
Amazing with Your Life [You are Raoul Moat],* London:
Scribe

Clifford Hanley (1980) *The Scots,* London: Sphere

Luke Harding (2014) *The Snowden Files: The Inside Story of
the World's Most Wanted Man,* London: Vintage

Tom Harper (2022) *Broken Yard: The Fall of the
Metropolitan Police,* London: Biteback

Shirley Harrison (2010) *The Diary of Jack the Ripper: The
Chilling Confessions of James Maybrick,* London:
John Blake

Roy Hattersley (2004) *The Edwardians,* London:
Little, Brown

Roy Hattersley (2007) *Borrowed Time: The Story of Britain
Between the Wars,* London: Little, Brown

Frances Heidenson (1994) *Women and Crime,* Basingstoke:
Palgrave Macmillan

Richard Henriques (2020) *From Crime to Crime: Harold
Shipman to Operation Midland, 17 Cases that Shocked
the World,* London: Hodder & Stoughton

Billy Hill (1955) *Boss of Britain's Underworld*, London: Naldrett Press

James Hinton (2006) *Seven Lives from Mass Observation: Britain in the Late Twentieth Century*, Oxford: Oxford University Press

Alan R. Hurndall (2022) *The Crooked Spire Killings*, independently published

Ian Jack (1987) *Before the Oil Ran Out: Britain 1977–1987*, London: Secker & Warburg

Chris Jenks (1996) *Childhood*, London: Routledge

Yvonne Jewkes (2004) *Media & Crime*, London: Sage

Victor Pierce Jones (1988) *Saint or Sensationalist: The Story of W. T. Stead*, Chichester: Gooday

Michael Kammen (1972) *People of Paradox: An Inquiry Concerning the Origins of American Civilisation*, New York: Alfred A. Knopf

Jack Katz (1990) *Seductions of Crime: Moral and Sensual Attractions in Doing Evil*, New York: Basic Books

Stephen Kelly (2020) *Margaret Thatcher, the Conservative Party and the Northern Ireland Conflict, 1975–1990*, London: Bloomsbury

Michael Khan (2002) *Basic Freud: Psychoanalytic Thought for the Twenty First Century*, New York: Basic Books

Anne-Marie Kilday and David Nash (eds) (2010) *Histories of Crime: Britain 1600–2000*, Basingstoke: Palgrave Macmillan

Bernard Knight (2016) *Murder, Suicide or Accident: The Forensic Pathologist at Work*, London: Endeavour Press

Stephen Knight (2010) *Crime Fiction Since 1800: Detection, Death, Diversity*, London: Palgrave Macmillan

David Kynaston (2021) *On the Cusp: Days of '62*, London: Bloomsbury

John Lahr (1978) *Prick Up Your Ears: The Biography of Joe Orton*, London: Allen Lane

Julia Laite (2021) *The Disappearance of Lydia Harvey: A True Story of Sex, Crime and the Meaning of Justice*, London: Profile

Erik Larson (2020) *The Splendid and the Vile: Churchill, Family and Defiance During the Bombing of London*, London: William Collins

Paul Lashmar (2020) *Spies, Spin and the Fourth Estate*, Edinburgh: Edinburgh University Press

Molly Lefebure (1958) *Murder with a Difference: The Cases of Haigh and Christie*, London: Heinemann

Molly Lefebure (1959) *Evidence for the Crown: Experiences of a Pathologist's Secretary*, London: Heinemann

Penny Legg (2017) *Crime in the Second World War: Spivs, Scoundrels, Rogues and Worse*, London: Sabrestorm

Clare Leigh (2010) *Massacre in Cumbria: The Day Gunman Derrick Bird Brought Terror to the Lake District*, London: John Blake

Frank Leishman and Paul Mason (2003) *Policing and the Media: Facts, Fictions and Factions*, London: Routledge

Alison Liebling, Shadd Maruna and Lesley McAra (eds) (2017) *The Oxford Handbook of Criminology*, sixth edition, Oxford: Oxford University Press

Jack Lule (2001) *Daily News, Eternal Stories: The Mythological Role of Journalism*, New York: Guilford Press

Adam Lynes (2017) *The Road to Murder: Why Driving is the Occupation of Choice for Britain's Serial Killers*, Winchester: Waterside Press

Stuart McAnulla (2006) *British Politics: A Critical Introduction*, London: Continuum

Alexander McGregor (2022) *The Law Killers: True Crime from Dundee*, Edinburgh: Black & White

Sigurður Gylfi Magnusson and Istvan Szijarto (2013) *What Is Microhistory? Theory and Practice*, London: Routledge

Robert Mark (1978) *In the Office of Constable*, London: Collins

Andrew Marr (2009) *The Making of Modern Britain: From Queen Victoria to VE Day*, London: Macmillan

Diane Morgan (2004) *Lost Aberdeen: Aberdeen's Lost Architectural Heritage*, Edinburgh: Birlinn

Rod Morgan and Tim Newburn (1997) *The Future of Policing*, Oxford: Clarendon

Belinda Morrissey (2003) *When Women Kill: Questions of Agency and Subjectivity*, London: Routledge

Blake Morrison (1998) *As If*, Cambridge: Granta

H. V. Morton (1929) *In Search of Scotland*, London: Methuen

Harry Mount (2012) *How England Made the English*, London: Viking

J. F. Moylan (1929) *Scotland Yard and the Metropolitan Police*, London: G. P. Putnam's Sons

Edwin Muir (1935/1979) *Scottish Journey*, Edinburgh: Mainstream

Owen Mulpetre (2024) *W. T. Stead and the New Journalism:*

How a Northumbrian Maverick Transformed Nineteenth-Century British Journalism, n.p.: W. T. Stead Resource Site

Martin O'Brien and Majid Yar (2008) *Criminology: The Key Concepts*, London: Routledge

David O'Donoghue (2010) *The Devil's Deal: The IRA, Nazi Germany and the Double Life of Jim O'Donoghue*, Dublin: New Island Books

Maggie O'Neil and Lizzie Seal (2012) *Transgressive Imaginations: Crime, Deviance and Culture*, Basingstoke: Palgrave Macmillan

Mark Olden (2011) *Murder in Notting Hill*, Winchester: Zero Books

Leonie Orton (2016) *I Had it In Me*, Watlington: Quirky Press

George Orwell (1941) *The Lion and the Unicorn: Socialism and the English Genius*, London: Secker & Warburg

Jeremy Paxman (1998) *The English: A Portrait of a People*, London: Penguin

Geoffrey Pearson (1983) *Hooligan: A History of Respectable Fears*, London: Macmillan

Alison Plowden (1974) *The Case of Eliza Armstrong: A Child of 13 bought for £5*, London: BBC Books

Clive Ponting (1993) *1940: Myth and Reality*, Chicago: Ivan R. Dee

Neil Postman (1994) *The Disappearance of Childhood*, New York: Vintage

Adrian Raine (2013) *The Anatomy of Violence: The Biological Roots of Crime*, London: Allen Lane

Simon Read (2008) *The Blackout Murders: The Compelling True Story*, London: JR Books

Simon Read (2010) *Dark City: Murder, Vice and Mayhem in Wartime London*, Stroud: The History Press

Gareth E. Rees (2020) *Unofficial Britain: Journeys Through Unexpected Places*, London: Elliott & Thompson

Robert Reiner (1992) *The Politics of the Police*, Hemel Hempstead: Harvester Wheatsheaf

Nick Rennison (2022) *1922: Scenes from a Turbulent Year*, Harpenden: Oldcastle

Hallie Rubenhold (2019) *The Five: The Untold Lives of the Women Killed by Jack the Ripper*, London: Doubleday

Andrew Rutherford (1984) *Prisons and the Process of Justice: The Reductionist Challenge*, London: Heinemann

Dominic Sandbrook (2005) *Never Had It So Good: A History of Britain from Suez to the Beatles*, London: Little, Brown

Dominic Sandbrook (2006) *White Heat: A History of Britain in the Swinging Sixties*, London: Little, Brown

Dominic Sandbrook (2010) *State of Emergency: Britain, 1970–1974*, London: Allen Lane

Michael J. Sandel (2013) *What Money Can't Buy: The Moral Limits of Markets*, London: Penguin

Simon Schama (2002) *A History of Britain: The Fate of Empire, 1776–2000*, London: BBC Worldwide

Raymond Schultz (1972) *Crusader in Babylon: W. T. Stead and the Pall Mall Gazette*, Nebraska: University of Nebraska

Åsne Seierstad (2015) *One of Us: The Story of a Massacre and its Aftermath*, London: Virago

Gitta Sereny (1999) *Cries Unheard: The Story of Mary Bell*, London: Macmillan

Mary L. Shanley (1989) *Feminism, Marriage and the Law in Victorian England*, Princeton: Princeton University Press

James Sharpe (2016) *A Fiery & Furious People: A History of Violence in England*, London: Random House

Keith Simpson (1978) *Forty Years of Murder*, London: Harrap

Neil J. Smelser (2007) *The Faces of Terrorism: Social and Psychological Dimensions*, Princeton: Princeton University Press

Robert Smith (1989) *The Granite City: A History of Aberdeen*, Edinburgh: John Donald

T. C. Smout (1986) *A Century of the Scottish People, 1830–1950*, Glasgow: William Collins & Son

A. J. P. Taylor (1965) *English History, 1914–1945*, Oxford: Oxford University Press

E. P. Thompson (1980) *Writing by Candlelight*, London: Merlin

Laura Thompson (2007) *Agatha Christie: A Mysterious Life*, London: Headline

Laura Thompson (2018) *Rex v Edith Thompson: A Tale of Two Murders*, London: Head of Zeus

Alex S. Vitale (2017), *The End of Policing*, London: Verso

Judith R. Walkowitz (1994) *City of Dreadful Delight: Narratives of Sexual Danger in Late Victorian England*, London: Virago

E. R. Watson (1922) *The Trial of George Joseph Smith*, London: William Hodge & Co.

René Weis (1988) *Criminal Justice: The True Story of Edith Thompson*, London: Hamish Hamilton

Colin Wilson (2012) *Dreaming to Some Purpose,*
London: Arrow

David Wilson and John Ashton (2001) *What Everyone in Britain Should Know About Crime & Punishment,*
Oxford: Oxford University Press

David Wilson, John Ashton and Douglas Sharp (2002) *What Everyone in Britain Should Know About the Police,*
Oxford: Oxford University Press

David Wilson (2007) *Looking for Laura: Public Criminology and Hot News,* Winchester: Waterside Press

David Wilson (2009) *A History of British Serial Killing,*
London: Sphere

David Wilson (2013) *Mary Ann Cotton: Britain's First Female Serial Killer,* Winchester: Waterside Press

David Wilson (2014) *Pain and Retribution: A Short History of British Prisons, 1066 to the Present,* London:
Reaktion

David Wilson (2021) *A Plot to Kill,* London: Sphere

John G. Wilson (ed.) (1953) *The Trial of Jeannie Donald* (Notable British Trials), London: William Hodge & Co.

Simon Winlow (2003) *Badfellas: Crime, Tradition and New Masculinities,* Oxford: Berg

Tom Wood (2020) *Ruxton: The First Modern Murder,*
Glasgow: Ringwood

Lucy Worsley (2022) *Agatha Christie: A Very Elusive Woman,* London: Hodder & Stoughton

Fenton Wyness (1965) *City by the Grey North Sea: Aberdeen,*
Aberdeen: Alex P. Reid & Son

Fenton Wyness (1971) *Aberdeen: Century of Change,*
Aberdeen: Impulse Books

Ray Wyre and Tim Tate (1995) *The Murder of Childhood: Inside the Mind of One of Britain's Most Notorious Child Murderers*, Harmondsworth: Penguin

Elizabeth Yardley (2017) *Social Media Homicide Confessions: Stories of Killers and Their Victims*, Bristol: Policy Press

Hugo Young (1989) *One of Us*, London: Macmillan

Acknowledgements

I would like to thank the following people who were interviewed during the research and writing of the book, and who'd often suggest looking at issues that I hadn't previously considered: Alan Hurndall, Bas Javid, Sam Lundrigan, Diarmid Mogg, Laura Thompson, Isla Traquair and John Treanor. In that context I would also like to thank Dr Sarah Pemberton, who accompanied me on one of my research trips to Whitehaven in Cumbria. At Birmingham City University (BCU) the following colleagues kindly discussed with me issues at the heart of the book, and I should also acknowledge that I have often borrowed from our written work: Professors Michael Brookes and Elizabeth Yardley; Drs Liam Brolan and Dan Rusu. Michael also read an early draft of the book and commented on it, as did Dr Peter Bennett. In the wider academy I would like to thank Professors Steve Hall and Simon Winlow, who both also read early drafts, and I am happy to acknowledge my ongoing debt to their own work.

At Sphere my thanks, as ever, to Kirsteen Astor and Zoe Gullen, and special mention has to go to Tig Wallace with whom I'm working for the very first time – it has been a wonderful experience, and we have to do it again. It's always a pleasure to work with Antonia Hodgson and this book reminded me of old times when she sat me down for the very first time to discuss how to write true crime as opposed to academic criminology. The book has benefited enormously from her insight and experience.

At Curtis Brown my thanks, as always, to Jacquie Drewe and Gordon Wise – how many books have we now worked on together? – and I hope that you enjoy the references to Aberdeen. A number of discussions about cases at the heart of the book also took place with colleagues at Alaska during the filming of Channel 4's *In the Footsteps of Killers* and especially with Louis Bennett, Sam Dean, Graham Hill, Emilia Fox, Melissa Mayne and Paul Sommers, and I benefited from those talks particularly with regard to matters surrounding the murder of Rita Ellis. I also co-presented the podcast *If it Bleeds, It Leads* with Emilia and several people who appeared on the podcast helped me to think about issues raised within the text, especially Professor Julia Laite. A number of the other cases featured began life as lectures to students at BCU – particularly about the circumstances surrounding the murders of James Bulger and Jimmy Mizen, which are both cornerstones of my survey course – and I would like to thank successive generations of students who have continued to shape my thinking about these matters. The staff and librarians of Cambridge University Library were unfailingly helpful to me during my various research trips.

It's rarely mentioned that I started my academic life as a historian – my journey into criminology stemmed from an incident at university on the rugby pitch (but that's another story) – and the late, great Professor William R. Brock, FBA, who died in 2014, guided my historical studies from my days as a callow undergraduate all the way through to supervising my doctoral thesis at Cambridge. I owe a great debt to William and a photograph of him smiling down at me sits on my bookcase reminding me of these formative years. It has taken too long to acknowledge publicly that personal and professional debt.

This book is, as ever, written with the support and love of my family and friends. It's always a delight to thank Anne, Hugo & Suzi and Fleur & Ollie – and now our two grandchildren Cillian and Ronan. Over the years they've had to listen to countless accounts about the worst of humanity which, I suppose, family – however grudgingly – has to indulge. However, I'm always amazed and very grateful that so many of my friends are willing to allow me to bang on about violent crime and murder which, if I am honest, is really a way that helps me to process so much of that darkness. The book is dedicated to four such special friends or, as I prefer to call them, 'chosen family'.

Notes

Introduction

1. Gerrard, *Soham*. All quotes are taken from the book.
2. The term 'ideal victim' was first coined by the Norwegian criminologist Nils Christie. Put simply, an ideal victim is one who generates the most sympathy from society because they're perceived as having the 'legitimate status' of being a victim. A 'little old lady' being mugged, or a child who is killed, will be seen to have legitimate victim status, which will be denied to, for example, a drug dealer or a sex worker who might have been murdered. The story of murder more broadly has been told through these ideal victims, rather than those who are murdered on a more regular basis.
3. If this was intended as a criminology book I would, at this stage in the narrative, spend the next few pages defining what is meant by 'murder', and how that definition is, for example, different from what we call 'manslaughter'. I might then consider how 'homicide' relates to murder. I'd describe *mens rea* – a 'guilty mind' – and how the various definitions that we use capture only some of the cases where a person comes to be killed. I would then go on to discuss state-sanctioned murders, such as when someone in the armed forces kills another person, when the state itself takes lives, or the numbers of people who die as a result of industrial accidents, pollution, global warming and so forth. These are all important issues, but they're not the focus of this book. Those wishing to read about murder in this more criminological context should consult Fiona Brookman, *Understanding Homicide*. However, just for ease of reference, murder is the unlawful killing

371

of a human being by another human accompanied by the legally required state of mind – the *mens rea*, or as it is sometimes termed, 'malice aforethought'.

4. For a general introduction to micro-history see Sigurður Gylfi Magnusson and Istvan Szijarto, *What Is Microhistory? Theory and Practice*, and John Brewer, 'Microhistory and the Histories of Everyday Life', *Cultural and Social History*, 7:1 (2010), pp. 87–109. 'Microhistory' is also sometimes spelled as 'micro-history' – the form I prefer.

5. Gaskill, *The Ruin of All Witches*, p. 234.

6. Jack, 'Finished With Engines', in *Before the Oil Ran Out*, p. 2.

7. The obvious example here is the use made of Sir Winston Churchill, who, more than anything that he did in his lifetime, has now become a site around which memories can 'accumulate to create a publicly sanctioned platform for understanding'. See Fielding, Schwarz and Toye, *The Churchill Myths*, p. 1. On the other hand, as I conducted my research in various libraries, I became acutely aware that I was often the first person to borrow the book that I was consulting about a historical figure from the period I was interested in. This struck me as odd and surprising. Books are commercial enterprises – the author must convince the publisher that there's a market for their work and that readers will buy a copy. That does at least suggest that the author and their material have something about them that is worthy of historical scrutiny. However, time after time, I would appear to have been the very first person to have read – or at least to have borrowed – the book. The characters being written about were historical 'winners' – after all, they had books being written by or about them – but no one seemed to care. It got to the stage that the staff at Cambridge University Library would joke with me as they slipped a formal 'checked' slip into the book's inside cover, 'So who is this that you're reading about now that no one has ever heard of?'

8. David Olusoga, 'Another Voice', *New Statesman*, December 2021, p. 51.

9. Rubenhold, *The Five*.

10. I benefited here from reading Graham Baxendale's unpublished PhD thesis, 'The Discursive Production of Homosexual Regulation', University of Southampton, 2013.

11. Grayling, *The Frontiers of Knowledge*.

12. Cobain, *The History Thieves*. The secrecy of the British state was something which was picked up on by an earlier generation of writers – see, for example, Peter Calvocoressi, *The British Experience, 1945–1975*. Calvocoressi was in a good position to judge this secrecy as he had worked as an intelligence officer at Bletchley Park during the Second World War. From a rather different political tradition, in 1980 the Marxist historian E. P. Thompson observed in his collection of essays called *Writing by Candlelight* that 'British security operations are distinguished by their invisibility and their lack of accountability.' For my generation of young historians, Thompson played the role that Slavoj Žižek plays for many younger academics today. Not quite as 'rock 'n' roll' as Žižek, Thompson nonetheless was a significant figure in the New Left, and then the Campaign for Nuclear Disarmament. His 1963 book, *The Making of the English Working Class*, remains for me insightful and inspirational. It might also be described as a work of micro-history, as Thompson set out to 'rescue the poor stockinger, the Luddite cropper, the "obsolete" hand-loom weaver, the "utopian" artisan, and even the deluded followers of Joanna Southcott, from the enormous condescension of posterity'. I confess that I still greatly admire the phrase 'the enormous condescension of posterity'. Thompson died in 1993.

13. See my *A Plot to Kill*, for example, an account of the murder of Peter Farquhar, a retired English teacher and lecturer in Buckingham. In conducting research for that book I attempted to navigate the various quasi-legal procedures that exist so as to read the account of the coroner's inquiry into Peter's death. This is a public document. However, I failed – a failure which seemed to me to have more to do with protecting and upholding the coroner's system that had viewed Peter's death as one stemming from natural causes, rather than as a murder. I've also joked that it is easier for me to enter Putin's prisons in Russia than it is to get access to jails in Britain.

14. Allport, *Britain at Bay*, p. 4.

15. George Orwell – and see below – would famously see the 'decline of the English murder' as being caused by the 'Americanisation' of English (by which he meant British) life and culture as a result of the war. As much as I admire Orwell, this is of course total nonsense. Geoffrey Pearson's *Hooligan: A History of Respectable Fears* is a very useful, if now dated way of putting this 'othering'

into a more historical perspective. Pearson describes it as a 'myth' that the 'British way of life' has been founded on stability and decency, and shows how various 'foreign' groups, or influences, came to be seen as the cause of British troubles. One useful, more recent, corrective to the trope that we love the rule of law and are peaceable is James Sharpe, *A Fiery & Furious People: A History of Violence in England*. Sharpe uses 'England' here in the accepted sense – in other words, he is not discussing Scotland, Northern Ireland or Wales.

16. See Lule, *Daily News, Eternal Stories*.

17. This section follows the arguments contained in Edgerton, *The Rise and Fall of the British Nation*.

18. I am again thinking of George Orwell, *The Lion and the Unicorn: Socialism and the English Genius*. Orwell debates at some length, and not always successfully, whether or not 'England' can be used interchangeably with 'Britain' and therefore justify the title of his book. He also – again I think incorrectly – suggests that 'the gentleness of the English civilization is perhaps its most marked characteristic'. Of course, he was writing this when Britain was at war with Hitler's Germany, and that simple reality must have had an impact on his judgement. Even so, as David Edgerton has been at pains to point out, Britain during the twentieth century was much more characterised by warfare than welfare. A small measure of support for Orwell's wartime England/Britain debate comes in the unlikely shape of architectural expert Harry Mount. In *How England made the English*, Mount notes: 'Most British troops fighting on the Continent came from our industrial towns and cities, but the propaganda link identifying England with rural England – and the patriotic images do tend to be English, rather than British – still went unquestioned.'

Chapter One

1. 'The Whitechapel Murders' is the name of the police files for the sequence of murders that took place there between 3–4 April 1888, when Emma Smith was murdered, and 13 February 1891, when Frances Coles was killed. The murders committed by, or attributed to, Jack the Ripper are therefore only a subset of the Whitechapel Murders. I prefer to use this title as it allows for a consideration of other women who were killed, and not just the

so-called 'canonical five': Mary Ann Nichols, Annie Chapman, Elizabeth Stride, Catherine Eddowes and Mary Jane Kelly.

2. This claim was made during her lifetime in *One of Us*, a biography written by Hugo Young, where it is suggested that Mrs Thatcher believed that no one but her cared about the fate of these 'wretched women'. Young's story wasn't refuted at the time of the book's publication, or later, and we can therefore infer its veracity. Sutcliffe's crimes, and the failure of the police to catch him, were dramatised in the ITV series *The Long Shadow* (dir. Lewis Arnold) in 2023 and the series was based on the true crime account by Michael Bilton, *Wicked Beyond Belief: The Hunt for the Yorkshire Ripper* (London: HarperCollins, 2003). The television series laid bare the sexism of West Yorkshire Police at the time and the misogyny more broadly that created the context for Sutcliffe to get away with murder.

3. Rubenhold, *The Five*, p. 16.

4. 'Jack the Ripper Tour with "Ripper-Vision" in London', TripAdvisor, as of December 2021.

5. See Baxendale, 'The Discursive Production of Homosexual Regulation'. An amendment to the Act by Henry Labouchere would also become a basis on which to prosecute Oscar Wilde in 1895 on twenty-five counts of gross indecency, and therefore the Act – even if the Labouchere Amendment was not central to its main provisions – made it clear that male same-sexual activity had no legitimate space either in public or in private. This state of affairs would continue until 1967 and helped to create the context in which many gay men were murdered.

6. For a good starting point for all matters related to W. T. Stead, there is an online resource centre at www.attackingthedevil. co.uk, which was launched by Owen Mulpetre in 2001. Much of the material reproduced comes from original sources, and the full text of 'The Maiden Tribute of Modern Babylon' can be found on the site. Mulpetre graduated with a master's from the University of Teesside in 2010 – his dissertation was 'W. T. Stead and the New Journalism'. All quotes used in this section are taken either from Mulpetre's website, or his thesis, which was published as an ebook in 2024. Mulpetre's thesis is mostly concerned with Stead's journalistic style and how it is – or is not – 'new journalism', although he does also offer a number of biographical details about Stead. These are to be welcomed for there are still relatively

few secondary works about Stead's life, although those who are
interested might find Raymond Schultz, *Crusader in Babylon: W.
T. Stead and the Pall Mall Gazette*, Victor Pierce Jones, *Saint or
Sensationalist: The Story of W. T. Stead* and Judith R. Walkowitz,
*City of Dreadful Delight: Narratives of Sexual Danger in Late
Victorian England* of use. Walkowitz is particularly critical of
Stead and suggests that he was voyeuristic and melodramatic.

7. A fading memorial still exists on the wall of the house where he
    was born, but on a visit in the autumn of 2022 no one seemed to
    know much about Stead and frankly seemed surprised that I was
    even asking.

8. I have written about Mary Ann Cotton in a number of places.
    See, in particular, *Mary Ann Cotton: Britain's First Female Serial
    Killer.* This book became the basis for the 2016 ITV series *Dark
    Angel*, starring Joanne Froggatt as Cotton. Cotton killed by
    using arsenic to poison her victims, and so it is difficult to be
    precise about the numbers of people she may have killed, as the
    arsenic would mimic the symptoms of other Victorian ailments.
    Estimates of Cotton's 'body count' have been as low as four and
    as high as twenty-five. In my own research I've suggested that she
    killed seventeen people, including her mother, various children
    and stepchildren, several lovers, two husbands and a female
    friend. Whatever the number – and seventeen seems most likely –
    she was a prolific serial killer.

9. Mulpetre, *W. T. Stead and the New Journalism*, p. 34.

10. Laite, *The Disappearance of Lydia Harvey*, p. 118. Lydia Harvey
    was a sixteen-year-old girl from New Zealand who in 1910, after
    a stint in Buenos Aires, was found selling sexual services on the
    streets of London. Lydia's story is unusual only in that those who
    had trafficked her were caught and tried at the Old Bailey, and
    Lydia herself returned home to New Zealand. The geographical
    background to this compelling story brings to life the more
    academic points made by David Edgerton (see Introduction, notes
    17 and 18) about Britain being international and cosmopolitan in
    late Victorian and Edwardian times.

11. W. T. Stead's closing statement, quoted in Plowden, *The Case of
    Eliza Armstrong.*

12. For example, it has been said that O'Connor had one of his
    journalists write a series of letters purporting to be from the
    murderer, and that it was they who had even coined the name

'Jack the Ripper'. This claim is well covered in Paul Begg, *Jack the Ripper: The Facts*, pp. 203–16. It has also been asserted that most of the Ripper letters were written by the artist Walter Sickert – see Patricia Cornwell, *Portrait of a Killer: Jack the Ripper – Case Closed*. Typical of the new journalism, the *Star*'s coverage of the murders was graphic and pulled no punches. However, the paper also attacked Sir Charles Warren, the Commissioner of the Metropolitan Police, for the 'outrages committed on the citizens of London', and 'the autumn of terror' in Whitechapel. The *Star* saw itself as the voice of the downcast and never missed an opportunity to attack government policies.

13. So badly did West Yorkshire Police handle the investigation into the murders committed by Peter Sutcliffe – who was interviewed eleven times by the police but never arrested – that Sir Lawrence Byford, HM Chief Inspector of Constabulary, was asked to investigate their handling of the investigation. Byford presented his report to the House of Commons in 1982, but it was so damning that successive governments suppressed its contents until 2006. HOLMES was introduced as a result of the Byford Report in 1985.

14. The College of Policing states that the SIO – who will usually have the rank of at least detective chief inspector – manages 'the investigative response, and all resources associated with the investigation. They develop and implement strategies, procedures and systems that underpin the investigation and ensure the management and assessment of threat, risk and harm.' ('Police Professional Profile: Senior Investigator – Serious and Organised Crime (PIP3)').

15. *Jack the Ripper – The Case Reopened*, BBC 1, 4 April 2019. In this documentary Professor Sam Lundrigan of Anglia Ruskin University geoprofiled the murder locations, starting with where Martha Tabram was murdered. She concluded that Sion Square was one of two 'hot-spots' where the killer was likely to have lived.

16. Harrison, *The Diary of Jack the Ripper*. I have cited most of the other books related to this section of the chapter within the text. For those who are new to this subject area, Paul Begg, *Jack the Ripper: The Facts*, and Stewart Evans and Keith Skinner, *The Ultimate Jack the Ripper Sourcebook*, are two good starting points.

17. I am thinking here of 'Wearside Jack' – the nickname given to John Humble, who pretended to be the Yorkshire Ripper in

several letters and an audio recording that he sent to the police between 1978 and 1979. Humble was eventually uncovered in 2006 through DNA evidence found on the envelope of one of the letters and sentenced to eight years in prison for perverting the course of justice. He died in 2019.

18. See Canter, *Mapping Murder: Walking in Killers' Footsteps*. This excellent popular book is a good way in to understand the science of what is now known as 'geographical profiling' – often shortened to 'geoprofiling'. As Canter explains, geoprofiling is 'the use of crime locations to understand the offender and propose where he might be living ... the secret of geographical profiling is to go beyond the dots on the map to understand the significance of the places the offender is choosing, and the meaning to him of the journey he is making' (pp. 8–9). Canter, the first of the generation of British profilers, who unlike most of their American counterparts were trained and worked in academia, also geoprofiled the crimes of Jack the Ripper, although he didn't include the murder of Martha Tabram. He noted that the pattern of the murders reflected within the canonical five suggested that the killer lived 'somewhere a little north of where Commercial Road meets Mitre Square' (p. 131).

19. See Begg, *Jack the Ripper*.

20. I am thinking here of the five murders committed in Ipswich between 30 October and 10 December 2006: Tania Nicol, Gemma Adams, Anneli Alderton, Annette Nicholls and Paula Clennell. All of the women were street sex workers, and each of them was addicted to Class A drugs. A local man, Steve Wright, was arrested on 19 December 2006 and convicted of their murder in February 2008. He is serving a whole life tariff. In June 2024 Wright was charged with the 1999 murder of a schoolgirl called Victoria Hall – his trial is due to start in 2026.

Chapter Two

1. See Saul Dubow, 'Britain's Imperial History Deserves Better than Petty Culture Wars', *Guardian*, 13 August 2021.

2. This portrait of Clifford has been built up using a variety of online sources and, in particular, Lizzie Seal and Alexa Neale, 'Race, Gender and Bourgeois Respectability: The Execution of Percy Clifford, 1914', *Irish Jurist*, 60 (2018), pp. 144–53.

3. Laite, *The Disappearance of Lydia Harvey*, p. 149.

4. Ibid., pp. 124–9.
5. A good starting point to understand coverture and the legal position of women in Victorian culture more generally is Mary L. Shanley, *Feminism, Marriage and the Law in Victorian England*. I have relied on Shanley's conclusion.
6. The trial papers are collected in Watson, *The Trial of George Joseph Smith*.
7. Dalrymple, *Crippen*, p. 109.
8. Evans, *The Father of Forensics*, p. 5.
9. See Hattersley, *The Edwardians*, pp. 416–17.
10. Reported in Robert Booth, 'UK More Nostalgic for Empire than other Ex-Colonial Powers', *Guardian*, 11 March 2020.
11. Rohan Deb Roy, 'Decolonise Science – Time to End Another Imperial Era', *The Conversation*, 5 April 2018.
12. 'All UK "Must Be on DNA Database"', BBC News, 5 September 2007.
13. Human Genetics Commission, 'Nothing to Hide, Nothing to Fear? Balancing Individual Rights and the Public Interest in the Governance and Use of the National DNA Database', November 2009.
14. Aaron Opoku Amankwaa and Carole McCartney, 'The Effectiveness of the UK National DNA Database', *Forensic Science International: Synergy*, 1 (2019), pp. 45–55.

Chapter Three

1. Knight, *Crime Fiction Since 1800*.
2. An entire episode of Radio 4's iconic *Woman's Hour* was devoted to 'True Crime: Five Reasons Why Women Love It': www.bbc.co.uk/programmes/articles/5BQCFMQd3mPqj7YT4hlvdCL/true-crime-five-reasons-why-women-love-it. These five reasons were: fear of crime; compassion for victims; a fascination with motives; true crime provides puzzles to work out; and, finally, escapism. The idea that true crime provides puzzles to work out takes us back to the sorts of murder mysteries written by Christie and others. However, what's perhaps more interesting about these five reasons is how they could be applied to men as much as to women. This gender disproportionality I've described can be explained in more evolutionary psychological terms. After all, it is usually women who have to manage the violence of men, and therefore understanding when and in what circumstances

men will be violent was probably an adaptive survival strategy for many women. In other words, the roots of their interest in crime fiction and true crime go deep and transcend whatever current fashions and preoccupations dominate a particular zeitgeist.

3. 'Crime (and Thrills) Pay in the UK Book Market', Neilsen Book Data, 20 October 2023.

4. See 'Who is Tommy? Where Does the Term "Tommy" Come From?', Royal British Legion, www.rbli.co.uk/wp-content/uploads/2021/07/Tommy-10k-Who-is-Tommy-A5.pdf.

5. Worsley, *Agatha Christie*, p. 98.

6. This account is drawn from edithjessiethompson.com, a website maintained by the Shakespearean scholar René Weis. For anyone interested in the case, the website is a 'one-stop shop' of materials, including all of the surviving letters that Edith wrote to Freddy Bywaters. It has almost obsessive levels of detail – including photographs and street plans – of everything that one might want to know in relation to Percy's murder. Weis has also written about the case, in *Criminal Justice: The True Story of Edith Thompson*.

7. Thompson, *Rex v Edith Thompson*, p. 50. Laura Thompson – no relation to Edith Thompson – also spoke about her book on the podcast *Most Notorious!* which was broadcast on 3 January 2020.

8. Ibid., p. 250.

9. In an unproduced screenplay called *One Little Hour*, written by Rene Weis (see note 5, and below) and Philip Horne, colleagues at University College London, Percy is described in the script as 'stolid and awkward, unauthentic and self-conscious; he couldn't dance', while Bywaters is a 'striking figure, only of medium height, but broad-shouldered, muscular and self-assured'. *One Little Hour* is reproduced on edithjessiethompson.com.

10. Thompson, *Rex v Edith Thompson*, p. 365.

11. A good example here is the case of the murder of Peter Farquhar by his former student Ben Field in Buckingham in 2015. At Field's trial the prosecution submitted several written texts, including emails exchanged between the pair. Of particular note were six poems that Field had written called 'Truest Jest', and which he'd presented to Peter after the pair had gone through a betrothal ceremony. These poems were cruel, abusive and hurtful about Peter, and also seemed to threaten him, although in the witness stand at Oxford Crown Court Field claimed that they were simply preparations for 'rap battles'. The poems included lines such as:

'there's nothing in your future when I do you', and 'the hospitality I'll give him's a hospital visit', both of which implied that Field was going to hurt Peter, with the first suggesting that he was going to kill his partner. Field would ultimately be found guilty of murder. For further information about their exchanges see Wilson, *A Plot to Kill*, pp. 130–3.

12. See, for example, D. Wilson, E. Yardley and S. Pemberton, 'The "Dunblane Massacre" as a "Photosensitive Plate"', *Crime, Media, Culture*, 13:1 (2016), pp. 55–68. This article analysed the letters written by Thomas Hamilton to various groups, organisations and individuals – including Queen Elizabeth II – prior to his commission of mass murder.

13. For a general introduction to psychological autopsies, see C. Bartol and A. Bartol, *Introduction to Forensic Psychology*.

14. Quoted in Benjamin, *The Arcades Project*, p. 482.

15. Yardley, *Social Media Homicide Confessions*, p. 27.

16. See, in particular, Baym, *Personal Connections in the Digital Age*, and Chambers, *Personal Relationships and Social Media*.

17. E. Yardley and D. Wilson, 'Making Sense of "Facebook Murder"? Social Networking Sites and Contemporary Homicide', *Howard Journal of Criminal Justice*, 54:2 (May 2015), pp. 109–34.

18. Thompson, *Rex v Edith Thompson*, p. 164.

19. My thinking here has been shaped by the writing and speeches of the historian John Taylor. See, in particular, a chapter in a Russian book published in 2024, *Agatha Christie's Novel 'The Secret Adversary' and Britain's Twentieth-Century Decline*, https://www.elibrary.ru/item.asp?id=65064450. Taylor had delivered a speech on this same subject to the British Book Centre in St Petersburg, Russia on 11 November 2018, entitled 'The Secret Adversary'.

Chapter Four

1. Diarmid Mogg, 'Crime Scene Aberdeen', Medium, 21 December 2017.

2. Hattersley, *Borrowed Time*, p. 174.

3. Edgerton, *The Rise and Fall of the British Nation*, notes that by the 1930s there were 'hundreds of thousands of unemployed miners' (p. 85).

4. Ibid., p. 232, for example, produces a very interesting table outlining how central government expenditure increased between 1920 and 1938 on financing old age pensions (OAP), contributory

pensions, unemployment benefit and health insurance. Spending on OAP, for example, increased from £19.3 million in 1920 to just over £40 million by 1938.

5. Twelve leaders of the Communist Party were arrested in October 1925, just prior to the General Strike, and imprisoned for between six and twelve months. Edgerton, *The Rise and Fall of the British Nation*, pp. 161–4 has a very interesting account of 'Anglo-Marxism' during this period.

6. See, for example, A. J. P. Taylor, *English History, 1914–1945*. Taylor noted that before the outbreak of the First World War, a 'sensible, law-abiding Englishman could pass through life and hardly notice the existence of the state' (p. 25), but this would change as a consequence of the war and developments throughout the 1920s and 1930s that saw the state taking on a bigger role in people's lives.

7. I rather liked the way that Simon Schama, in *A History of Britain: The Fate of Empire, 1776–2000*, compares the rustic sentimentalism of the journalist H. V. Morton travelling around in his motor car in *In Search of England* – published in 1927 – with the observations that George Orwell would make in *The Road to Wigan Pier* published ten years later. Orwell and Morton both wanted to capture something about England (in this case, although Morton would also write about Scotland) but come to very different conclusions about what they observe.

8. Circulation figures taken from Wilson, *A History of British Serial Killing*, p. 91.

9. I have written about *Brighton Rock* in *A Plot to Kill*, pp. 221–6. Note how the teenager – a recurring source of fear in our post-war culture – is successfully used by Greene before 1939 to suggest uncontrollable danger.

10. I have discussed these questions previously in *A History of British Serial Killing*, pp. 84–110.

11. Joe Hicks and Grahame Allen, *A Century of Change: Trends in UK Statistics since 1900*, Research Paper 99/111, House of Commons Library, 21 December 1999.

12. Moylan, *Scotland Yard and the Metropolitan Police*, p. 176.

13. Howard Taylor, 'Rationing Crime: The Political Economy of Criminal Statistics since the 1850s', *Economic History Review*, 51:3 (1998), pp. 569–90. The disparity of active serial killers between Germany and the UK has been described in Phillip Jenkins, 'Serial

Murder in England, 1940–1985', *Journal of Criminal Justice*, 16 (1988), pp. 1–15.

14. Marr, *The Making of Modern Britain*, p. 310.

15. Clifford Hanley in *The Scots* describes them as 'never monolithic like the Bolsheviks' and that their socialism 'brought together an electrifying variety of opinions and intellects, maybe unique in political history' (pp. 221–2). Hanley also argues that Scotland can be best summed up by 'small inconsequentialities – the day-to-day trivia mean as much as the great sweeps of history' (p. 260) – a conclusion not out of place with micro-history.

16. Devine, *The Scottish Nation*, pp. 316–17. As for daily sales of newspapers, the circulation of the Dundee-based *Sunday Post*, founded in 1914, was once so high that by the late 1960s it had the highest per capita readership in the world, with an estimated 2.9 million readers – more than 80 per cent of the total population of Scotland over the age of sixteen.

17. Marr, *The Making of Modern Britain*, p. 311.

18. Figures taken from Smout, *A Century of the Scottish People, 1830–1950*, pp. 85–114.

19. Devine, *The Scottish Nation*, p. 269.

20. Smout, *A Century of the Scottish People, 1830–1950*, p. 33.

21. de Beauvoir, *Force of Circumstance*, p. 248.

22. Blake, *The Heart of Scotland*, p. 49.

23. For those interested in a very readable introduction to murder in Dundee, see Alexander McGregor, *The Law Killers: True Crime from Dundee*.

24. See Morgan, *Lost Aberdeen*.

25. Wyness, *City by the Grey North Sea*. See also Wyness, *Aberdeen*, and Smith, *The Granite City*.

26. See 'On the Artistry of Architecture', Claire's Travels Through Architecture, 14 February 2016, www.builtadventures.wordpress.com/2016/02/14/on-the-artistry-of-architecture/.

27. Wyness, *City by the Grey North Sea*, p. 1.

28. Muir, *Scottish Journey*, p. 158.

29. Blake, *The Heart of Scotland*, p. 52.

30. Morton, *In Search of Scotland*, p. 150.

31. This account of the murder is built from Wilson (ed.), *The Trial of Jeannie Donald*; various newspaper accounts, including Reg McKay, 'Bad Blood and the Vile Death of Little Helen', *Daily Record*, 19 October 2007; Mogg, 'Crime Scene Aberdeen';

and several descriptions about the case on the website www.
murderpedia.org.

32. I am presuming that this term was being used in a way that was
different in the 1930s and in Scotland to how it would be used
today when it is now intended as a racial slur.

33. For a general introduction see Erin Blakemore, 'FBI Admits
Pseudoscientific Hair Analysis Used in Hundreds of Cases',
Smithsonian Magazine, 22 April 2015; 'Hair Analysis – Science or
Objective Opinion?' CaseGuard, 13 May 2020.

34. Wilson (ed.), *The Trial of Jeannie Donald*, p. 45.

35. 'Murder By Mistake? Helen Priestly and Jeannie Donald',
Wattpad.com on www.murderpedia.org.

36. Glasser, *Growing Up in the Gorbals, Gorbals Boy at Oxford* and
Gorbals Voices, Siren Songs. I used an omnibus edition of all
three books, *Growing Up in the Gorbals*, published in 2006 by
Black & White Publishing Ltd, and subsequent quotes are taken
from that edition. See also Frank Kermode's review of *Gorbals
Boy at Oxford* in the *London Review of Books*, 10:11, 2 June 1988.
I searched in vain for a contemporary account of tenement
life in Aberdeen in the 1930s, although I think that it's safe to
generalise from Glasser about what conditions were like at the
time. Glasser – who died in 2002 – worked for the British Council
after 1945 and is one of those Scots whose work deserves to be
much better known. I particularly enjoyed his insight about
life at Oxford, which he 'romantically' imagined was going to
be 'sweetness and light' after his life in Glasgow. Not a bit of it,
for 'behind the shallow refinement it could be as ferocious as
the Gorbals, and in some ways more so, for the Gorbals did not
pretend to be other than it was!'

37. Quotations taken from *Growing up in the Gorbals*, pp. 19–20, 68
and 139.

Chapter Five

1. I'm applying the idea of there being a national origin myth in a
common sense, rather than in a theoretical way. For those who
might want to pursue this more analytically the best starting
point remains Roland Barthes, *Mythologies*. Barthes sees a myth
as a fixed system of signs which perform a symbolic function
for a society, and which are essentially depoliticised. However,
we could equally argue that a myth is malleable and contingent,

and therefore constantly reacting to events, stresses and tensions within society. In that way myths *are* political. These two understandings don't have to be mutually exclusive but that's an issue for another day – see Steven Fielding, Bill Schwarz and Richard Toye, *The Churchill Myths.*

2. Lina Mann, 'The Enslaved Household of President Thomas Jefferson', The White House Historical Association, 20 November 2019. I first became interested in this paradox while still an undergraduate and read the Pulitzer Prize-winning book by the late American historian Michael Kammen, *People of Paradox: An Inquiry Concerning the Origins of American Civilisation.* Kammen described how 'The myth of the melting pot is precisely that: a myth' and how 'guilt and insecurity have played a major part in keeping contradictory tendencies inherent in our style. First we wiped out the Indians whose land it was; then we emasculated the Africans brought to work the land. Few cultures in history have had to bear this kind of double collective culpability' (p. 293).

3. The Scotland team sings 'Flower of Scotland' before every rugby or football international, after the song was adopted as the national anthem for those sports. Written in the 1960s by Roy Williamson of the folk group The Corries, it contains the lines 'O flower of Scotland, when will we see your like again, that fought and died for your wee bit hill and glen, and stood against him, proud Edward's Army and sent him homeward, tae think again.'

4. Martin Gilbert (ed.), *The Churchill Documents, Volume 15: Never Surrender, May 1940–December 1940* (Hillsdale, MI: Hillsdale College Press, 2011), p. 368. Churchill was careful to use 'Britain' in his speech, but as the historian Alan Allport has suggested, 'Symbolically it was never Scotland's war in quite the same way as it was England's' (*Britain at Bay*, p. 278), and therefore how recent appeals (see note below) to the 'spirit of the Blitz' or the Battle of Britain have been unable to transcend Celtic nationalism.

5. Of course, it might be argued that this continues to underplay how this is an English, rather than an Irish, Welsh or Scots origin myth – and we should remember that the pre-war years did see the growth and formal creation of various political parties interested in independence for Wales and Scotland. See, for example, Angus Calder, *The Myth of the Blitz.* Also of relevance is Clive Ponting, *1940: Myth and Reality.*

6. Allport, *Britain at Bay*, p. 8.

7. Ibid., p. 331.

8. Connelly, *We Can Take It*, p. 131.

9. Ibid., pp. 335–50.

10. Early in the COVID-19 pandemic, for example, the then Health Secretary, Matt Hancock, writing in the *Sunday Telegraph* on 15 March 2020, thought: 'Our generation has never been tested like this. Our grandparents were, during the Second World War, when our cities were bombed during the Blitz. Despite the pounding every night, the rationing, the loss of life, they pulled together in one gigantic national effort. Today, our generation is facing its own test, fighting a very real and new disease.' Fifteen years earlier, after the 7 July 2005 terrorist bombings in London – the worst bombing attack on the capital since the Second World War – the 'spirit of the Blitz' was similarly invoked by several politicians and commentators, although not altogether successfully. See, for example, Darren Kelsey, 'Remembering to Forget: Supporting and Opposing the War on Terror through the Myth of the Blitz after the 7th July Bombings', *Critical Approaches to Discourse Analysis across Disciplines*, 6:1 (2012), pp. 23–37.

11. Hill, *Boss of Britain's Underworld*. This is a rather marvellous, ghost-written 'con's account' (rather than a 'straight's account') of Hill's life and times. It deserves to be better known, and I was intrigued that I was the first person ever to borrow the book at Cambridge University Library in 2023, almost seventy years after it had been acquired (also see Introduction, note 7).

12. His autobiography was ghostwritten by Duncan Webb, the enigmatic crime correspondent of the *People* – see Duncan Campbell, 'Criminal Confessions', *Guardian*, 3 July 2011. The launch party for the book was held at Gennaro's – now the Groucho Club – and Campbell describes how the party 'made even Soho gasp'. A more traditional biography of Hill is offered by Wensley Clarkson, *Billy Hill: Godfather of London*. A recent account of the work of a crime correspondent is also useful – see Martin Brunt, *No One Got Cracked Over the Head for No Reason: Dispatches from a Crime Reporter*.

13. It's rarely discussed that the opposite also held true – prisoners serving less than three months were immediately pardoned at the outbreak of war in the hope that many would join the military.

14. It is worth remembering that official statistics about crime tend to *underestimate* the amount of offending that's going on at any

given time, which is why criminologists talk about 'the dark figure of crime' – those crimes which for various reasons don't get reported. The question of 'How much crime is there?' is one of the standard lectures for new students of criminology. Any introductory textbook will cover this topic – see, for example, Liebling, Maruna and McAra (eds), *The Oxford Handbook of Criminology*, Chapter 7. I've discussed this issue at some length in Wilson and Ashton, *What Everyone in Britain Should Know About Crime & Punishment* and Wilson, Ashton and Sharp, *What Everyone in Britain Should Know About the Police*. In the latter book we suggested that 'some [police] officers attempt to manipulate the crime figures. The favoured method in relation to crime rates is known in police slang as "cuffing", because the crimes in effect disappear, as if secreted up the cuffs of the officer's uniform. The technique simply involves the non-recording of certain crimes' (p. 58). The manipulation of the recorded crime statistics and the reality that many people for various reasons might not want to report crimes that had been committed against them or others means that greater reliance has historically been placed on victim surveys to extrapolate the actual rate of crime in any given year.

15. The figures cited and the quotations used come from a variety of sources: Jose Harris, 'War and Social History: Britain and the Home Front during the Second World War', *Contemporary European History*, 1: 1 (March 1992), pp. 17–35; Juliet Gardiner, *Wartime Britain, 1939–1945*; Clive Ponting, *Myth and Reality*; Duncan Campbell, 'London in the Blitz: How Crime Flourished under Cover of the Blackout', *Guardian*, 29 August 2010; Mark Ellis, '10 Facts about Crime on the Home Front in the Second World War', *History Extra*, 12 March 2018. The private papers of the Reverend John Markham can be accessed at the Imperial War Museum, and other contemporary accounts of attitudes towards the Blitz can be found in the Mass Observation Archive, online at www.massobs.org.uk. A useful secondary work about these attitudes is Becky Brown, *Blitz Spirit: Voices of Britain Living Through Crisis, 1939–1945*, which also details issues related to looting.

16. Quote taken from Larson, *The Splendid and the Vile*, p. 18.

17. Quotes taken from ibid., pp. 387–8.

18. 'Eighty Years On: Café de Paris, 8 March 1941'. The Drinker, 2

March 2021. Ballard Berkeley would later find fame playing the bumbling Major Gowen in the BBC sitcom *Fawlty Towers*.

19. See Lefebure, *Murder with a Difference*, pp. 172–7; Wilson, *A History of British Serial Killing*, pp. 125–32.

20. Allport, *Britain at Bay*, p. 169.

21. Lefebure, *Murder with a Difference*, pp. 42–6; Wilson, *A History of British Serial Killing*, pp. 117–24.

22. My observations about the civilian population reflect an interest in how prisons were organised during the Blitz and how prisoners coped with this experience. One prison governor remembered in his autobiography that 'with the coming of night bombing and the Blitz, fear and a certain amount of hysteria were only to be expected'. This same governor acknowledged that some prisoners felt that they were being left to 'die like rats in a trap', although he tried to assure them that their cells were 'first-class air-raid shelters'. See Grew, *Prison Governor*.

23. Lefebure, *Evidence for the Crown*, p. 58. This book was republished by Sphere in 2013 as *Murder on the Home Front: A True Story of Morgues, Murderers and Mysteries during the London Blitz* and serialised in the *Daily Mail*, headlined 'Molly in the Morgue', two months after Molly Lefebure's death. Other details about Rachel Dobkin are taken from Read, *Dark City* and Bechhofer Roberts, *The Trial of Harry Dobkin*.

24. Read, *Dark City*, p. 24.

25. Simpson, *Forty Years of Murder*; Lefebure, *Evidence for the Crown*. All quotes in this section are taken from these books.

26. There's a good, technical account of Simpson's investigation in Amy Bell, 'The Development of Forensic Pathology in London, England: Keith Simpson and the Dobkin Case, 1942', *Canadian Bulletin of Medical History*, 29:2 (2012), pp. 265–82.

27. See Wood, *Ruxton: The First Modern Murder*, for a general introduction to the case. Ruxton – the so-called 'savage surgeon' – was an Indian-born doctor who practised in the town of Lancaster. He was hanged in 1935 for the murders of his common-law wife Isabella Ruxton and the family housemaid Mary Rogerson. Their bodies, which had been extensively mutilated, were found under a bridge near the town of Moffat in Scotland and the case became known as 'the jigsaw murders' because of the painstaking efforts of forensic scientists to re-assemble and then identify the victims.

28. See, most recently, a podcast about the case by the social historian Hallie Rubenhold and the journalist Alice Fiennes called *Bad Women: The Blackout Ripper*.

29. The best book remains Simon Read, *The Blackout Murders: The Compelling True Story*, and I use it throughout this section. There are chapters about the Blackout Ripper in several other books about the Home Front – see in particular Penny Legg, *Crime in the Second World War: Spivs, Scoundrels, Rogues and Worse*. Of the true crime documentaries, as far back as 2012 *Fred Dinenage: Murder Casebook* covered the Blackout Ripper – the series is still available to view on YouTube. I was co-presenter on the first two series of the show. There are several podcasts about this sequence of attacks and murders – *Bad Women* is mentioned above, but the case is also covered in the *Dark Histories* podcast and in a variety of other history podcasts. Of the many useful other sources about and accounts of the case, Fred Cherrill, *Fingerprints Never Lie: The Autobiography of Frederick Cherrill* is particularly useful as the author attended several of the crime scenes and took the fingerprints that would ensnare Cummins. Scotland Yard's own case files are now kept at the National Archives in Kew and are available to consult – see TNA HO 144/21659: Criminal Cases: Cummins, Gordon Frederic.

Chapter Six

1. Reality Check Team, 'Unexploded Bombs: How Common Are They?', BBC News, 14 February 2018.

2. Dominic Sandbrook even uses the phrase within the title of his 2005 book: *Never Had It So Good: A History of Britain from Suez to the Beatles*.

3. This reality wasn't lost on prisoners serving sentences at this time. Peter Baker, for example, an MP imprisoned for fraud in 1954, wrote in his autobiography that the food at HMP Wormwood Scrubs was 'not fit for pigs to eat' and lost three stone during his first six months in custody. He thought that conditions in the prison were worse than he'd experienced in a German prisoner-of-war camp, which had been 'less formalised than the deadening sordid uniformity of exercise at Wormwood Scrubs in 1954' (*Time Out of Life*, p. 24).

4. Quoted in Wilson, *Pain and Retribution*, p. 109.

5. For general overviews about the development of prison regimes at

this time see Victor Bailey, *The Rise and Fall of the Rehabilitative Ideal, 1895–1970*, and Andrew Rutherford, *Prisons and the Process of Justice: The Reductionist Challenge*.

6. This maximum penalty has resulted in some remarkable decisions. For example, Norway's only serial killer, a man called Arnfinn Nesset – who murdered twenty-two elderly patients at the nursing home he managed between 1981 and 1983 – was released in 1993 after serving only ten years of his twenty-one-year sentence. Nesset then spent the remainder of his sentence under supervision in the community, living under an assumed name.

7. The account that follows is taken from Olden, *Murder in Notting Hill*. There are several useful reviews of this book, including Ian Thomson, 'Dark Days in the Dale', *Spectator*, 17 September 2011, and Harmit Athwal, 'The Worst Kept Secret in Notting Hill', Institute of Race Relations, 25 August 2011. Also of use is Raphael Rowe, 'Who Killed Kelso Cochrane?', BBC News, April 2006, an account of the case used to promote a BBC 2 documentary called *Who Killed my Brother?*, which was broadcast on 8 April 2006 and follows the journey of Stanley Cochrane coming to London to seek justice for Kelso. See too Thomas Kingsley, 'The Horrific Notting Hill Murder of Kelso Cochrane and Why Carnival Can Never be Cancelled', MyLondon, August 2022.

8. This account follows that provided in Olden, *Murder in Notting Hill*. See also Louise Boyle, 'Man who Stabbed Antiguan Carpenter through the Heart in Notting Hill "Race Killing" Finally Named after Fifty Years', *Daily Mail*, 8 September 2011.

9. Mark, *In the Office of Constable*, p. 83.

10. Olden, *Murder in Notting Hill*, p. 150.

11. See Lizzie Dearden, 'A UK Teen Became Fixated on Extreme Violence. But Was It Terrorism?', *New York Times*, 30 January 2025; 'Families "Shocked" at Missed Chances to Stop Killer', BBC News, 28 January 2025; and Josh Halliday and others, 'Axel Rudakubana: A "Ticking Timebomb" who Murdered Three Girls in Southport', *Guardian*, 20 January 2025.

12. Professor Geoffrey Pearson, one of the most gifted criminologists to emerge after the Second World War, stated that 'the Teds took Britain by storm' in the 1950s. Their name came from the 'Edwardian' style of dress that they adopted, which included long drape jackets, thick-soled 'brothel creepers', slim ties and

drainpipe trousers. Their hair was cut into a 'duck tail' and was heavily greased. See Pearson, *Hooligan*, pp. 17–24. The various suggestions about the cause of the riots can be followed in Sandbrook, *Never Had It So Good*, pp. 313–25.

13. Christopher Hilliard, 'Mapping the Notting Hill Riots: Racism and the Streets of Post-war Britain', *History Workshop Journal*, 93:1 (spring 2022), pp. 47–68. All quotes are taken from this article.

14. Quoted in Olden, *Murder in Notting Hill*, p. 6. Mack Charles Parker was a black man accused of raping a white woman and had been abducted from his jail cell by white men in hoods who shot him in the head. The story of Little Rock begins with the Little Rock Nine – a group of black students who enrolled in the formerly all-white Central High School in Little Rock, Arkansas. On the first day of the new school term in 1957 the state governor ordered the Arkansas National Guard to block their entry to the school. This resulted in President Eisenhower sending federal troops to escort to the nine black students into the school. In retaliation, in September 1958 the governor closed all of Little Rock's high school pending a public vote to prevent integration, and the schools did not re-open until August 1959.

15. Quoted in Olden, *Murder in Notting Hill*, p. 48.

16. See 'Family of Britain's "First Racist Murder" Denied Access to Police Files', Hickman & Rose, 8 February 2024, https://www.hickmanandrose.co.uk/family-of-kelso-cochrane-denied-access-to-police-murder-files/

Chapter Seven

1. Both *A Hard Day's Night* (1964) and *Help!* (1965) had been directed by Lester and, given that Paul McCartney was a fan of his work – he had invested money in Orton's play *Loot* – Lester had approached Orton to write a screenplay. However, the script was rejected and the third film that the Beatles made was *Magical Mystery Tour* (1967). They would go on to make *Yellow Submarine* (1968) and *Let It Be* (1970).

2. Lahr, *Prick Up Your Ears*, pp. 168–9. Also see Orton, *I Had it In Me*.

3. Co-defendants Gwynne Evans and Peter Allen were executed at HMP Strangeways and at HMP Liverpool on 13 August 1964, having been found guilty of murdering a van driver called John

West in April of that year. The last execution in Scotland took place on 15 August 1963, when Henry Burnett was hanged at HMP Craiginches in Aberdeen for the murder of a merchant seaman called Thomas Guyan.

4. Good starting points which act as standard accounts of the history of the 1960s are: David Kynaston, *On the Cusp: Days of '62*, and Dominic Sandbrook, *White Heat: A History of Britain in the Swinging Sixties*.

5. Philip Larkin, 'Annus Mirabilis', from *High Windows* (London: Faber & Faber, 1974).

6. This secret language was called Polari, which was made up of Italianate phrases and rhyming slang. See Paul Baker, *Fabulosa: The Story of Polari, Britain's Secret Gay Language* and also 'Polari: The Code Language Gay Men Used to Survive', BBC Online, 12 February 2018.

7. Fone, *Homophobia*.

8. For an excellent and recent account of these murders, see Alan R. Hurndall, *The Crooked Spire Killings*, which is self-published but available on Amazon.

9. E. S. Bradshaw, 'The Carbon Copy Murders, or Murder in Triplicate', *Police Journal*, 50:2 (April 1977), pp. 116–41 and *Police Journal*, 50:3 (July 1977), pp. 260–79. Bradshaw was formerly Detective Chief Superintendent of Derbyshire Constabulary and worked on the case.

10. Fulcher, *Catching a Serial Killer*. Also see Steven Morris, 'Becky Godden Detective: Why I Broke Rules over Christopher Halliwell', *Guardian*, 20 September 2016. Fulcher, whom I have met and interviewed, remains controversial but comes out of these accounts with honour and dignity.

11. Quotes taken from Bradshaw, 'The Carbon Copy Murders', p. 263.

12. See Jake Hall, 'A Definitive Guide to Dogging', *Cosmopolitan*, 11 November 2019.

13. A 'peeping Tom' is a male voyeur, and the original 'peeping Tom' is supposedly a Coventry tailor who spied on Lady Godiva as she rode naked through the town. See Jonny Wilkes, 'Why Do We Say "Peeping Tom"', *History Extra*, 14 September 2021.

14. Bradshaw, 'The Carbon Copy Murders', p. 124.

15. Hurndall, *The Crooked Spire Killings*, pp. 93–102.

16. For a good introduction to this subject area try David Canter, *Mapping Murder: Walking in Killers' Footsteps*. For an

explanation of how geo-profiling might be applied in a specific case see Laurence Alison and Marie Eyre, *Killer in the Shadows: The Monstrous Crimes of Robert Napper*.

17. This account follows Bradshaw's verbatim notes in 'The Carbon Copy Murders', pp. 267–71. All direct quotes are taken from this source.

18. I concentrate on the murders of William and George given that the focus of the book is about Britain. However, those interested in the murder of Guenther Helmbrecht should follow the account contained in Hurndall, *The Crooked Spire Killings*, pp. 70–89.

19. Quoted in ibid., p. 116.

20. Ibid., p. 117.

21. In one of our conversations, I asked Alan directly who 'they' were and he simply replied, 'The authorities: the Police and the CPS.'

22. This comment was made to the journalist Sam Dean by Rita's sister Tina Streeter on the fiftieth anniversary of Rita's murder. Sam, who at the time was working for the *Bucks Herald*, which was covering the 2017 appeal into the murder, interviewed Tina as part his newspaper's cold case review. Sam subsequently worked as a researcher on the Channel 4 series *In The Footsteps of Killers* which featured Rita's case. I am grateful to Sam for the many conversations that we have shared about what might have happened to Rita.

23. These stories are shared on the website www.rafmuseum.org and www.rafstories.org – 'The Female Experience'.

24. See 'Sister Appeals for New Information in 1967 Murder of Rita Ellis', *Guardian*, 9 November 2017; Shruti Sheth Trivedi, 'Fresh Appeal Launched on 50th Anniversary of RAF Halton Servicewoman Rita Ellis' Brutal Murder', *Bucks Free Press*, 13 November 2017; and Dave Doyle and Rachel Sloper, 'Rita Ellis: A Savage Murder, a Cold Case and a Sealed File', BuckinghamshireLive, 2 October 2021.

25. I met with Thames Valley Police – in the company of my co-presenter Emilia Fox – to ask them to participate in our Channel 4 series, which was going to feature the case. We offered to share all of our research, contacts and information. Their cold case unit were polite but couldn't have been less helpful and then seemed to be rather nonplussed that, despite their lack of cooperation, we were still going ahead with the documentary. They were wrong-footed and, whether or not prompted by the prospect of

the Channel 4 documentary, quickly put out a *Crimewatch Live* appeal on BBC1 about Rita's murder. As far as I am aware, no new leads emerged as a result of that appeal.

26. Through familial DNA Watson is one of the two hundred men who have seemingly been ruled out as a suspect (personal communication obtained during filming).

27. This account follows that in Cobain, *The History Thieves*, pp. 16–63. It should also be noted that Le Queux wasn't the first to write about Britain's unpreparedness for war, with Erskine Childers's 1903 *The Riddle of the Sands*, for example, ploughing a similar furrow. However, Le Queux's influence was undoubtedly strongest, to the extent that Christopher Andrew, in *The Defence of the Realm*, describes him as 'the alarmist-in-chief', but noted that the evidence on which he made his claims about German spies was 'flimsy' (p. 20).

28. See Paul Lashmar, 'Official Secrets Act: UK Government has a Long History of Suppressing Journalism to Hide its Misdeeds', *The Conversation*, 27 July 2021.

29. Quotes taken from Cobain, *The History Thieves*, pp. 154–6.

30. Ibid.

31. Ibid., pp. ix–x. The novelist and journalist John Lanchester was given access to the leaked GCHQ materials in New York (which demonstrates the futility of destroying the hard drives of the *Guardian*'s computers in London) and concludes that what he saw 'makes clear that GCHQ's eavesdropping abilities are on a scale unmatched anywhere in the free world – yet nobody seems to care'. See John Lanchester, 'The Snowden Files: Why the British Public Should be Worried about GCHQ', *Guardian*, 3 October 2013.

Chapter Eight

1. Tom Tullett, 'Night of the Mugger', *Daily Mirror*, 17 August 1972.

2. See 'Waterloo's Dark Side (Waterloo Station Part 9)', View from the Mirror: A Cabbie's London, 12 July 2014, https://blackcablondon.net/2014/07/12/waterloos-dark-side-waterloo-station-part-9/.

3. Tullett, 'Night of the Mugger'.

4. Hall et al., *Policing the Crisis*, p. vii. Put simply, a moral panic occurs when a condition, episode, person or group of people emerge and come to be defined as a threat to society, but that

threat is out of all proportion to the actual level of threat that it entails. In other words, there is a 'panic'. The Italian Marxist Antonio Gramsci developed the concept of hegemony to describe how one social class achieves and maintains dominance in society. Hall et al.'s argument is that the figure of the mugger and the panic about mugging were specifically created to manipulate conditions in which it would be easier to gain consent to control urban space by more targeted and politicised forms of policing.

5. See Wilson and Ashton, *What Everyone in Britain Should Know About Crime and Punishment*, pp. 1–8, for a discussion and consult the graph on page 4 – 'Crimes Recorded in England and Wales, 1876–2000'. The figures in this section are also cited in Sandbrook, *State of Emergency*, p. 283. The official recorded crime rate can be manipulated in various ways and does not necessarily reflect how much crime is actually taking place, which is why more emphasis is placed on the figures produced by various victim surveys, such as the Crime Survey of England and Wales. This crime survey was first introduced in 1982 and, prior to Scottish devolution, was called the British Crime Survey. All this having been said, the crime rate over this period of time – measured in various ways – did increase.

6. The figures and specific examples which are described in this section are taken from a number of different places. Chief among these are: Beckett, *When the Lights Went Out*; Sandbrook, *State of Emergency*; Brown and Sparks (eds), *Beyond Thatcherism*; and McAnulla, *British Politics*.

7. For a general introduction see Jewkes, *Media & Crime*.

8. Laurie Calhoun, 'The Phenomenon of Paid Killing', *International Journal of Human Rights*, 6:1 (2003), pp. 1–18; quote taken from p. 2.

9. D. McIntyre, D. Wilson, E. Yardley and L. Brolan, 'The British Hitman: 1974–2013', *Howard Journal of Criminal Justice*, 53:4 (2014), pp. 325–40. The £200 hit was conducted by a young man called Santre Sanchez Gayle in March 2010 when he murdered Gulistan Subasi in Hackney, London. With his £200 he bought a fake Gucci hat.

10. There are various spellings of Henry MacKenney's name – 'McKenny' and 'MacKenny', for example. I've used the spelling which appeared in the Court of Appeal judgment in 2003.

11. These details are constructed from a variety of secondary sources:

'Murder Convictions Overturned', BBC News, 15 December 2003; Duncan Campbell, 'Hope of Freedom after 20 Years', *Guardian*, 5 April 1999; Jeff Edwards, 'The Only Way to Make Childs Laugh is Start Talking about Killing People', *Daily Mirror*, 23 February 2014; Mark Townsend, 'Hitmen for Hire: Academics Unlock the Secret Behaviour of Britain's Contract Killers', *Guardian*, 25 January 2014; 'Evil Hitman Who Butchered Six People Tells Penpal ... I would Do It All Again Tomorrow', *The People*, 2 March 1997; and *R v. Terence Pinfold and Henry MacKenney* [2003] EWCA Crim 3643. Also of use is Nick Appleyard, *Life Means Life: Jailed Forever*. Finally, there is a Sky TV documentary – shown in 2022 – called *Confessions of a Hitman: The John Childs Story* which is of interest and is available on YouTube. All quotes used in this section are taken from these various sources.

12. There were, however, claims that Terry Eve was in the witness protection scheme and living under an assumed name in west London.

13. Appleyard, *Life Means Life*, p. 85.

14. McIntyre et al., 'The British Hitman', p. 335.

15. See: Hall and Winlow, *Revitalizing Criminological Theory*; Hall, *Theorizing Crime & Deviance*; and Winlow, *Badfellas*.

16. Sandel, *What Money Can't Buy*.

17. This is a reference to E. P. Thompson's *Writing by Candlelight*, a book written, according to Thompson, 'to controvert, and if possible to discomfort, the purveyors of received wisdom, and to contest the official descriptions of reality presented in the media', p. vii.

Chapter Nine

1. All details and quotes within this section are taken from Patrick Bishop, *The Man Who Was Saturday: The Extraordinary Life of Airey Neave – Soldier, Escaper, Spymaster, Politician*. Also of use are Stephen Kelly, *Margaret Thatcher, the Conservative Party and the Northern Ireland Conflict, 1975–1990*, and Richard English, *Armed Struggle: The History of the IRA*.

2. Bishop, *The Man Who Was Saturday*, pp. 249–65, and also see Patrick Gysin and Chloe Kerr, 'Bloody Disgrace', *Sun*, 13 March 2019. Of note: Bishop is also critical of the secrecy surrounding this case and the failure of his Freedom of Information requests for access to the files.

3. See Martin Innes and Michael Levi, 'Making and Managing Terrorism and Counter-Terrorism: The View from Criminology', in Liebling, Maruna and McAra (eds), *The Oxford Handbook of Criminology*, pp. 455–77. This section is also influenced by Smelser, *The Faces of Terrorism*.

4. All the details in this section about the bombing of Coventry in 1939 are taken from Simon Shaw, 'Not Forgotten: The IRA Bomb Attack', Historic Coventry Articles, www.historiccoventry.co.uk; Jenny Scott, 'Coventry IRA Bombing: The "Forgotten" Attack on a British City', BBC News, 25 August 2014; and David O'Donoghue, *The Devil's Deal: The IRA, Nazi Germany and the Double Life of Jim O'Donoghue*.

5. Rebekah Poole, Jennifer Llewellyn and Steve Thompson, 'The Provisional IRA's Mainland Campaign', Alpha History, 2020.

6. For a recent account see Rory Carroll, *Killing Thatcher: The IRA, the Manhunt and the Long War on the Crown*.

7. This section is based on the obituary of Gavin Vernon, *Telegraph*, 26 March 2004; Olga Craig, 'Ian Hamilton on Stone of Destiny: I Felt I was Holding Scotland's Soul', *Telegraph*, 14 December 2008; and Elizabeth Quigley, 'My Dad Wouldn't Want Stone of Destiny at Coronation', BBC News, 17 March 2023.

8. See, for example, Steven Brocklehurst, 'Declaration of Arbroath: The Most Famous Letter in Scottish History?' BBC News, 6 April 2020. More scholarly accounts can be found in Edward J. Cowan, *For Freedom Alone: The Declaration of Arbroath*, and David Crouch, *Medieval Britain, c. 1000–1500*.

9. Elizabeth Quigley, 'The Day the Stone of Destiny Returned to Scotland', BBC News, 26 November 2021.

10. Sheena Goodyear, 'Scottish Stone Shouldn't be in Coronation, Says Son of Man Who Stole it Back from England', CBC Radio, 5 May 2023.

11. Devine, *Independence or Union*, p. 135.

12. Toby Helm, 'Margaret Thatcher Would Not Have Supported Brexit, Says Top Aide', *Observer*, 3 September 2016.

13. All quotes are taken from Devine, *Independence or Union*, pp. 166–8, 178. The issue of misogyny in Scotland and specifically within Scottish politics hasn't gone away. There have been suggestions that this is the root cause of criticism of the former First Minister Nicola Sturgeon. See, for example, Alistair G. J. Stewart, 'Nicola Sturgeon: Sexism is Behind Many Attacks

on First Minister and Other Female Leaders', *Scotsman*, 10 February 2023.

Chapter Ten

1. 'DJ Cox's Queen Mother Gaffe', BBC News, 4 August 2000.
2. Louise Donovan, 'The Rise and Fall of the Ladette', *Vice*, 8 March 2017. The ladettes can be viewed at the height of their cultural moment on *The Girlie Show* – a Channel 4 series from 1994–95, with Sara Cox one of the presenters. Episodes are still available on YouTube.
3. See Wilson and Ashton, *What Everyone in Britain Should Know About Crime & Punishment*, pp. 102–14. For a discussion about female aggression over this period see Steve Muncer, Anne Campbell, Victoria Jervis and Rachel Lewis, '"Ladettes", Social Representation and Aggression', *Sex Roles*, 44 (2001), pp. 33–44.
4. For an overview of Lombroso's ideas see O'Brien and Yar, *Criminology*, pp. 125–8, and also of use is Raine, *The Anatomy of Violence*. Raine describes Lombroso as a 'straw man' who is too often held up for attack by those who oppose a biological theory of crime causation. His book can therefore be read as a defence of what is described by criminologists as 'biological positivism'.
5. Heidenson, *Women and Crime*.
6. O'Neil and Seal, *Transgressive Imaginations*.
7. Adler, *Sisters in Crime*.
8. Rene Chun, 'Female Fugitives: Why is "Pink-Collar" Crime on the Rise?' *Guardian*, 6 January 2020. More academic accounts can be found in Anette Ballinger, *Dead Woman Walking*; Shani D'Cruze, Sandra Walklate and Samantha Pegg, *Murder*; and Belinda Morrissey, *When Women Kill*.
9. Quoted in 'Campaign Launched to Catch Europe's Most Wanted Women', *Guardian*, 19 October 2019.
10. These details are taken from the podcast *The Storyteller: Violent Delights and Murder Most Foul*, which is written, presented and produced by the Scottish journalist Isla Traquair. I've interviewed Isla several times about the murder of Melanie Stourton and use text from these interviews within this chapter. Isla has presented a strand in ITV *This Morning*'s Women and Crime series about Melanie's murder in April 2023, which can be viewed on YouTube.
11. 'Life for Evil Killer Who Slit Throat of Victim Neighbour Murdered in Cold Blood', *Herald*, 10 March 2000.

12. Interview conducted in June 2022.
13. Berry-Dee, *Love of Blood*. As I've noted in the main text, Dennehy was a spree and not a serial killer.
14. See Louie Smith, 'My Devil in the Flesh: Accomplice's Shocking Love Notes from Prison to Serial Killer Joanne Dennehy', *Daily Mirror*, 22 March 2014.
15. Laurence Cawley and Laura Devlin, 'Joanne Dennehy's Sister Maria on Triple Killer's Childhood', BBC News, 12 February 2014.
16. 'Statistics on Women and the Criminal Justice System', Institute for Criminal Justice Policy Research, School of Law, King's College London, January 2009.
17. 'Homicide in England and Wales: Year Ending March 2023', Office for National Statistics, February 2024.
18. Sarah Corker, 'Sharp Rise in Women Caught Carrying Knives', BBC News, 8 August 2019.
19. See Manuel Eisner, 'Interpersonal Violence on the British Isles', in Liebling, Maruna and McAra (eds), *The Oxford Handbook of Criminology*, pp. 565–86.

Chapter Eleven

1. 'Homicide in England and Wales: Year Ending March 2022', Office for National Statistics, 9 February 2023.
2. Ash Sarkar, 'How Andrew Tate Built an Army of Lonely, Angry Men', *British GQ*, 15 August 2022; Maya Oppenheim, 'Figures That Lay Bare the Shocking Scale of Toxic Influences on Andrew Tate's Reach Among Young Men', *Independent*, 16 February 2023.
3. 'Milestones: Journeying into Adulthood', Office for National Statistics, 18 February 2019.
4. See Postman, *The Disappearance of Childhood* and Jenks, *Childhood*.
5. Stephen Bates, 'Teenager Jailed for Murdering Schoolboy Jimmy Mizen', *Guardian*, 27 March 2009. Copyright Guardian News & Media Ltd 2025.
6. For an introduction, see Khan, *Basic Freud*.
7. Gilligan, *Violence*.
8. Katz, *Seductions of Crime*.
9. See Owen Scott, 'Killed by Rap-Star', *Sun*, 16 January 2025; Harry Lowe, 'Killer Recalled to Prison after Murder "Boast"', BBC News, 17 January 2025.
10. The British crime drama series *Adolescence*, which was released

on Netflix in March 2025, is of relevance here. Created by Jack Thorne and Stephen Graham, *Adolescence* is about a thirteen-year-old schoolboy called Jamie Miller who murdered a girl at his school. The series received widespread critical acclaim and started a debate about the toxic nature of the social media 'manosphere'. With the support of the prime minister, the series has now been made free to view in all British secondary schools.

11. For accounts of the murder see Green, *When Children Kill* and Morrison, *As If.*

12. See the account in Henriques, *From Crime to Crime*. Henriques led the prosecution against Venables and Thompson.

13. Ibid., pp. 45–71.

14. There's some evidence to suggest that the murder may have been inspired by the video *Child's Play 3*. In it a possessed doll called Chucky comes to life in a military academy and abducts the youngest cadet. The demonic doll then tries to kill the cadet by pushing him under the wheels of a fairground ghost train. Chucky dies after being splattered by paint and having his face mutilated. This video was the last to be rented by Venables's father prior to the killing. See Henriques, *From Crime to Crime*, p. 63.

15. Quoted in Wilson, *Pain and Retribution*, p. 165.

16. Ibid.

17. Wilson and Ashton, *What Everyone in Britain Should Know About Crime & Punishment*, p. 47.

18. For a good overview see Sereny, *Cries Unheard*.

19. Davies, *Dark Heart*.

20. Ibid., p. 34.

21. Ibid., p. 288.

22. 'Suspensions and Permanent Exclusions in England', Department for Education, 21 November 2024.

23. Figures are taken from *Still Running: Children in the Streets in the UK* (London: The Children's Society, 1999) and *Still Running II: Findings from the Second National Survey of Young Runaways* (London: The Children's Society, 2005). Also useful are Libby Brooks, *The Story of Childhood: Growing Up in Modern Britain*, and Frank Furedi, *Paranoid Parenting: Abandon Your Anxieties and Become a Good Parent*.

Chapter Twelve

1. I wrote about the ongoing manhunt for Moat several times – see, for example, 'Twisted Mind of a Maniac', *Daily Mail*, 7 July 2010 – and Moat's various writings and recordings were later used by Andrew Hankinson in *You Could Do Something Amazing with Your Life [You are Raoul Moat]*.

2. Quoted in Helen Carter, 'Raoul Moat Facebook Tribute Page Taken Down', *Guardian*, 15 July 2010.

3. 'Day of Terror', *Whitehaven News*, 3 June 2010. There's one book-length account of these shootings: Clare Leigh, *Massacre in Cumbria: The Day Gunman Derrick Bird Brought Terror to the Lake District*. Much of what appears in this section is taken from newspaper accounts and noted from one of my own research trips to Whitehaven with a colleague, Dr Sarah Pemberton.

4. See Helen Pidd, 'Cumbria Shootings: Timeline of Witness Testimony', *Guardian*, 8 June 2010.

5. 'Carnage in West Cumbria', *Whitehaven News*, 3 June 2010.

6. Fox and Levin, *Extreme Killing*, pp. 17–18.

7. Leigh, *Massacre in Cumbria*.

8. D. Wilson, E. Yardley and S. Pemberton, 'The "Dunblane Massacre" as a "Photosensitive Plate"', *Crime, Media, Culture*, 13:1 (2016), pp. 55–68.

9. Richard Collier, 'After Dunblane: Crime, Corporeality, and the (Hetero) Sexing of the Bodies of Men', *Journal of Law and Society*, 24:2 (1997), pp. 177–98.

10. Aylward, *Understanding Dunblane and other Massacres*.

11. Brewer, *Ethnography*.

12. Hall, Winlow and Ancrum, *Criminal Identities and Consumer Culture*, p. 4.

13. Seierstad, *One of Us*, p. 515.

14. Gilligan, *Violence*, p. 111.

15. Andrew O'Hagan, 'Who's the Alpha Male Now, Bitches?' *London Review of Books*, 22 October 2015.

Chapter Thirteen

1. I have previously written about Todd's death in *Looking for Laura: Public Criminology and Hot News*, pp. 68–72. All quotes are taken from this account. A full copy of the report of the enquiry undertaken by Sir Paul Scott-Lee can be found in Neal

Keeling, 'Todd: The Official Verdict', *Manchester Evening News*, 12 January 2013.

2. Reiner, *The Politics of the Police*.

3. These quotes are taken from the blog posts of Alison Halford – also see note 14, below. Her 1993 autobiography, *No Way up the Greasy Pole*, is also of interest.

4. Vitale, *The End of Policing*.

5. Sam Levin, 'It Never Stops: Killings by US Police Reach Record High in 2022', *Guardian*, 6 January 2023.

6. Vitale, *The End of Policing*, pp. 2–3, 21–2.

7. Police Shootings', Inquest.org.uk, 12 January 2023.

8. 'IOPC Publishes Figures on Deaths During or Following Police Custody for 2023/24', IOPC, 17 October 2024.

9. David Spencer, 'What Do We Want from the Next Prime Minister? A Series of Policy Proposals for New Leadership: Crime & Policing – A Force Fit for the Future', Policy Exchange, 30 August 2022.

10. Mark Townsend, 'Crisis After Crisis: What is Going Wrong at the Met Police?' *Observer*, 18 July 2021.

11. Zoe Williams, 'Isn't it Frightening that a Lone Woman seeing a Policeman Now Feels Afraid, Not Reassured?' *Guardian*, 10 June 2022.

12. This account is drawn from a number of different newspaper sources, including Haroon Siddique, 'Sarah Everard's Family Haunted by the Horror of Her Murder', *Guardian*, 29 September 2021 and Matthew Cox, 'What Happened to Sarah Everard?' *Daily Mail*, 14 September 2023, as well as Tom Harper, *Broken Yard*, pp. 379–97.

13. See Miriam Kuepper, 'Women Arrested at Sarah Everard Vigil at Clapham Common Receive Payouts from the Met Police after Officers were Criticised for their Heavy-Handed Response', *Daily Mail*, 14 September 2023. Stevenson is quoted as saying: 'It has taken over two years to reach this conclusion, it's been a really tiring and difficult process but it has felt important to push for some form of accountability and justice for myself and all women who attended the vigil to express our anger and grief over the murder of Sarah Everard by a serving Metropolitan Police officer.'

14. A good example here is Alison Halford, who's a very insightful critic of her time as a police officer, joining the Metropolitan

Police in 1962 and eventually becoming Assistant Chief Constable of Merseyside Police in 1983. She was the first woman to hold this rank in the history of British policing. However, she failed to win further promotion and claimed that she'd faced discrimination because of her gender. Her autobiography, *No Way up the Greasy Pole*, is an excoriating account of what her life as a female police officer was like during this period and offers some eye-watering vignettes of her time within the force. She continued to make criticism of the culture of policing for a number of years through her many blog posts.

15. See Stuart Hoddinott, Nick Davies, Thomas Pope, Amber Dellar and Philip Nye, 'Austerity Postponed? The Impact of Labour's First Budget on Public Services', Institute for Government, 8 November 2024.

16. For a general introduction see: Clive Emsley, *The English Police*; Rod Morgan and Tim Newburn, *The Future of Policing*; Robert Reiner, *The Politics of the Police*; David Wilson, John Ashton and Douglas Sharp, *What Everyone in Britain Should Know About the Police*.

17. See Wilson, Ashton and Sharp, *What Everyone in Britain Should Know About the Police*, pp. 28–45.

18. A good starting point for the media portrayal of policing remains Marianne Colbran, *Media Representations of Police and Crime: Shaping the Police Television Drama*. Also of use is Frank Leishman and Paul Mason, *Policing and the Media: Facts, Fictions and Factions*.

19. See 'Police Powers: Stop and Search', House of Commons Library Research Briefing, 20 July 2022; Ben Bradford and Matteo Tiratelli, 'Does Stop and Search Reduce Crime?' Issue 4, UK Justice Policy Review FOCUS, 2019.

20. A very readable account of the effectiveness of stop and search can be found in 'Pros and Cons of Stop and Search', *The Week*, 22 June 2023, and in more detail in Nils Braakmann, 'Does Stop and Search Reduce Crime? Evidence from Street-Level Data and a Surge in Operations Following a High-Profile Crime', *Journal of the Royal Statistical Society Series A Statistics in Society*, 185:3 (July 2022), pp. 1370–97.

21. I have known Bas for a number of years, and this anecdote and the interview that he provided in relation to the vigil on Clapham Common was recorded for an episode of the podcast that I

co-presented with Emilia Fox called *If It Bleeds, It Leads* on 19 July 2021.

22. Damian Gayle, 'Thousands March in London in Fourth Anti-Lockdown Protest', *Guardian*, 24 October 2020.

23. Bas Javid, 'Why I Joined the Police', *Spectator*, 3 October 2020.

24. 'Sarah Everard: It Will Take Years to Repair Trust – London Mayor', BBC News, 3 March 2024.

25. Quotes taken from Jack Wright, 'Unrepentant Met Cops Justify Heavy-Handed Arrests at Sarah Everard Vigil', *Daily Mail*, 7 June 2022.

26. Quotes taken from Vikram Dodd and Emine Sinmaz, 'David Carrick Jailed for Life Over Series of Rapes While Met Police Officer', *Guardian*, 7 February 2023.

27. Bethan Bell, 'Sarah Everard: Daughter, Sister, Friend and Colleague', BBC News, 9 July 2021.

At the End of a History

1. A British Social Attitudes Survey reported in 2023 that there'd been a 'near revolution' in attitudes towards a range of social and moral issues since the 1980s. From attitudes towards gay sex and single parenting, to views about the role of women in society and abortion, Britain had 'evolved into a more liberal-minded country'. See Patrick Butler, 'Britain is Much More Liberal-Minded than it was 40 Years Ago', *Guardian*, 21 September 2023.

2. My thoughts about this were sharpened by reading Alice Hunt, *Republic: Britain's Revolutionary Decade, 1649–1660* (London: Faber & Faber, 2025). Outside of my time frame, Hunt's book considers the 1650s, after the execution of Charles I, the establishment of a republic and then the restoration of the monarchy. So, England (at least) went from being an absolute monarchy to republicanism but returned to monarchy, albeit a constitutional variety. In other words, what England was and who the English were was contingent on what the state wanted, rather than any underlying, ingrained historical and cultural values. More recently, we've been an empire, but are now a commonwealth; and once 'at the heart of Europe' but now no longer.

3. See, for example, Frances Perraudin, 'English People Living in Wales Tilted it Towards Brexit', *Guardian*, 22 September 2010.

Index